Black Curators Matter

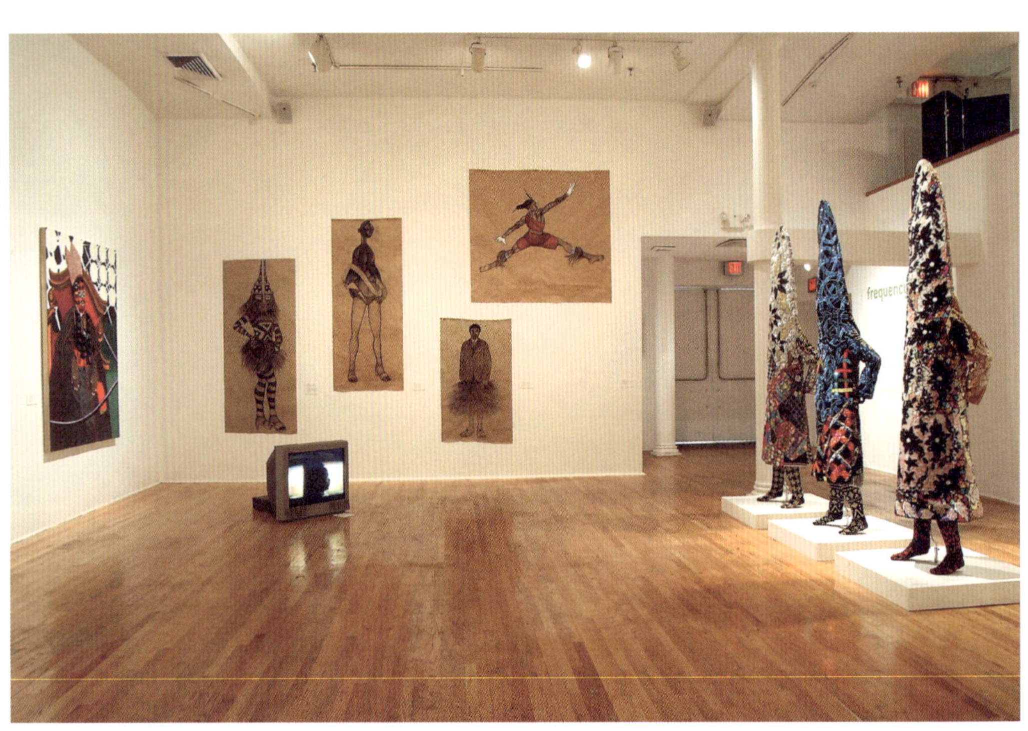

Black Curators Matter

Conversations on Art and Change

Edited by
Kellie Jones and
Tumelo Mosaka

Getty Research Institute
Los Angeles

Published by the Getty Research Institute, Los Angeles
Getty Publications
1200 Getty Center Drive, Suite 500
Los Angeles, California 90049-1682
getty.edu/publications

Adriana Romero, *Editor*
Jon Grizzle, *Designer*
Victoria Gallina, *Production*
Karen Ehrmann, Jennifer M. Harley, and Ardel'Paschal Sampson, *Image and Rights Acquisition*

Distributed in the United States and Canada by the University of Chicago Press

Distributed outside the United States and Canada by Yale University Press, London

Printed in China

Type composed in Rand

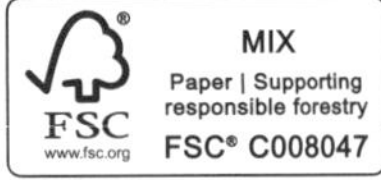

Library of Congress Cataloging-in-Publication Data
Names: Jones, Kellie, editor. | Mosaka, Tumelo, editor.
Title: Black curators matter : conversations on art and change / edited by Kellie Jones and Tumelo Mosaka.
Description: Los Angeles : Getty Research Institute, [2026] | Includes bibliographical references and index. |
Summary: "The transformative impact of Black curators on American art museums since the 1970s as told by the visionaries at the forefront of the change"—Provided by publisher.
Identifiers: LCCN 2025043734 | ISBN 9798887120140 (paperback) | ISBN 9798887120164 (pdf) | ISBN 9798887120157 (epub)
Subjects: LCSH: African American art museum curators—Interviews. | Art museums—Curatorship—United States. | Art museums—Social aspects—United States. | Museums and minorities—United States. | Art, Black—Exhibitions. | Art and race.
Classification: LCC N406.A1
LC record available at https://lccn.loc.gov/2025043734

Authorized Product Safety Representative in the European Union: Easy Access System Europe, Mustamäe tee 50, 10621 Tallinn, Estonia, gpsr.requests@easproject.com

CONTENTS

ABOUT THE INTERVIEWS

Black Curators Matter: Conversations on Art and Change is part of Columbia University's Mellon Arts Project in African American and African Diaspora Studies in partnership with the Columbia University Center for Oral History Research. This book is drawn from extensive oral histories recorded between 2021 and 2023. Originally planned as in-person interviews, the conversations were conducted and recorded on Zoom due to the COVID-19 pandemic. Despite the distance and challenging circumstances, the interviews maintained their vibrancy, which made it all the more exciting when participants could gather in person for the public programs related to the project.

Each narrator participated in two interview sessions of varying lengths. The six interviews were recorded and audited by Ornella Baganizi, Chris Pandza, Jarrett Payne, Kayleigh Stack, and Auriana Woods. They were transcribed by the Audio Transcription Center. From these full transcripts, the interviews were carefully condensed and edited for clarity, consistency, and narrative cohesion following the *Chicago Manual of Style* 18th edition and Columbia University Center for Oral History Research's *Oral History Transcription Style Guide.* To enhance readability while preserving each narrator's voice and story, the following editorial decisions were made: verbal fillers and mannerisms were removed; names were fact-checked and standardized; dates, small clarifications, and short editorial insertions were added in brackets; repetitive information was omitted; and language was streamlined in cases where interjections or trailing thoughts obscured meaning.

The complete audio files and transcripts of the original interviews are available at the Getty Library and the Schomburg Center for Research in Black Culture.

INTRODUCTION

Kellie Jones and Tumelo Mosaka

In 1899 the Philadelphia Museum of Art purchased *The Annunciation* (1898) by the African American expatriate artist Henry Ossawa Tanner; it is perhaps the first acquisition by an art museum in the United States of a work by an African American artist.[1] *The Annunciation* diverges from conventional biblical imagery: Mary is portrayed as an ordinary girl in Middle Eastern attire, while the angel Gabriel, the messenger of her divine child, is depicted simply as a powerful ray of light. More than a century later, in 2023, the museum launched the Brind Center for African and African Diasporic Art. Led by Imani Roach, the initiative seeks to expand such collections and related art histories and, in its own way, carries forward Tanner's ray of light.

This development also points to the increasing presence of Black curators across major art institutions. In 2020, Naomi Beckwith was named deputy director and chief curator of the Guggenheim Museum and, four years later, was tapped as the next artistic director of Documenta, the contemporary art exhibition that takes place only twice per decade in Kassel. Koyo Kouoh was selected as the artistic director of the 2026 Venice Biennale to become the first African woman to lead one of the most prestigious and long-standing international art exhibitions of its kind. Beckwith's and Kouh's appointments have been part of a recent broader wave of Black curatorial leadership at prominent art institutions, including Thomas Jean Lax, Smooth Nzewi, and Oluremi Onabanjo (Museum of Modern Art [MoMA]), Valerie Cassel Oliver (Virginia Museum of Fine Arts), and Adrienne Edwards, Rujeko Hockley, and Meg Onli (Whitney Museum of American Art). A new generation of Black leaders has also emerged at culturally specific institutions. Key Jo Lee is chief of Curatorial Affairs and Public Programs at San Francisco's Museum of the African Diaspora, and Cameron Shaw serves as the executive director at the California African American Museum (CAAM) in Los Angeles.

All this activity comes some fifty years after Black artists protested their exclusion from exhibitions at the Metropolitan Museum of Art, the Whitney, and MoMA, among others, calling for museums across the United States to hire Black curatorial talent. In response to continual institutional rejection, their advocacy helped lay the groundwork for the birth of museums and cultural organizations dedicated to promoting Black art and culture, such as the Studio Museum in Harlem, the Museum of the National Center of Afro-American Artists, and CAAM. Beginning in the 2000s, Black Lives Matter activism brought issues of racial equity into public discourse once again. After historic protests and demonstrations against police brutality following the murder of George Floyd in 2020, art museums in the United States began to listen.

Black Curators Matter: Conversations on Art and Change takes up the call of the Black Lives Matter movement to examine the complex history of Black cultures in museums and spotlight Black curators who have transformed the visual arts landscape since the 1970s. This book presents illuminating conversations with six pioneering figures—Lowery Stokes Sims, Deborah Willis, Richard J. Powell, Kellie Jones, Thelma Golden, and Franklin Sirmans—and a younger cohort of professionals including Ashley James, Kalia Brooks, Aaron Bryant, Lax, Hockley, and LeRonn P. Brooks. These curators have not only witnessed but driven significant change in the curatorial field and museum world, paving the way for institutional reckoning that museums are finally undertaking today. By fostering intergenerational dialogue, these conversations offer firsthand accounts of the curators' experiences, aspirations, and achievements, alongside candid reflections on their struggle for acknowledgment in the field. The interviews take stock of civil rights–era influences to the more recent protests led by the Black Lives Matter movement, touching on issues of race, identity, aesthetics, and power.

Each term in the project title—*Black, curators,* and *matter*—inhabits meaningful entry points into understanding the impact Black curators have had on the visual arts. With museums finally taking steps to rectify gaps in their exhibition and hiring programs, it is crucial to document how Black curators paved the way for such changes. This oral history amplifies the journeys of curators who have reshaped not only the art historical canon but also the lives of many neglected and forgotten artists, while celebrating the institutions that have committed to writing new histories of the curatorial field.

The relationship between Black Americans and American art museums has historically been fraught, uneasy, and hard-won over the course of the twentieth and twenty-first centuries. While American art museums have traditionally been known for curating and cementing ideals of beauty and national identity, they have also been sites of ongoing negotiation and conflict regarding the inclusion and exclusion of Black artists, administrators, and audiences. As Bridget Cooks writes in *Exhibiting Blackness: African Americans and the American Art Museum,* "African American artists still face an art world in which the exhibition and reception of their work can depend upon proof of their value as artists despite their racial identity."[2] The exhibition model of American museums has proven to be both a way to uphold dominant understandings of race and racial difference and a catalyst for the inclusion of Black American artists and voices within the museum. In the early part of the twentieth century, figures such as Arturo Alfonso Schomburg in New York and Miriam Matthews in Los Angeles began curating with African American and African diaspora artists and histories in mind. (Schomburg's extensive collection became the foundation for the Schomburg Center for Research in Black Culture, whereas Matthews was the first African American librarian employed by the Los Angeles Public Library.) Throughout the twentieth century, artists and art historians at historically Black colleges and universities—such as James V. Herring and James A. Porter (Howard University), and Hale Woodruff and Nancy Elizabeth Prophet (Spelman College)—along with other artists and scholars, like David Driskell and Samella Lewis, continued this critical work of cultural preservation and documentation.

How has Blackness been represented in the American art museum? From the scholarship that has focused on the exhibitionary model and inclusion of Black voices, American art museums have never been race neutral. In fact, the ways that the work of Black artists have been exhibited in American museums in the twentieth and twenty-first centuries can be seen as a bellwether for national grappling with social, political, and cultural transformations. *Black Curators*

Matter explores this historical context by positing that the individual experiences of Black curators is another important part of the story that has not been thoroughly told or examined.

One signature moment of important Black critique of American art museums was ignited by the Met's infamous exhibition *Harlem on My Mind: The Cultural Capital of Black America, 1900–1968* (1969). Deemed by many to be unrepresentative of the Harlem community the exhibition purported to represent, *Harlem on My Mind* spurred a flurry of artist activism as the show did not feature a single Black artist. In response, a group of Black artists formed the Black Emergency Cultural Coalition (BECC), which influenced how Black artists in New York interacted with and approached major arts institutions. Tracing the role Black curators have played in shaping and transforming American arts institutions reveals the deeper roots of this history. Mabel O. Wilson has examined how, beginning in the nineteenth century, the exhibition of Black culture and creation of exhibitions by Black curators and organizers at American world's fairs aimed to transform both the American public and African American community life. Wilson writes of the Black American *counterpublic* that formed in response to the systemic exclusion of Black Americans from political and public life, creating necessary spaces of self-determination and community beyond dominant spheres.[3] Culturally specific institutions like the Studio Museum and the Schomburg Center represent large-scale attempts to establish world-class cultural institutions that serve the Black community in Harlem as well as national and international audiences. Culturally relevant and specific spaces have also developed in other locales and at different scales, led by vanguard curators and artists working with few resources. In this vein, Jones has considered how Black artists and curators in postwar Los Angeles had to form their own "exhibitionary complex," finding new ways of displaying art by Black artists for Black audiences that broke out of traditional and restrictive practices of other institutions.[4] In this light, many Black curators have often juggled between working within historically, predominantly white institutions and cultivating autochthonous spaces where Black creativity can flourish. The stories shared by the participating seasoned curators—the narrators of *Black Curators Matter*—reveal transformative strategies, critical interventions, and boundary-breaking exhibitions that reshaped the exhibitionary model of American art museums toward greater inclusivity and experimentation.

Black curators have been central to reimagining the representation of Black Americans in American art museums. They have initiated and expanded the call for a more diverse and inclusive art world to bring new scholarship and ideas to light as well as to promote the work and value of Black American artists. In the United States, curators demographically have been predominantly white. A survey conducted by the Mellon Foundation with the Association of Art Museum Directors in 2018 found that 84 percent of curators in American art institutions were white, with African Americans representing only 4 percent of all intellectual leadership roles in American institutions.[5] In this context, the Black curator becomes essential to broadening the discourse around the endeavors of Black artists and for providing the frameworks in which depictions of the Black experience are perceived, historicized, and reviewed. Even though Black Americans have traditionally made up a small percentage of curators in the United States, Black curators have long been engaged in countering the narrow reception that Black artists receive from the mainstream art world.

The growing recognition of diverse perspectives in curatorial departments makes documenting the contributions of Black curators through oral history even more essential. *Black Curators Matter* follows the oral history model that has been used by our partner the Columbia University Center for Oral History Research since its founding in 1948. We also take inspiration from the artists and archivists Camille Billops and James Hatch who, in 1970, began their Hatch-Billops Oral History of Black Culture in the milieu of New York cultural activism.[6] Black curators have fundamentally transformed the art world through their work and determination. *Black Curators Matter* documents this transformation by capturing firsthand accounts of Black curatorial leadership and its impact on American art institutions.

PERIODS OF INQUIRY

Black Curators Matter is focused by design, following a chronological structure. This oral history project foregrounds the histories of six vanguard curators who rose to prominence in the curatorial field in the period from the 1970s to the 2000s. Their exhibitions and writing unify aesthetic qualities with social politics, initiating new critical dialogues about beauty, diversity of resources, alternative histories, and modes of looking that interrogate the systems of power that define and assign value.

1970S–1980S

The first two curators featured in this project are Lowery Stokes Sims and Deborah Willis. Both entered the field following their coming of age during the civil rights and Black power movements of the 1960s and 1970s. Sims began working at the Met in 1972 in the Community Programs Department and then became the museum's first Black curator. Her tenure at the museum lasted until 1999, after which she served as director of the Studio Museum until 2007. Willis served as the curator of photography and prints at the Schomburg Center for Research in Black Culture from 1980 to 1992. She became associate director for Research and Collections and exhibitions curator at the Center for African American History and Culture from 1992 to 2000, now known as the National Museum of African American History and Culture. Willis is currently a professor of photographic history at New York University's Tisch School of the Arts.

1980S–1990S

The narratives of Kellie Jones and Richard J. Powell showcase how they carved out careers by beginning in community institutions that supported Black artists. Jones's early positions at the Studio Museum and the Jamaica Arts Center positioned her to be an advocate for contemporary Black artists. Her role as both a curator and academic has led to innovative and scholarly research on previously underrepresented Black artists, including David Hammons, Senga Nengudi, Maren Hassinger, Dawoud Bey, and Lorna Simpson. Since 1989, Powell has been a member of the art history faculty at Duke University. His research, including his important survey text *Black Art: A Cultural History* (2021), has been influential in the field of African American art history. His early position in the 1980s as program director at the Washington Project for the Arts, an alternative art space in Washington, DC, set the stage for his career-long engagement with both historical and contemporary Black artists.

1990S–2000S

The careers of Thelma Golden and Franklin Sirmans demonstrate how the growing significance of multiculturalism, audience diversity, and academic critical and theoretical engagement made an impact on the art world during this last decade of the twentieth century. An increasingly globalized art world in the late 1990s and early 2000s gave Black exhibitionary projects a wider Black diasporic platform. Golden began her career at the Studio Museum in 1987, later becoming the first Black curator at the Whitney in the early 1990s. Among her shows, *Black Male: Representations of Masculinity in Contemporary American Art* (1994–95) at the Whitney was groundbreaking, offering unprecedented representation of Black artists and incisive sociopolitical commentary within a predominately white institutional context. Golden is currently the director and chief curator of the Studio Museum; she is the longest-serving director in the institution's history. Sirmans's early role in publications at the Dia Art Foundation starting in 1993 and work as an international art critic helped launch his curatorial career. In 2006, he was appointed curator of modern and contemporary art at the Menil Collection in Houston. He then served as department head and curator of contemporary art at the Los Angeles County Museum of Art. Sirmans is currently the director of the Pérez Art Museum Miami.

The work of the curators showcased in this oral history project as well as those that came before them reminds us not only of our past but also our potential futures. Their experiences illuminate the curatorial process and its connections to other forms of scholarship responsible for accurately retelling American and global histories. Their voices and personal observations have been instrumental in shaping the current curatorial field, illuminating the profound ways Black curatorial perspectives have enriched the art world and culture at large. We understand the project can expand and develop in many ways, regionally or internationally, and hope to inspire others to document more aspects of a broader, worldwide curatorial and museum story.

Notes

1. Timothy Rub, foreword to *Represent: 200 Years of African American Art in the Philadelphia Museum of Art*, by Gwendolyn DuBois Shaw, exh. cat. (Philadelphia Museum of Art, 2014), vii.
2. Bridget R. Cooks, *Exhibiting Blackness: African Americans and the American Art Museum* (University of Massachusetts Press, 2011).
3. Mabel Wilson, *Negro Building: Black Americans in the World of Fairs and Museums* (University of California Press, 2012).
4. Kellie Jones, *South of Pico: African American Artists in Los Angeles in the 1960s and 1970s* (Duke University Press, 2017).
5. Mariët Westermann, Liam Sweeney, and Roger C. Schonfeld, *Art Museum Staff Demographic Survey 2018* (Andrew W. Mellon Foundation and Ithaka S+R, 2018), https://doi.org/10.18665/sr.310935.
6. The Camille Billops and James V. Hatch Archives, Stuart A. Rose Manuscript, Archives, and Rare Book Library, Emory University, Atlanta, Georgia, http://rose.library.emory.edu/collections/african-american-history-culture/billops-hatch-archives.html.

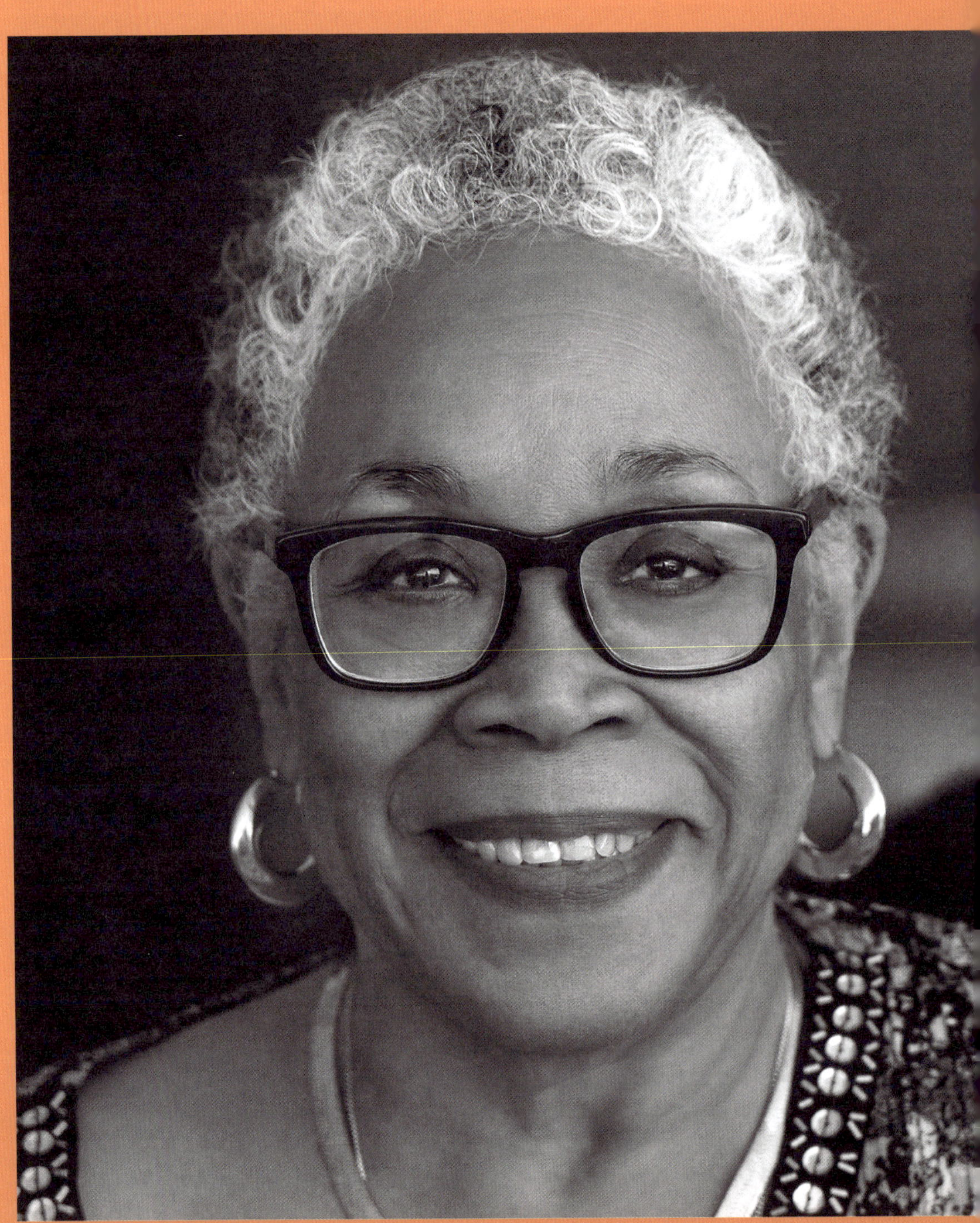

Lowery Stokes Sims

INTERVIEWED BY ASHLEY JAMES
28 April and 6 May 2022

ASHLEY JAMES (AJ): I'm very interested in your upbringing and, more generally, the kinds of upbringing that Black curators have had to get into this very specialized field. Even for a white person, it's hard to get into the curatorial field, let alone a Black child who grew up middle- and working-class.

LOWERY STOKES SIMS (LSS): I was born in Washington, DC, in 1949, when my father was attending Howard University's architecture school and simultaneously working in an ice cream factory during the day to support my mother and me. He had been raised in Tennessee on a farm and left to join the war, rather late because he was the only son in the family. He met my mother when he was stationed at Camp Shanks in upstate New York. I have about seventy letters that I'm working on that chronicle their romance and interactions between 1943 and 1946.

We moved to New York in 1950. We first lived in a Quonset hut. I have some unusually vivid memories of the circular dome of that house. Soon after, my brother was born and, by that time, we had moved to the newly inhabited Harlem River Houses. We stayed there until I was six. In the meantime, my sister was born. There are about two years between the three of us. Then we moved out to Queens and were all enrolled in Catholic school. We were all baptized Catholic, which I never understood because my mother's family seemed to have been Episcopalian and my father's family was Baptist. My father later revealed himself to be an avowed atheist, although he was confirmed in the Episcopal Church when he married my stepmother many, many years later. I think he was just a religious roamer. From the very beginning, my parents had us all involved in the arts, obviously because my father was an architect. He worked in various architecture firms throughout the 1950s.

My mother was an interesting case because she came from a rather prosperous family in Virginia. We've done some genealogy and discovered that the family seat was in Farmville, Virginia. In the late 1990s, I went down with my mom and met some cousins. I found out that the family owned a lot of land at some point and there is a road named after my family, Stokes, which is my middle name and my grandmother's maiden name. My grandmother instilled in my mother the value of culture. When my mother was raising us, her credo was, "Culture is free and available. You can get standing room at the opera, you can go to museums for free, libraries for free."

When I was fourteen, I trudged into Manhattan to see the *Mona Lisa* when it came to the Metropolitan Museum of Art. When I was sixteen, my mother took me to get a job at Woolworth's as a saleswoman, which I think was her strategy for me to understand that that was not how I was supposed to spend my career. I took the money I earned and purchased a membership at the Met. I once described myself as a real art nerd.

In 1970, I came down to Baltimore for graduate school after getting my BA in art history at Queens College and studied art history for two years at Johns Hopkins University with a fellowship from the Ford Foundation. I was recruited by the head of the art history department, the art historian John White. I didn't focus on it at the time, but clearly they were interested in adding Black students to the program. In a way, I followed my longtime friend and fellow troublemaker Leslie King-Hammond, who preceded me by a year. I was enrolled in the PhD program, but after two years I got restless. I kept meeting students who were taking ten years to finish their doctoral program and I decided that I was not interested in deferring getting a job. By my first year in grad school, I had already applied for a job at the Met through one of my former classmates at Queens College who worked in the museum's High School Programs Department. I went and interviewed with Philip Yenawine, who's still a friend today. He told me he loved me and that I was fabulous, but on reconsideration, he wanted to hire an artist, so he hired Randy Williams.

A year later, in 1972, after I'd decided to finish my MA at Johns Hopkins University and had sent out a few resumes, I was contacted by the Met about another position in the Community Programs Department, which was part of the larger Education Department. I had my interview with the then-incoming head of the department, Cathy Chance, and we agreed we could work together. Then I had an interview with Harry Parker, who was the vice president of education. Harry was a great guy. At one point in our conversation, he said to me, "You know, Lowery, I just want you to know that sometimes situations can get a little difficult. I hope that if you run into any problems that you'll come talk to us first before going to the press." So, I said, "Oh, sure, no problem. And I hope if I say anything untoward that you will call me on the carpet."

He looked at me, and I said, "Harry, not all Black people like all white people, you know what I mean?" I found out later that my hiring was a stopgap measure following the departure of another Black woman who had left the Met under less-than-ideal circumstances. So, I started working in community programs and found a very congenial, multi-cultural group of people to work with. I used that platform to establish relationships with individuals working in various communities and organizations throughout New York City, outside the Met. In the wake of the controversies around the exhibition *Harlem on My Mind: The Cultural Capital of Black America, 1900–1968* [1969], the Community Programs Department was to provide a kind of decentralized access to the Met's resources. As I look back on it now, I realize that I had been primed for this type of experience through a job I previously had with the Education Department at the Brooklyn Museum for six months in early 1970, where I worked with Joy Sales to bring African art objects to art classes in public schools. The art had been donated by Merton Simpson, one of the best-known African art dealers, who was also a well-known mid-twentieth-century Black artist [fig. 1.1].

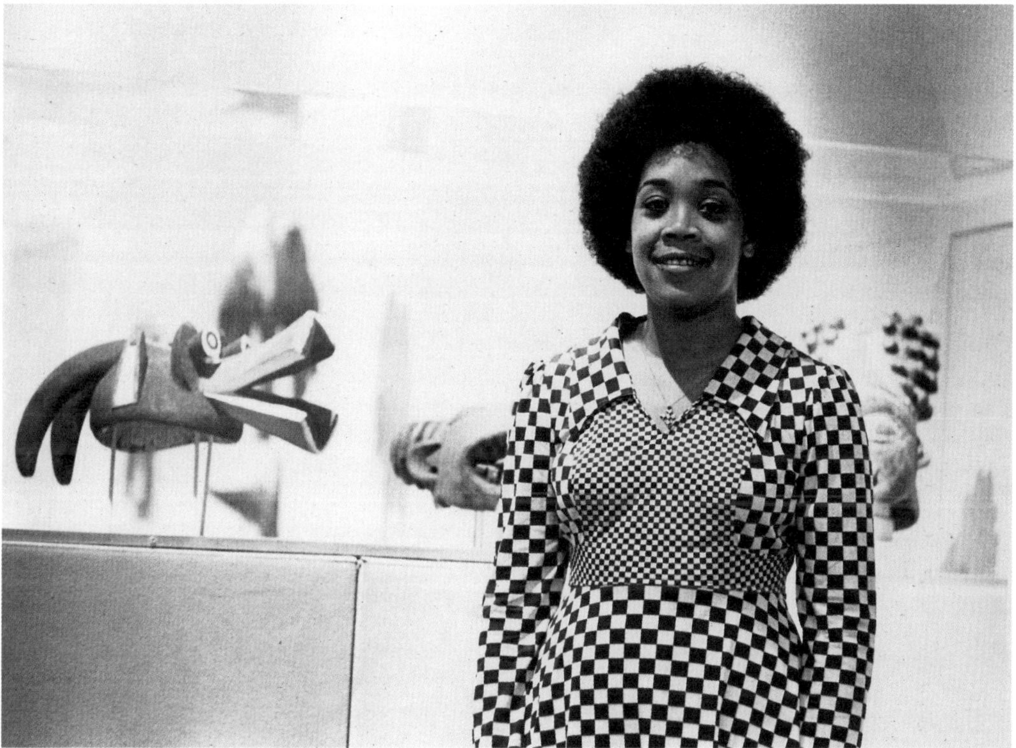

Fig. 1.1 Lowery Stokes Sims in the Arts of Africa galleries at the Metropolitan Museum of Art, New York, 1972.

Through my position in community programs, I worked with organizations such as the Studio Museum in Harlem, the Queens Museum, El Museo del Barrio, the American Indian Community House, and the Basement Workshop in Chinatown. That's really how I developed my cohort of colleagues who are still with me today, and who really helped me form a sense of what my mission would be if I stayed at the Met; this all involved what we now call "diversity and inclusion." My goal became to get as many artists of color, women, and underrecognized white male artists as I could into the museum.

After a couple of years, I looked around the job market because I really wanted to get into a position where I could have a real impact. Even by 1972, 1973, 1974, it became clear that all those kinds of community outreach programs in museums had a limited shelf life. So, I thought, "Well, the thing to do is enter curatorial work because there you would have an impact on the collections, artists, and exhibitions." I just willy-nilly applied for every curatorial assistant job that came up. After all, I was a Phi Beta Kappa graduate of Queens College, had my master's in art history from Johns Hopkins University, and had studied regular white people's art history; however, given the resources available to me, I had to teach myself African, African American, and Caribbean art history. But I kept getting the reaction: "You don't have any experience." So, my question became, "Who's going to give me the experience?"

AJ: Who's going to give you the experience?

LSS: The answer came in the person of Henry Geldzahler, who was then the curator of twentieth-century art at the Met. In 1975, his longtime assistant, Kay Bearman, was leaving, so there was a position coming up in his department. There, it got political again. Eleanor Holmes Norton, the congresswoman representing Washington, DC, was then head of the Equal Employment Opportunity Commission of the City of New York. She put an affirmative action lean on the Met.

AJ: Oh, wow.

LSS: So guess who became the poster child [*laughs*], with the potential to be vaulted into this curatorial position but *moi.*

It all worked out, but I would say for the first year or two that I was in the curatorial position, I was trying to catch up, get the thing going. Most of my curatorial colleagues just looked at me and said, "Well, you just got the job because you're Black." So I said, "Okay." You know, not that anyone would recognize that I knew any art history. I mean, God forbid. [*Laughs.*]

Another thing I did during the 1980s was go back to graduate school. I did that because when I first went back to New York and was first working in community programs, I had enrolled at Columbia University because I still had the fellowship from the Ford Foundation. I ran into trouble because I was working at the Met, teaching at the School of Visual Arts, and taking coursework. I was given the distinct message that if I were not enrolled in Columbia full-time, I was not serious and couldn't continue. So, I quit. I think I took courses for two semesters. But by the late 1970s, thankfully, the Graduate Center of the City University of New York [CUNY] had opened, so I was able to reunite with professors that I had had as an undergraduate at Queens College, which was also part of the CUNY system.

It took me about fifteen years of coursework and writing to finish, but, ultimately, I did it. In the meanwhile, Henry had left the museum in 1978 to become the commissioner of cultural affairs for New York City. Thomas Hess, the famed editor at *Art News* and the then-newish *New York Magazine,* assumed chairmanship of the department. He died after only a few months, so I was appointed acting head of the department. That lasted for about eighteen months until William Lieberman left the Museum of Modern Art [MoMA] to be the chairman of the department in 1979. His arrival heralded the opening of a new wing for modern and contemporary art in 1987. In 1988, I got my first real serious exhibition assignment: the artwork of Stuart Davis. The exhibition, *Stuart Davis: American Painter,* opened in 1991 [fig. 1.2].

This was also the time during which I was dealing with the nitty-gritty of curatorial work and how my personal interests interfaced with institutional priorities. Because of all the personal professional contacts I had, I developed a strong alternative career of writing and curating outside of the Met. The impetus for this was an experience I had in the late 1970s when I was first working with Henry. The Bedford

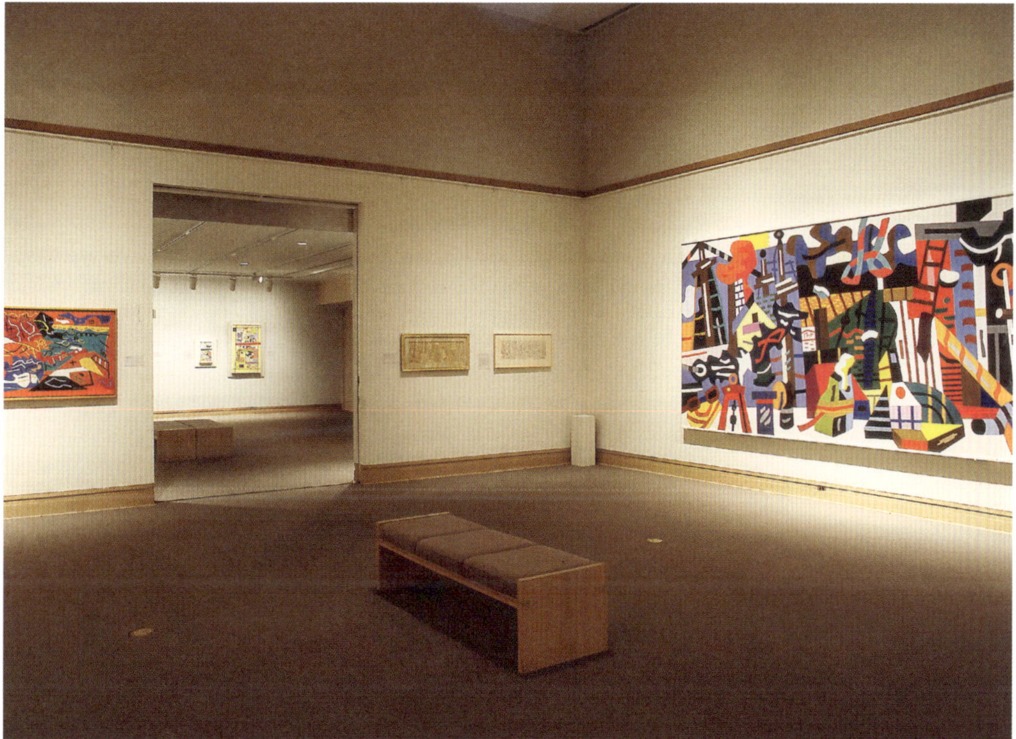

Fig. 1.2 Installation view of *Stuart Davis: American Painter,* curated by Lowery Stokes Sims, Metropolitan Museum of Art, New York, 23 November 1991–16 February 1992.

Stuyvesant Restoration Corporation asked us to do a small exhibition in their gallery of works by Black artists in the Met's collection [*Selected Works by Black Artists from the Collection of the Metropolitan Museum of Art* (1976)]. I was given that assignment and I wrote an essay for the accompanying publication [fig. 1.3]. It was an analysis of the situation of Black artists and what it would take to promote them to the position they should have been in, which would require the work of a coalition of critics, curators, collectors, et cetera, et cetera. I guess it was a little too political because it was not accepted. If you tell me it's too political, that's fine, but then the higher-ups tried to tell me that I could not write. The one thing I knew was that I can write. So, I wrote some nebulous sort of thing and they were happy. But that experience really spurred me to accept and seek curatorial and writing opportunities outside the Met so that I could get a sense of my skill set outside institutional politics.

Years later, I curated the Stuart Davis show with Bill [William C.] Agee, who was working on the catalogue raisonné of Davis's work at that time—it got finished much later. For the catalogue raisonné, Bill had been collaborating with a number of scholars, whom I then commissioned to write essays for the Met's exhibition catalog on Davis. During the installation for the show, I was in the galleries, and Philippe de Montebello came down and he said, "I've just heard from the College Art Association that you have been awarded the Frank Jewett Mather

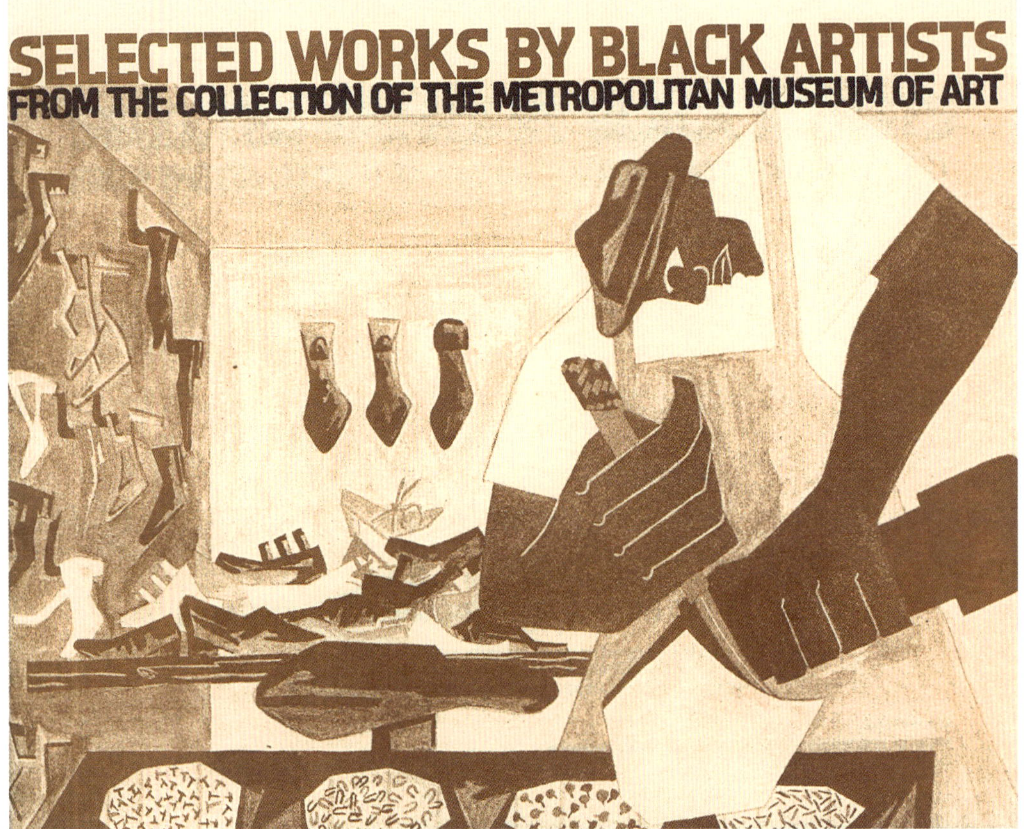

Fig. 1.3 Cover of *Selected Works by Black Artists from the Collection of the Metropolitan Museum of Art*, exh. cat. (Metropolitan Museum of Art, 1976).

Award for distinction in art criticism." And I knew the next question on his mind—and he was trying to figure out how to say it—was "What did you get it for?" Right? [*Laughs.*]

AJ: Yes.

LSS: I said to him, "I got it for all the outside work I've been doing over the years." Then the museum started embracing my activities. Throughout the 1990s, I spent my time finishing my graduate courses, writing my dissertation, and doing some exhibitions and some traveling. I did a lot of the traveling as a courier for loans from the Met. Some of these aided and abetted in financing my research trips to Paris for my dissertation on Wifredo Lam, which I published as a book with the University of Texas Press in 2002. In the meantime, many other things were going on in my life, including dealing with my father's poor health before he died in 1999. I was also moving around the art world, and various people associated with the Studio Museum would kind of whisper in my ear, "You know, we want to talk to you about the Studio

Museum." In 1999, the Studio Museum announced that the then-director Kinshasha Holman Conwill was leaving for another job and so they approached me. At that point, I said would never be a wife or a director. [*Laughs.*] But, I was fifty years old and had achieved about everything I wanted at the Met: I had finally gotten promoted to full curator, thanks to the museum's associate director, Jennifer Russell.

My father was also dying, and when your first parent dies, the gate that separates you from your own mortality starts to open. You think, "Well, better go for it!" So, I had conversations with the Studio Museum. At that same time, Thelma Golden was facing challenges at the Whitney Museum of American Art with Maxwell Anderson, who was the new director. I said to the Studio Museum, "Well, I don't want to do this forever and I think Thelma would be a good candidate." I think the makeup of the Studio Museum board at that time wasn't conducive to that proposition, but I knew that the board president could fix the situation in a couple of years and Thelma could take over. I accepted, but I said, "I'm hiring Thelma." And Thelma said, "I'd love to come on as your chief curator." I told her, "No, you're going to be deputy director for exhibitions and programs." This was because I had always observed that, at the Met, education was an afterthought. I wanted to make sure that curatorial and education work together smoothly.

Thelma then recommended that I hire Sandra Jackson-Dumont, who ran the Lucas Museum of Narrative Art from 2020 to 2025, as the head of education. People used to call me and Thelma the "dynamic duo," but it was really a tripartite force: me, Thelma, and Sandra. We revitalized the Studio Museum and supervised the building renovation that had already been in the works. After about four years, we had a board retreat, and I said, "I'm exhausted. It is time to make the change." They didn't want to quite let me go, so they created a presidency for me, and Thelma came on as director. I worked in that position for about a year. I had become chair of those famous Cultural Institutions Groups [CIG]. I was very involved in the advocacy and the lobbying around the city budget and learned a lot from that. I worked very closely with Janet Schneider, who was the most savvy executive director for the CIGs. It was a very political moment. This was, let me see, 2004 or 2005.

AJ: Was this toward the end of your time at the Studio Museum?

LSS: Yes, I stayed until 2007. I have often said that leaving the Met, directing the Studio Museum, and working with the CIGs were experiences that really prepared me for the rest of my life. I learned how to really maneuver politically—and that became important as I was taking care of aging parents and figuring out how to get what I needed for my life. Those experiences were really stellar. So here we are, 2006, 2007, and I wanted to segue away from the Studio Museum to give them space.

Then Holly Hotchner and the Museum of Arts and Design [MAD] entered my life through my relationship with Barbara Karp Shuster, a MAD board member who was also on the Studio Museum's acquisition committee. They had just recently rebranded themselves from the American Craft Museum to the Museum of Arts and Design to explore the interaction among the fine arts, craft, and design. They wanted a person who would cover the fine arts aspect but also had a sensibility for and perspectives on design and craft and could work along with the curators in those areas. Holly and I had lunch and discussed all this, and she said, "I'll take you any way you want. Do you want to come on part-time? Do you want to come as a consultant?" I went home and thought, "Well, maybe I could work part-time here, part-time there." But at that time, my fifty-eight-year-old knees were failing me and I was going to have knee replacement surgery. I thought to myself, "What, are you crazy? You're going to be running all over the city. Take the freaking job at MAD." So I did. I started working part-time on alternate weeks when I wasn't going to Minneapolis because I'd committed to teach in the art department at the University of Minnesota Twin Cities with Clarence Morgan and Tom [Thomas] Rose. I had told Holly that I wouldn't be able to start until January 2008, but she said, "No, we need you now, because we're opening up a new building in a year, and we need you to have input and be in our inaugural exhibition." I started full-time in January 2008 and had my knees replaced in April.

I would describe MAD as the best curatorial experience of my career because they let me do anything I wanted to. I just had to raise the money, which I did. The first show I worked on after the inaugural exhibition *Second Lives: Remixing the Ordinary* [2008–9] in MAD's new building was *The Global Africa Project* [2010–11]. Immediately, I pulled in Leslie, who had transitioned from the dean of graduate studies at the Maryland Institute College of Art to the founding director at the institute's Center for Race and Culture. Leslie and I had done a lot of projects together, including the exhibition *Art as a Verb: The Evolving Continuum* [1988–89], which looked at performance and installation work by Black artists [fig. 1.4]. From 2021 to 2023, there was a gallery installation in MoMA dedicated to the idea of *Art as a Verb.* I find that astonishing.

When Leslie and I worked on *The Global Africa Project* together, it was 2008 [figs. 1.5–1.7]. Due to the economic crisis, we had no travel money. But it was interesting, because contemporary African art had gained enough of a foothold in this country that we could find works here. I worked with a fantastic development person at MAD, Judith Kamien, who sourced out support from the Robert Sterling Clark Foundation, because Peggy [Margaret] Ayers, the foundation's program officer, was interested in intercultural exchange. So, we got a big chunk of money from them and we also got support from Darren Walker at the Ford Foundation. We were able to use that money to bring about thirty of maybe ninety artists that we had in the show to the opening. The timing was rather exquisite because when we did *The Global Africa Project,* it was right when South Africa was hosting the World Cup.

I also have to single out the incredible support that Darren has given me during my professional life, back to when I was the director of the Studio Museum and he was the CEO of the Abyssinian Development Corporation. I would also be remiss if I didn't mention Erana Stennett, a stalwart force at Bloomberg.

After *The Global Africa Project,* I decided to tackle design, craft, and art in Latin America for my next exhibition, *New Territories: Laboratories*

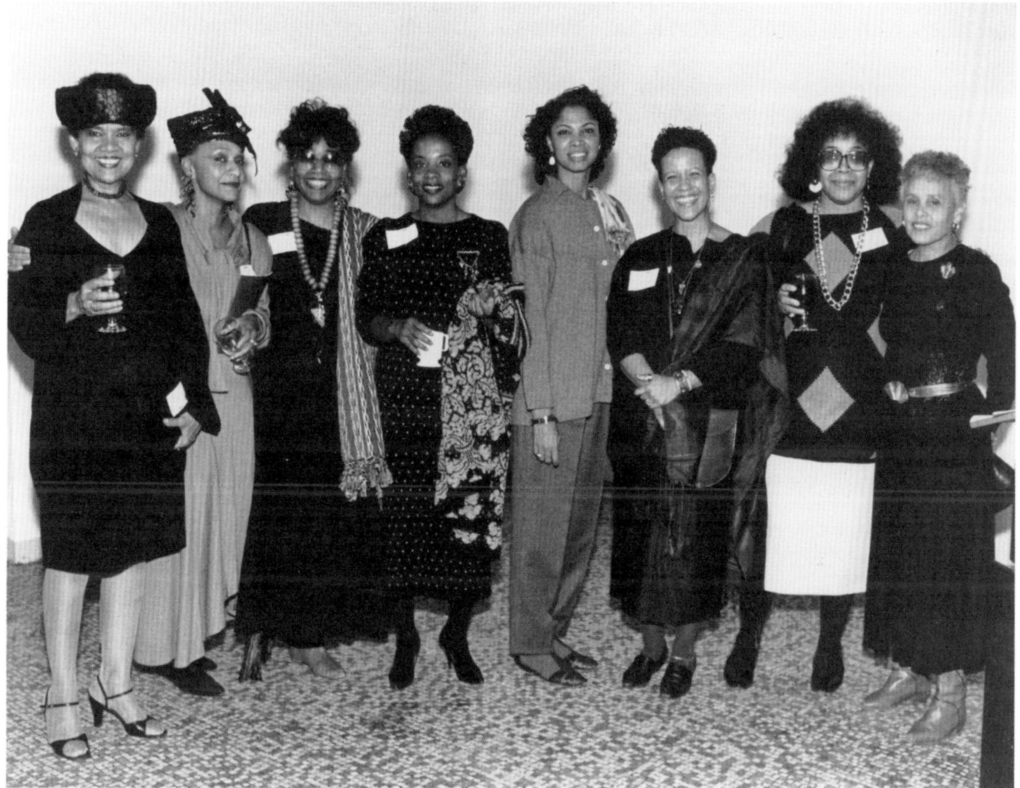

Fig. 1.4 *Left to right:* Lorraine O'Grady, Joyce Scott, Leslie King-Hammond, Martha Jackson-Jarvis, Candace Hill-Montgomery, Kaylynn Sullivan TwoTrees, Lowery Stokes Sims, and Betye Saar, at the opening of *Art as a Verb: The Evolving Continuum,* Maryland Institute College of Art, Baltimore, 1988–89.

for Design, Craft and Art in Latin America [2014–15]. After attending a panel discussion at the Americas Society, I decided that for *New Territories,* I should have a more formal advisory committee. I put together an advisory committee of about six people and got some more money from the Robert Sterling Clark Foundation to do three convenings. We did two in New York and one in Mexico City. I decided on the exhibition title because I'd seen that an installation by the noted Italian designer Gaetano Pesce was featured at the Collective Design Fair. In this installation, Pesce had a statement about how the exploration of the relationship between art and design would lead to new territories in art.

By the time I opened *New Territories* in 2014, I was sixty-five and had applied for Social Security and Medicare. So I retired. However, I was contacted by Suzanne Isken, who was the director of what was then the Craft and Folk Art Museum, now Craft Contemporary, in Los Angeles. Suzanne asked me to work with her to conceive a project for the upcoming Pacific Standard Time festival being organized by the Getty across Southern California from 2017 to 2018. The theme was Latin America and Latino art in Los Angeles. My first thought was to

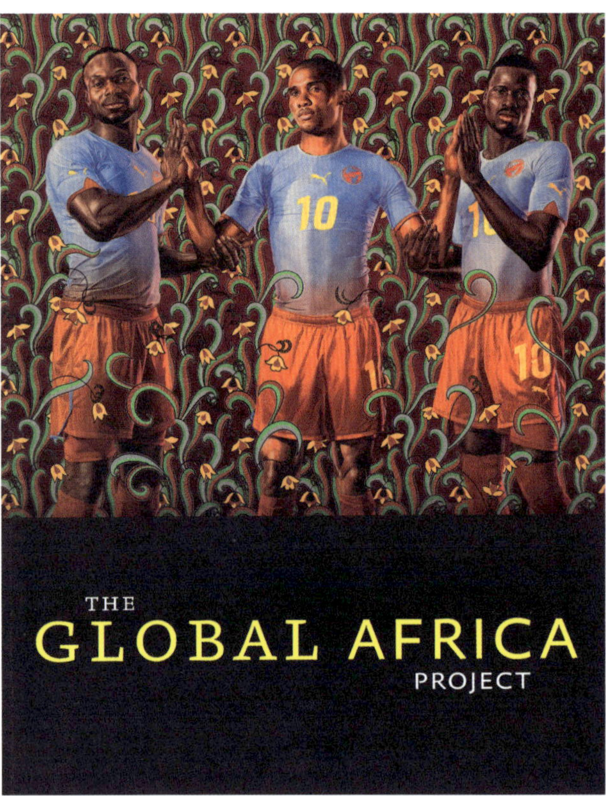

Fig. 1.5 Cover of *The Global Africa Project*, ed. Lowery Stokes Sims et al., exh. cat. (Museum of Arts and Design, 2010).

Fig. 1.6 Installation view of *The Global Africa Project*, curated by Lowery Stokes Sims and Leslie King-Hammond, Museum of Arts and Design, New York, 17 November 2010–15 May 2011.

Fig. 1.7 Installation view of *The Global Africa Project*, curated by Lowery Stokes Sims and Leslie King-Hammond, Museum of Arts and Design, New York, 17 November 2010–15 May 2011.

suggest an exhibition about Latin American design sensibilities in the United States since *New Territories* dealt with designers working in the various countries and areas of Central and South America. Suzanne and I met up when I did a ten-day compressed visiting professorship at the University of California, Irvine. We put together a preliminary proposal that got us started, and then right after I retired in 2015, Suzanne brought me out to Los Angeles and I started planning things with her very savvy and smart staff. The amazing Chicana artist, Amalia Mesa-Bains, who was a longtime friend of mine, was one of the advisors, along with Tanya Aguiñiga, who is a designer working on and across the Mexico-US border. Eventually, we realized that what we were talking about was border culture. The result was the exhibition *The US-Mexico Border: Place, Imagination, and Possibilities* [2018]. It was a fantastic experience for a New Yorker like me to visit El Paso and Tijuana and experience in-between spaces with the border fence, meet all the intrepid artists, and visit valiant art organizations in the area.

Among the other projects I've worked on over the last decade include: a retrospective of Joyce Scott at Grounds for Sculpture with Patterson Sims [*Joyce J. Scott: Harriet Tubman and Other Truths* (2018)] and the show *Home, Memory, and Future* [2016–17] to commemorate the Caribbean Cultural Center African Diaspora Institute's opening of their new space in East Harlem. What else did I do? I worked with the Baltimore Museum of Art recently on *Guarding the Art* [2022] as a mentor to the security staff who curated the exhibition from the

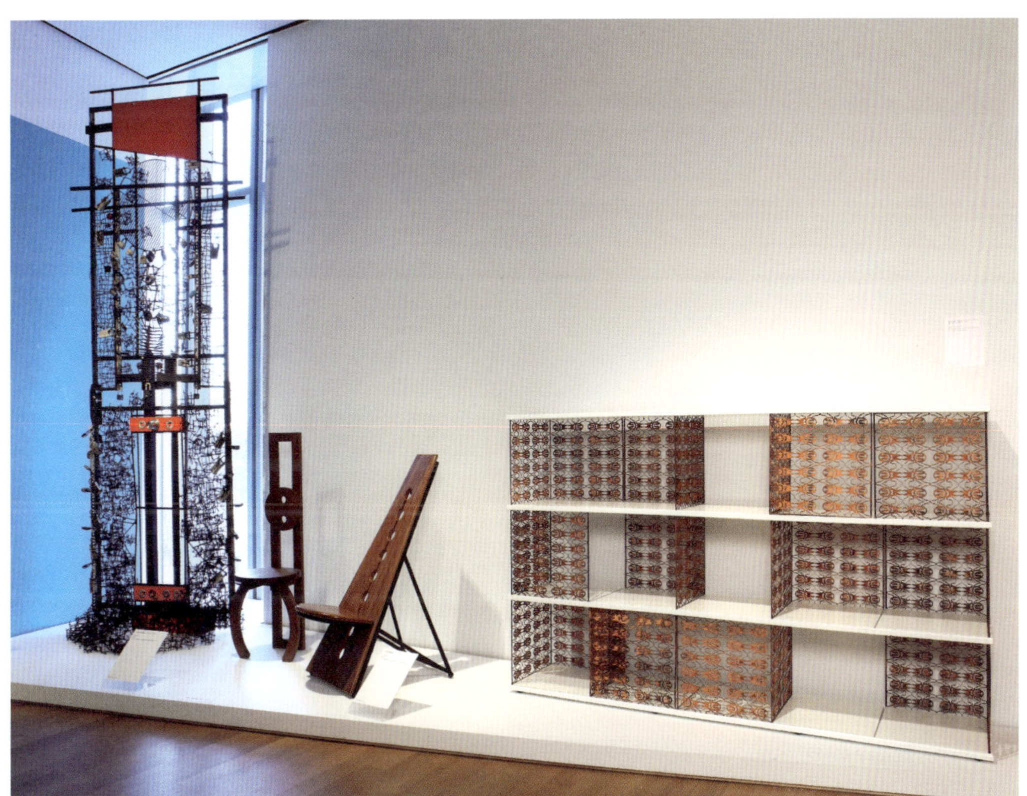

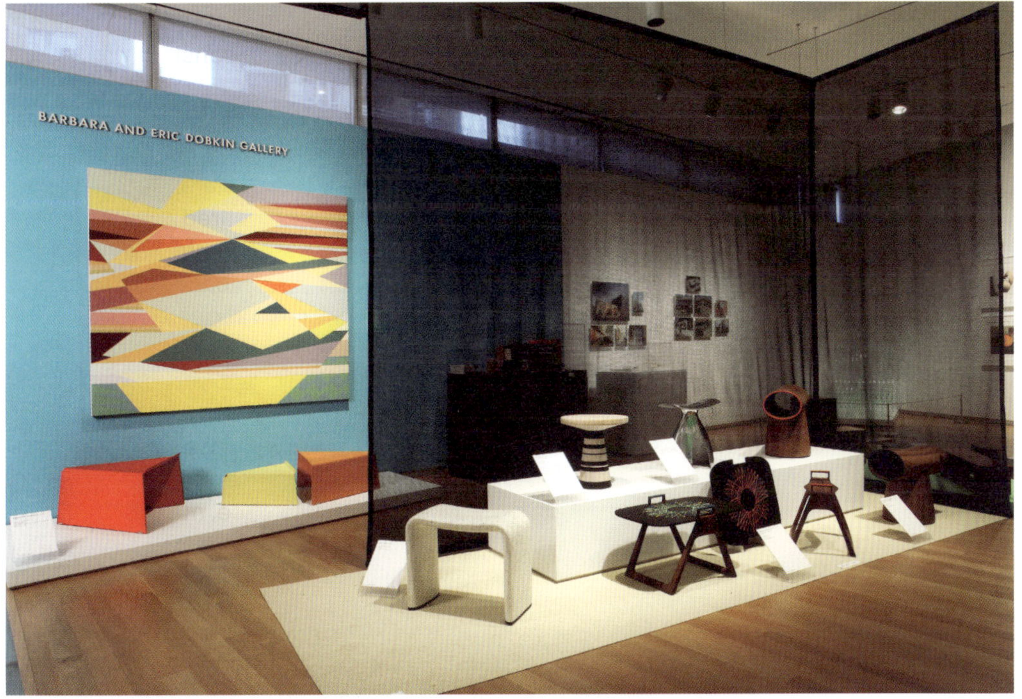
BARBARA AND ERIC DOBKIN GALLERY

permanent collection. I did a whole bunch of other stuff, including a retrospective on Oletha DeVane at the University of Maryland, Baltimore County, in 2022, so I guess that brings us up to today.

AJ: Oh gosh, oh yes, absolutely. That's amazing, I think it points to the way that you have been able to think multigenerationally *and* collectively. I have many follow-up questions, but I want to bring it back to the beginning, to think about your family and how they brought you up as a person. I'm so fascinated by the confidence, integrity, and ethics around the way that you've moved through the art world. I would love to hear about how you continued to interact with your family throughout these different phases. Did they give you advice? Were you telling them all about what was happening? What was that kind of exchange?

LSS: It was kind of interesting because when I was working at the Met early on, my mother decided to go back to work after years of being a stay-at-home mom. She was working for Upward Bound, a program for preschoolers, and quickly became tired of the librarians telling her what books to read with the kids because she had taught my brother, sister, and me how to read even before we entered kindergarten. She was very dedicated to literacy, and when I meet people I grew up with in our neighborhood, they say, "Oh, your mother, she was always throwing books at us." I have a little plaque that she received in recognition for her work in adult literacy. When she went back to get her master's degree in library science, we shared a lot of information, and I could tell her how to do things. My father was as much a builder as he was an architect in the old, traditional sense of Black architecture, going back to the turn of the century, like at Tuskegee and Howard Universities. My brother gravitated towards science, acting, and building. But he dropped out three credits short of his degree—which he eventually finished and started a career in contracting and building in San Francisco, where he's been ever since. Finally, at the age of forty-five, he put down his tools and became a building inspector. And, of course, my sister became a classical ballet dancer in the 1970s and danced in Canada, Switzerland, and Germany before coming back to the United States and eventually being hired by the American Ballet Theatre in 1978. She then crafted a post-ballet career in costume design and worked at Disneyland Paris until her retirement in 2018.

The other day when my sister and I were talking, she said, "I remember dad told me that life was like a long corridor with a lot of doors. And all through your life, you're going to try different doors, some will open, some won't. Some you can go through, you get there, you don't fit, you go out, and you find another one that opens." I think that was an excellent metaphor for what he gave us. He helped me through the management/staff relations I first faced. I remember he told me, "You may think that something is happening to you because you're Black and a woman. But look at what is happening to the white person working next to you." He really instilled a sense of pragmatism in me.

I would be remiss in not mentioning the fact that I was really fortunate in having a lot of people who supported me along the way. During my years at the Met as a curator, there were several women dealers who listened to me, discussed art with me, and took me to dinner—whether I bought art from them or not: Jill Kornblee, Rosa Esman, Bella Fishko, Joan Washburn, Grace Borgenicht Brandt, Terry Dintenfass, and Rachel Adler. I benefited from learning about their experiences as women in the art world. Then there's my eternal cohort of people whom I met through community programs and through the early discussions of multiculturalism in the 1980s—not only Leslie but also Jaune Quick-to-See Smith, Margo Machida, Napoleon Jones-Henderson, Edgar Heap of Birds, and Amalia Mesa-Bains. These are all people with whom I shared aspirations, cultural dreams. We remarked on the commonalities of our experiences and perspectives and respected our differences. I'm lucky that I'm still in contact with them to this day. And we're still fighting the same battles.

AJ: I face certain things as a Black curator in 2023, but I can only imagine what the late 1960s were like, showing up as a young Black girl in these spaces. I'm curious about the racial dynamics, for example, when you visited the Met and other museums as a young child or when you were first employed by the Met in 1972. How did you navigate all this? What was the culture or the feel of the atmosphere like on a racial level?

LSS: You know, that's interesting. When I became a curator and had to visit different collectors and patrons on Park Avenue, Fifth Avenue, and Madison Avenue, very often the doorman directed me to the service entrance around the corner. I would tell them, "No, I'm from the Metropolitan Museum of Art and I am here to see so-and so. Please call up." Then they would call up and direct me to the elevator. It must have been in the 1990s when a young Black woman from the Columbia University Graduate School of Journalism interviewed me and asked, "How can you work in a place where you know that everybody hates you?" I said, "I don't think that everybody hates me, actively. And if I worried about what people thought about me, I would not get out of bed in the morning. I just don't care. You just have to respect me."

Now with the increased presence of young African Americans working in museums, there are questions about how to integrate them into institutional life. I think it's really simple: They want to be taken seriously and respected, and not have you second-guess them, patronize them, or be outright hostile toward them for no reason. When I first entered the field, I didn't have expectations about the art world and the larger world and how I would be received, so you knew you were going to face resistance and have to navigate unexpected circumstances. One of my favorite memories is a courier trip I took to Japan. I had ten days' notice and didn't know quite what to expect, but that didn't stop me. The Met had been doing a lot of exchanges with Japan, and the men in particular would come back with these tales of being pampered by geishas and stuff like that. [*Laughs.*] But when I got off the thirteen-hour flight and found my way to the luggage area, three people were there to meet me—I think a woman and two men with my name on a sign. I smiled and, as I approached them, I could see on their faces what they're thinking: "Oh God, she's a woman, and she's Black." [*Laughs.*]

When I went to Cuba for the first Havana Biennial, in 1984, I gave a presentation on Wifredo Lam, whom I had just started researching for my doctoral studies. I mentioned his association with proponents of anticolonialism such as Léopold Sédar Senghor, Léon-Gontran Damas, and Aimé Césaire. During the feedback session, I was challenged for associating him with individuals who were considered "imperialist lackeys," so I had to reiterate that I was focusing on them in the 1930s and 1940s when their politics were more leftist. When I got down off the stage, the woman whom I'd met the night before came to me and said, "Can you come with me?" And in the back was a whole group of Black Cubans, students and people, and they told me that they couldn't believe I'd associated Lam with negritude because any illusion to race or racism was not accepted in Cuban society at that point.

These experiences made me aware of different cultural perceptions, even when I shared a racial presentation with people. When Howardena Pindell and I were in Nigeria in a group taxi in 1973, and this pompous Englishman got out, the cab driver was chuckling. We asked him, "Well, what are you laughing at?" He says, "I'm going to tell you a funny thing about white people." And he turned around and said, "You all are Negros, aren't you?" Howardena and I looked at each other and said, "Yes, last time we looked." When I went to Brazil in 2013, I hired Adriana Kertzer, whose father was from Brazil, to be my guide and interpreter. I deliberately did not speak Portuguese, so it was interesting as people tried to figure out who or what I was. [*Laughs.*]

AJ: Have a little fun with it.

LSS: Yes. Why not?

AJ: Speaking of Howardena, who I know you've known for a very long time, and traveled to Africa with, gets me back to another question around this idea of the cohort and who was in the orbit. I know that Howardena also had her own and maybe similar experiences as the first Black woman curator at MoMA. I wanted to get a sense from you—you spoke a little bit about community engagement—who were the various people you met that became your cohort? I'm also wondering, once you moved into the curatorial space, was there a kind of new cohort? How did those formations happen? Did you feel like you were more flying solo when it came to the curatorial side?

LSS: I used to do studio visits with Howardena and we'd hang out. Sometimes she'd let me squeeze paint through templates she created from the dots on the surface of her paintings. Let me think about the answer to your question a bit more.

AJ: Let's begin with the Met in the 1970s. You mentioned that you came in the aftermath of the *Harlem on My Mind* exhibition, which was a disaster for the institution, and they recognized that they had to do something differently. So, starting at the Met roughly three years after that exhibition, what was the feeling? What was the mood in your department? How did you digest that occasion and the aftermath of it? Was it something that you felt you had to respond to? How did it inform your work?

LSS: That's an interesting question. By the time I got there in 1972, they had started the Department of Community Programs and had established a number of programs that encompassed decentralizing the museum and doing outreach. I was assigned to something called the Borough Exhibitions Program, which was essentially a program whereby we worked with smaller arts organizations around the city to create exhibitions from the Met's collection. These organizations could have been Snug Harbor Cultural Center and Botanical Garden, the Queens Museum, or the Bronx Museum of the Arts; in fact, the Met had a lot to do with bringing the latter two into existence. In a sense, I was involved in curatorial work from the beginning. I was not necessarily curating the shows myself because people would say, "Well, we'd like this, or that," but I would negotiate with the appropriate curatorial department to see if they had work that could travel and be available to different organizations. So that's the way it started.

The second program that I was responsible for was something called the Senior Citizen Slide Lecture Program, which was precipitated by an organization—I can't remember the name—that dealt with senior centers. From today's perspective, I would say that the concept of aging and what we now call "assisted living" and things like that were still rather primitive back in the 1970s. But they always wanted some kind of programming for their residents. I was informed about a group of retired teachers—women mostly, and men—who wanted to volunteer at the Met. They had traveled extensively and were not necessarily art people; however, they had visited many cultural institutions in Europe and the United States and were interested in being docents. But the docent cohort, of course, was very upper-class, exclusive, et cetera. This program put together two needs: the needs of senior citizens to have programming and the needs of other retirees who wanted to be involved in the museum. I don't know if it was thought that the retired teachers could relate to older people better, but the program worked. I hired Bob [Robert] Friedman to be an instructor and guide for the volunteers.

This is how I got to know a wide group of people in the city who were associated with a variety of organizations, including El Museo del Barrio, the Studio Museum, the American Indian Community House, and the Basement Workshop. I was sort of swimming in all these conversations about what museums were and how they related to nontraditional communities. I think that really shaped my perspective on things. I didn't have a kind of theoretical or critical approach to museum work, but because I was at the Met, I was aware I had this unique opportunity and I was going to do everything I could to not only promote what we now call diversity but also to make sure that a lot of different voices were heard.

There were a lot of people—like John R. Kinard, who was at Anacostia Community Museum, the filmmaker Topper Carew, and Joan Sandler—who were really smart community activists I met at different conferences and gatherings. We were all comparing notes. I also had a cohort in New York, but I was slowly beginning to get a sense of a national movement, particularly during that time. Philip Morris, which became the Altria Group, was also sponsoring exhibitions of Black artists nationally, so I got to know Caroline Goldsmith, who was a principal there through ArtTable. I got involved with ArtTable through Patricia Hamilton, who was a dealer, and I was one of the founding board members of the organization. So, I would say I was looking outside the Met to get a sense of what my job should be, how I could garner support for what I was doing, and to have an idea of what kinds of steps and principles that I should be espousing as I went through my career. After a couple of years in community programs, I decided that the way I could really have an impact was to go to the curatorial arena.

AJ: I think it's so critical that in your trajectory you began as part of Community Programs in the Education Department at the Met. As you've mentioned, the idea of diversity and community outreach was so organic to that work from the beginning that you didn't even have to theorize it. It was what you were meant to do at that moment. And you've talked also about multiculturalism before it was called *multiculturalism,* of this heterogeneous cohort. I'm wondering how that played out a little bit more specifically, just in thinking about the demographics of New York City. And, in thinking about *Harlem on My Mind,* was there specific talk about outreach to Black populations in general, as in Harlem versus Brooklyn? Was there a sense of who this audience was that the Met needed to reach, or was it really a broad understanding of community outreach? Was that connected to some of the political movements that were happening at the time? I'm wondering how you navigated all this as a Black woman who, of course, was interested in many disparate populations and continues to be.

LSS: One of the concrete things that came out of *Harlem on My Mind* was the founding of the Community Programs Department and putting Arnold Johnson on the board, who was a businessman from Harlem. I don't remember necessarily a specific focus on Harlem; we were going all over the place. I think that goes back to what was expected of the museum through the New York Board of Estimate, whose members were borough presidents. There was a sense of accommodating the needs of many different kinds of communities. Also, at the time—I don't know if they still do—each borough had a representative on the Met board who was not necessarily a borough president but someone prominent in their community. For instance, Muriel Silberstein-Storfer, who was from Staten Island and a very influential and innovative art teacher. She initiated a program of classes for parents and children at the Met that was part of this whole way of how people were looking at art and education and making things a lot more accessible and integrated. Through the years, she worked with an educator named Jane Norman, who then developed a whole course system she taught at the Met based on mathematics and art.

Then Philip Yenawine, who was my contemporary, directed the high school program and created the Arts Awareness Program that brought high school students into the galleries and used dance, music, and poetry to enhance their experience of the arts. There's a great film recorded at the Met that I showed for years after when I was teaching that shows Jeanette Cole playing the harpsichord in front of a Jackson Pollock painting, while the students drew, and Jennifer Muller, the dancer, taking students into the Greek and Roman Art Department, many of them binding their bodies to mimic the broken statuary.

From the beginning, I knew the Art Workers' Coalition, Faith Ringgold's Women Students and Artists for Black Art Liberation, "Where We At" Black Women Artists, the Weusi Artist Collective, and others because the other program that I worked on at the Met, before I went into curatorial work, was the Junior Museum Exhibition Program. If you enter the Met at East Eighty-First Street and you turn right, there's a corridor. In the 1970s, beyond that corridor was the Junior Museum—an installation for children about art and artistic methods and techniques. Off that was a cafeteria. So, what I did was, I organized exhibitions of real, live artists and groups like En Foco, the Black Photographers Annual, and other community arts groups. The work would be installed along that entry corridor, around the walls, and the rest of the cafeteria because those were the only blank walls. And of course, Benny Andrews wrote an article taking me to task for promoting what he called "kitchen art." But for me personally, this experience was invaluable for learning about installing work, getting to know all these different artists and community groups involved in the arts, and getting to know their perspectives, needs, and positioning with regard to larger institutions.

AJ: Eventually, you decide that curatorial "proper" was the place to make your next step. Can you talk about that decision in terms of these questions around impact, and how you can make an impact?

LSS: I think it was very simpleminded. I was thinking, How can a person in the museum make the biggest impact on the future? And I said, "Well, you build a collection, because by bringing works of art into the collection, they then enter the conversation about the larger creativity of humanity." I know that sounds kind of stupid and corny, but that was basically it.

AJ: It's true.

LSS: So how could I do that? By becoming a curator. So, I started applying for curatorial jobs, which kind of shocked everybody. What I didn't realize at the time was that there was this kind of hidden understanding that people did not move from education to curatorial. But I just really kept at it. And I guess, again, the way I'm sort of moving around the world in the Met, I started to get to know people. One of them was Henry Geldzahler, whom I met at the staff cafeteria that was very democratic and open—anybody could sit anywhere. Henry and I just started chatting, probably about some artists that I was working with that he knew, or was interested in, because Henry was another person about town. You know, some things sort of came together. As I mentioned earlier in our conversation, Kay Bearman, who had lived through founding the department with him, was about to take another job in the director's office. So, we talked about my interest in curatorial work and the possibilities for me. Somehow, and I'm not quite sure how, our conversation got up to the director's office. This was the moment when Percy Sutton was running for Manhattan borough president, so he would have a say on the budget, and he was a Harlem luminary. Eleanor Holmes Norton was also on the EEOC at the time and she made affirmative action demands on the Met. I guess I was perfectly positioned to be an agent for that.

The time came to apply for the job. I remember, I picked up the phone and it happened to be Henry looking for a coworker of mine. He said to me, "Oh, by the way, I'm posting the job for assistant curator." And I said, "Okay. But you know, I'm going to Jamaica for a week. Can I interview the week after?" He said, "The week after, I'll be in Europe." I said, "Oh Henry, what are we going to do?" There had been all this kind of mishmash—he was interested in hiring Penelope Hunter-Stiebel, the assistant curator in the European Sculpture and Decorative Arts Department who was having problems with her personal life intersecting with her professional life. In the meanwhile, Hoving was making all these promises about being affirmative and hiring a Black person, so it got complicated. At some point, I had a copy of the letter that Hoving had sent to the city with these promises and I had a meeting with Philippe de Montebello. And Philippe said to me, "Do you have a copy of the letter?" And I said, "Yes." He said, "Don't worry about a thing." [*Laughs.*]

You know, I'm sure there were other conversations that were happening that I knew nothing about, but I was ready to respond to whatever they decided to do. Henry called the Human Resources Department, and they made an appointment for me to see Henry before I left for Jamaica. My interview consisted mainly of him complaining about how Hoving was making him do the Andrew Wyeth show and how that was going to be detrimental to his reputation as a champion of advanced art. And I just listened to him for a half hour and then he said to me, "Did you see the job description?" I said, "Yes." He says, "Do you think you can do the job?" And I said, "Well, I guess we'll see." And I left. [*Laughs.*]

I came back from Jamaica and he was in Europe. Then the head of Human Resources called me and said, "Henry called from Europe to offer you the job as assistant curator." And I said, "Oh, that's wonderful. I'll think about it." I took two hours and then I called him back: "I'll accept the position." [*Laughs.*]

So it began. By the way, Penelope was my rival for the position and we later became good colleagues and friends. We are still in contact with each other today.

AJ: So it began. You had a long tenure there, going through many phases of the department. You spoke a bit about how the department had an existential crisis at one point, that you were placed in the middle of. You're the first Black curator at the Met and you're a woman. It's interesting because you were already there in education. Did you know your colleagues in a way that maybe somebody who would have come fresh from another institution would not?

LSS: Yes.

AJ: Can you talk about how you experienced that shift socially and professionally? Were people kind to you? Did you feel like you were—I don't want to say "accepted"—but what was the kind of ethos of the department at that time with your colleagues?

LSS: Oh, I think there was some enthusiasm, particularly among my friends outside the museum [*laughs*]. Inside the museum, among the curatorial staff, I don't remember anybody reaching out specifically. In fact, somebody came and said, "The only reason why you got this job is because you're colored." We were a very small department: it was just Henry, me, and an administrative assistant. We shared the American Wing with the art handlers. I jumped in feet first to figure out the day-to-day running of the department. A lot was on me because Henry maintained a very relaxed schedule. I used to say his hours were Tuesday through Thursday, 10:00 a.m. to 2:00 p.m. [*Laughs.*] Henry was kind of—how would I describe it? He wasn't mean, but he wasn't overly friendly. He had odd ways that I knew he was mentoring me. For instance, one day out of the blue, he said, "Get your coat, we're going down to SoHo," and he took me to Semaphore Gallery and introduced me to Robert [Bob] Colescott's work. That led to a forty-year involvement with Bob's work [figs. 1.8, 1.9].

I worked with Henry from 1975 to 1977. By 1977, I was going back to graduate school, so I spent a lot of time doing research and writing papers. It was really kind of an interesting period. Just thinking about outgoing loans, as we were approaching the Bicentennial of American Independence in 1976, it was fascinating to see what works were requested for loans. When you were taught art history at that point, there was this very specific canon of artists that you learned about, although you knew there were tons of other artists. The works requested certainly were off the canonical grid. Then, all of a sudden, loan requests started coming in for all these artists that you never really studied at that time—Lamar Dodd, who was very important for Georgia, Florence McClung for

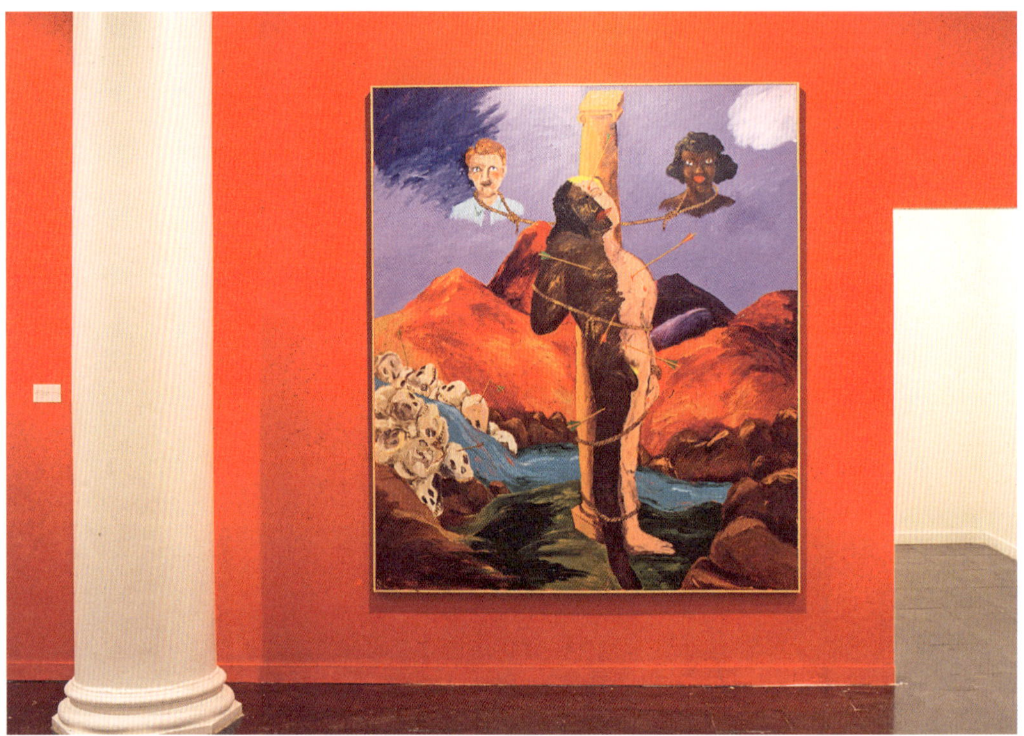

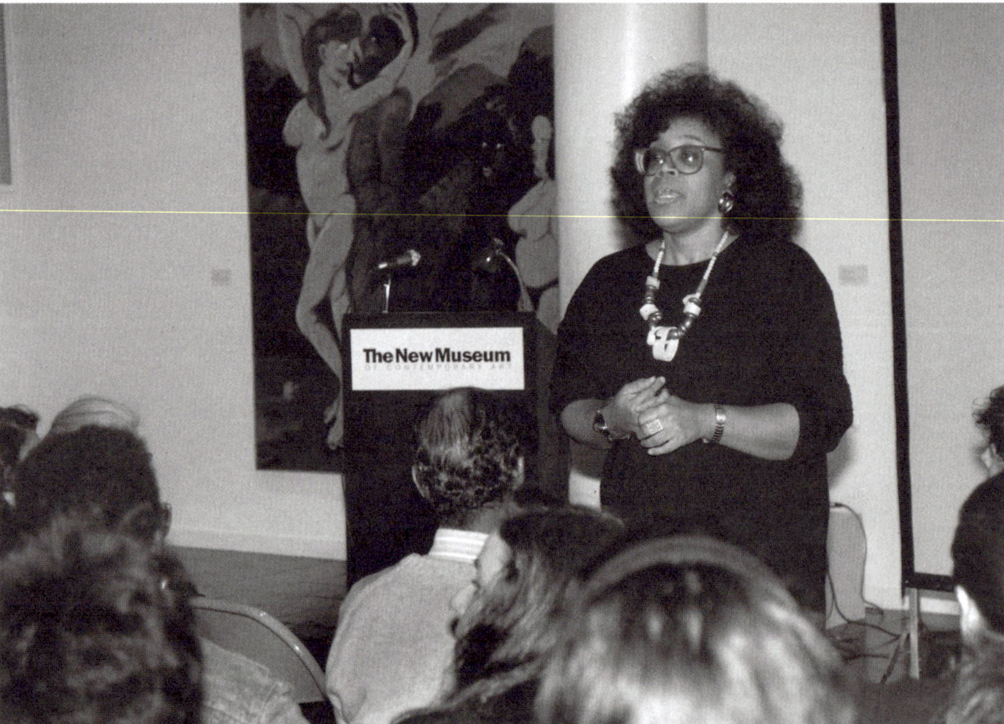

Fig. 1.8 Installation view of *Robert Colescott: A Retrospective,* curated by Lowery Stokes Sims and John Olbranz, New Museum, New York, 23 February–15 April 1989.

Fig. 1.9 Lowery Stokes Sims delivering the keynote lecture "The Unedited Robert Colescott," New Museum, New York, 1989.

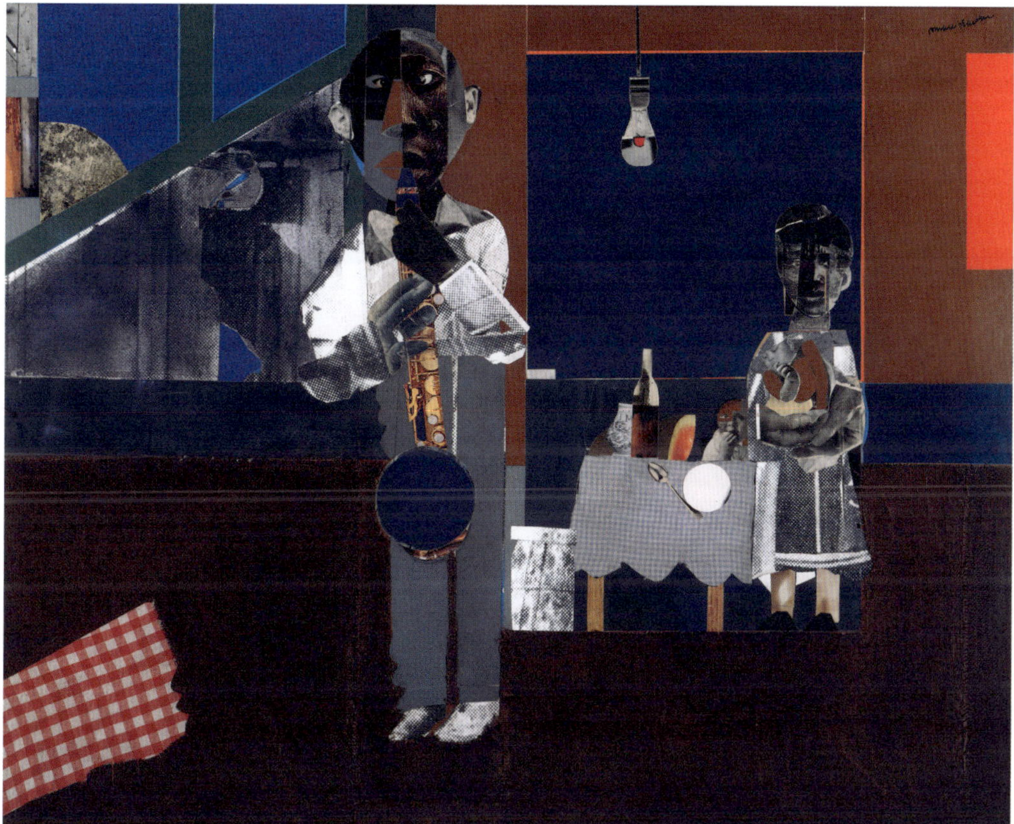

Fig. 1.10 Romare Bearden (American, 1911–88). *The Woodshed,* cut-and-pasted printed and colored papers, photostats, cloth, graphite, and sprayed ink on Masonite, 102.9 × 128.6 cm, 1969. New York, Metropolitan Museum of Art, 1970.19. Artwork shown in *The Figure in 20th Century American Art: Selections from the Metropolitan Museum of Art,* curated by Lowery Stokes Sims, traveling exhibition, 1985–86.

Texas, and Doris Lee in New York. I became interested and curious who these people were. As I was doing the loan paperwork for their works, I researched them and got a much broader sense of what art history was. This was in line with the fact I was teaching myself about Black artists with my friends, because there weren't any courses on Black art at that time. We had a kernel of a collection of Black artists at the Met that I was getting to know [fig. 1.10].

AJ: Very important. And to your point about how people really don't know what curators do, they also don't often know that curatorial exhibitions happen by assignment and for various reasons. I'm interested in how you navigated the assignments versus other interests of yours. I know you spoke about Stuart Davis as being one of the first exhibitions.

LSS: Stuart Davis—yes, but Stuart Davis is way down the line in the late 1980s. Early on, I organized shows like the portraits of Helena Rubinstein in the mid-1970s right after I became a curator. It was installed in the Costume Institute at the Met. But, I wrote a catalog for it and learned about all the artists—I mean, every situation was a learning situation, and you just accepted all your assignments, like doing the show on Black artists for the Bedford Stuyvesant Restoration Corporation. Then I got to work on exhibitions we sent to Russia in the years 1977 through 1979. After all, I had to know information about the works so that when I got to Russia, I could explain things to people. But I think after my experience with the Bedford Stuyvesant Restoration Corporation project, I really put it in my mind that I needed to do things in other venues, just to prove to myself what was going on.

AJ: Right. The fact that, at the time, we had this cohort of curators who are now doing this oral history is a testament to how a lot has changed in terms of the expansion of Black curators and networks. Initially, it was you at the Met and Howardena at MoMA. [Kynaston McShine was also at the Jewish Museum in the mid-1960s before moving to MoMA later in the decade.]

LSS: It was Howardena until she decamped to teach at Stony Brook University; Dewey Mosby in Detroit at the Detroit Institute of Arts; and Thelma at the Whitney. I think this was a bit before Roslyn Walker went to the Dallas Museum of Art, and then there were curators in African American–focused museums. But that was it for major white museums.

AJ: Were you having discussions among your peers in curatorial or education—the ones you first came up with professionally—about the question you were already asking yourself: What am I able to do here at the Met versus how do I find other outlets and exhibition spaces? Was that a conversation that was happening among all these folks? Or did you feel like you were going down your own curatorial road, through your own thoughts and paths?

LSS: My own thoughts and paths, but they were informed by my relationships with my colleagues and peers outside the Met.

AJ: Let's move to your transition to the Studio Museum. I'm interested in how you were philosophically thinking about culturally specific museums at the time, and what it looked like to go from an encyclopedic organization to one that was more specifically focused. Could you talk a little bit about the reasons for that move and if you were thinking through what that meant in terms of this mission-oriented, ethnically, and culturally specific institutionship?

LSS: I would say that the decision was situational. I had reached the limits of what I could do at the Met. I could have stayed there until I retired. But I was fifty-eight years old, and given my father's recent passing, I realized I needed to take the same kind of chance I did to get into the Met. The Studio Museum had always been a very important support for me outside the Met because I could go there and meet African Americans who were collectors, critics, curators, and directors. I also knew most of the board members.

AJ: I think that the transition from curatorial to leadership and directorship is fascinating, and people take different courses toward that transition. When you moved into that leadership capacity, how did you feel about curatorial? I mean, you were obviously still writing and working on long-term projects.

LSS: Yes. I always say one of the smartest things I did was to bring on Thelma because she had a curatorial reach that allowed us, for example, to attract Kerry James Marshall to do his show at the Studio Museum. He could have done his first show in New York at the Whitney, but he did it at the Studio Museum. Also, Yinka Shonibare could have done his first show in New York anywhere else, but he did it at the Studio Museum. I think that made people realize that something special was going on that marked my involvement with the Studio Museum.

AJ: Yes, and that has also, I think, offered different platforms for your intellectual journey in ways that are unexpected, too. Thinking now about your shift to MAD—and I know that also came about spontaneously—you weren't looking for a position, it sort of came to you. But it's fascinating that it returned you to thinking about Latin American art, and being able to work on exhibitions that you literally wouldn't have necessarily been doing at the Studio Museum if you were curating there—

LSS: Yes, or at the Met.

AJ: —or the Met, exactly.

LSS: I always say that I think for me, MAD was my best curatorial experience. After four or five years at the Studio Museum, I had checked off all the list of things I wanted to accomplish there. Frankly, Thelma was ready to take over, so I convinced the board that it was time. They appointed me president for a year and then I did a year as adjunct curator working on the permanent collection. I was trying to figure out what to do next. I thought maybe I'd go into teaching because I had some experience teaching here and there.

Then I found out that academia viewed me in a very specific way. Responses to my inquiries went something like, "Well, I think we'll have to start you out as an assistant professor, because you haven't taught that much." Now my last gig teaching was in 2005–6 at Hunter College, and in 2007 at Queens College I was an adjunct associate professor. Eventually I connected with William Clark, who had been one of my professors when I was an undergraduate at Queens College and was then chair of the art history department. We began discussions about how I could segue to a professorship at my alma mater. By the fall of 2007, I was teaching every Friday at Queens and commuting for four days a week every other week to Minneapolis because I'd made a commitment to teach in the art department at the University of Minnesota. Alternate weeks I was at MAD because they wanted me to start working immediately with the chief curator, David [Revere] McFadden, on the exhibition that would inaugurate the new building that would open in fall 2008.

I was full-time with MAD by January 2008. Immediately the pressure was on: what shows did I want to do? That was a new experience for me working institutionally—I was so used to being assigned shows as a curator, so here I am as a recovering curator, and they're asking me what I want to do. They already had a thought about an African design show, so I just picked that up and it developed into *The Global Africa Project.* That was a lot of fun, but it was a big challenge. The market had crashed in late 2008, so there was little money for development and travel. We were lucky to find a lot of resources here in the United States and had a great cohort of colleagues who gave us invaluable resources and contacts for the project.

I brought on Leslie as the co-curator and we came up with the idea of having the exhibition focus on the intersections among fine art, craft, and design. At that time, there wasn't really much information on African design, but our friends who were Africanists discouraged us from using verbiage around "tradition" and other stereotypical ideas about Africa. But the careers of the individual creators we identified did that just fine. In terms of finding a thematic organization, we benefited from a dialogue with Ousmane M'Baye, who was in Senegal. He sent me this article he was featured in, which included interviews with twelve thinkers on African design. They were talking about all the challenges and issues about African design, and that's where we found our subject themes, such as sourcing locally, cultural fusion, global reach, transformations in craft practices, et cetera. Despite many obstacles, we were able to get funding and figure out how to identify creators who worked in Africa, Europe, the United States, the Caribbean, and even in Japan and India.

AJ: That leads to my last question, which is a big question and one that curators and artists always get. I'm curious, particularly because of your beginnings in community engagement, How do you think about audience? Who is the imagined audience? Has that shifted over time? Is it something you were conscious of as a curator and in your writing? There are such marked differences in terms of the locations of the institutions you worked for and their missions.

LSS: I'm going to make a confession. Because of the time I came through, my focus had to be on the artists. Not that I ignored audiences, but at times it was just so much work to make sure artists had their voices heard so that they could communicate with audiences. I'm not going to pretend that I sit down and calculate what's happening with the audience. But in terms of the way I work—I had this conversation with Leslie—it's really us following the artists. What I find is that you can encourage artists to sort of be their own ambassadors to the audience.

You do your best to organize a show or to write an essay that provides an entryway for somebody else into the art. But, ultimately, you hope that people look at the work through their own eyes and have that experience. People often say they appreciate the fact that I write fairly clearly. And I say, "That's because when I used to give stuff to my sister to read, she'd hand it back to me and say, 'I don't understand one thing that you're saying.'"

My sister was a classical ballet dancer and then made it into costuming. She went through high school—did not go to college—but is a voracious reader and probably one of the most intelligent people I know. If she tells me it's crap, then I know it is. She was the one who sort of worked me through to say exactly what I mean and not just string words together, which can be tempting when you're trying to articulate your intentionality and positionality.

AJ: Absolutely. I think that's the idea of the curator as facilitator of experience, which seems to be a through line in your career. I have many more questions, but I want to make sure that there isn't anything else you want on the record. It's been really helpful to hear all this coming from someone as seasoned as you are.

LSS: I was listening to somebody the other day, and they were talking about what a privilege it is to have these kinds of jobs, to be able to think about some of the better aspects of humanity and their creativity. Curating is a cool job. It really is a privilege to be able to bring your experience and your point of view to art. I think that is really quite special. I continue to enjoy it to this day. I think that it still requires a lot of strategy. I tell young people, particularly African Americans who come to me for advice, that you have to be on your toes all the time and figure out what's behind any resistance or problem you run into. Then determine who can help you solve it. Never have an ego, it's not about you, it's not about your feelings. It's about considerations that are larger than you. And if you remember that, you will be able to make an incredible contribution to the story of human creativity.

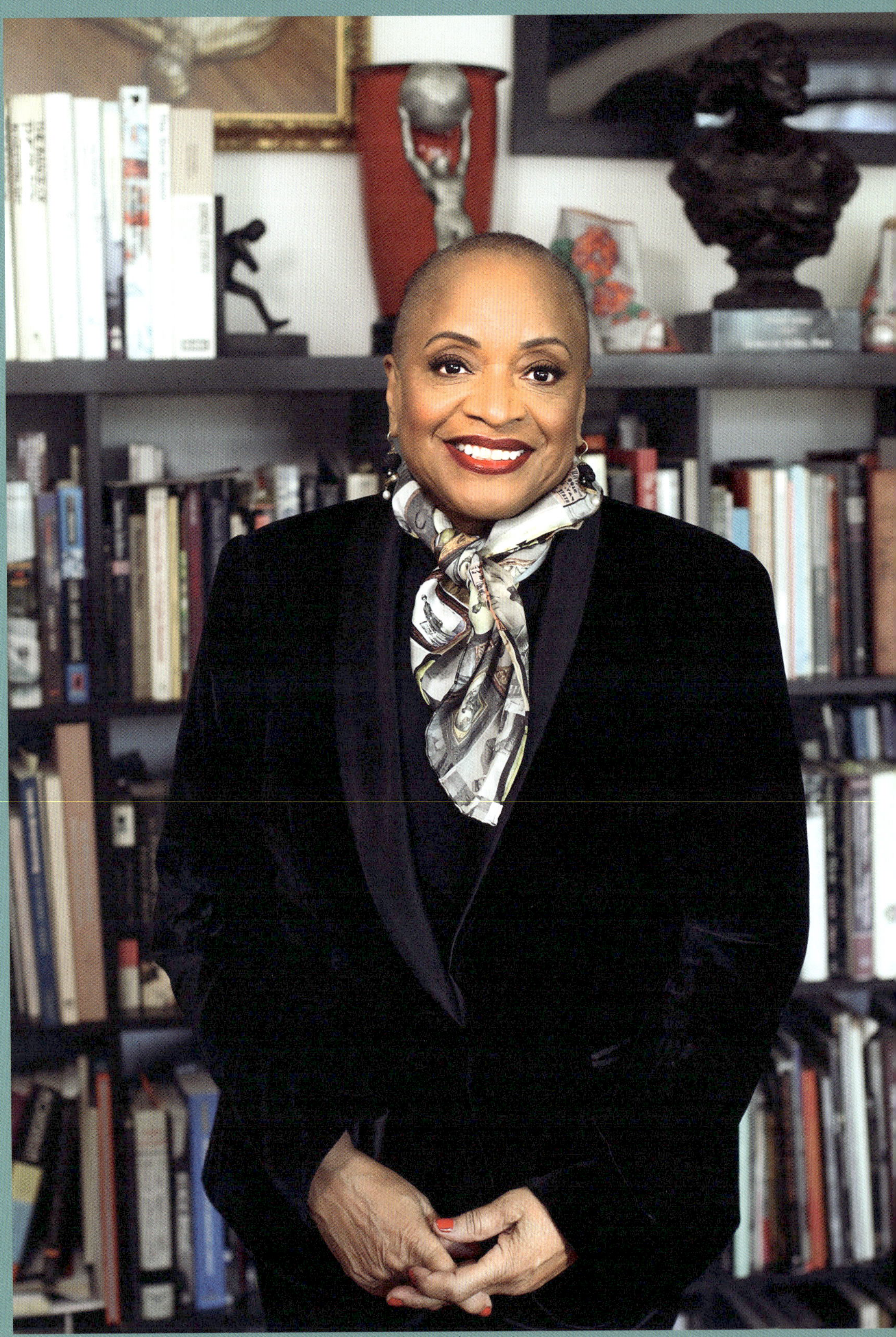

Deborah Willis

INTERVIEWED BY KALIA BROOKS
11 and 22 November 2021

KALIA BROOKS (KB): We get to kick off this historic initiative, which is really centered on an intergenerational dialogue about Black curators and the innovations they have brought to the field of visual culture and the arts. Our conversation, along with the other interviews in this book, is an incredible resource for future generations of artists, curators, and curious seekers. It's an important endeavor, and I can't think of anyone I'd rather be spending these initial moments with than you.

DEBORAH WILLIS (DW): Thank you. It's truly an honor. When I received the letter from Dr. Kellie Jones and you to consider this topic that *Black Curators Matter*—is that the correct title?

KB: *Black Curators Matter.* That's the title.

DW: You know, we know it, but no one else knows it. Having an opportunity to talk with curators about their experiences, desires, dreams, hopes, and disappointments is all a part of what it means to tell and create new narratives, so I really am honored by this opportunity.

KB: I'm going to start more broadly and then get into more specifics, so I'd first like you to start by describing who you are.

DW: I am Professor Deborah Willis. I am a curator. I am a teacher. I am a writer. I'm also a photographer and the mother of an artist. I am interested, in terms of who I am as a Black woman, in looking at ways to tell stories about Black people—women specifically—that have been ignored, through the visual experience. So, I am a Black woman, I am a photographer, I am a teacher, I am a mother, now grandmother, and I am a curator!

KB: I think we often neglect the dynamism and complexity of all the many facets of ourselves. One thing I really respect about you and your work is how you have been able to be multivocal; it's part of who you are and has become part of your practice. You being a mother, sister, and aunt—my aunt in particular—as well as an artist, curator, educator, and historian, says it all about the way you approach creative practice. Can you take us through the first time you saw a photograph and knew it was an important document? What was that like? What was that photograph and what was that experience like for you?

DW: If I can go back to childhood, the first experience I had with a photograph was my dad's own photographs of family members. He was an amateur photographer and loved taking photographs. He had a Rolleiflex. He also had a cousin who had a photography studio that was about two blocks from our home. I grew up with photographs. The first experience I recall was posing for my father with my sister, who is your mother. We were two daughters in a small family in North Philadelphia. We had pictures on calendars. We had pictures in frames. We had pictures in photo albums. When my father took photographs of us, he would pick them up either at the local drugstore, the five-and-dime store on Lehigh Avenue, or other places. I don't know where he had them processed, but I would always put them in the family album. Placing photographs in the "family book" to tell the story was my job. This was an exciting act for me because I began to think about picture books during that period. I loved opening them up and smelling the chemicals but also making sure that the negatives did not curl. I had no idea negatives curled and my father would always take them and put them away.

KB: That's incredible. I can envision how those early moments have led all the way through to the work that you do. It's enlightening to hear about those moments where you were enjoying handling a photograph and putting it in a book, and how you have continued to do this [*laughs*].

DW: It's fascinating because my sister Yvonne [Arlene Willis Brooks], who's eighteen months older, loved to read. She'd read in the dark. She'd read with a flashlight. I always wanted to look at photographs. I didn't read comic books, like my cousin often did. My sister read fairy tales. I wanted to create tales through photographs. Even though I've lived through some of the moments that my father photographed, I wanted to re-create the moments that were in the family album. My part was looking at photographs and placing them in a narrative in some format.

KB: In what city did you grow up?

DW: I grew up in Philadelphia, Pennsylvania, after World War II.

KB: What was Philadelphia like during that time? What was it like to grow up post–World War II?

DW: It was fun. I lived two blocks from my elementary school, the Rudolph Walton Elementary School. I had Black teachers at that time. In second grade, I remember my teacher was Mr. Toles. We had Black History Week in February and my birthday is in February, so that period was often a celebration for me at school. We grew up with the memory of Marian Anderson, who was living at the time, and also with the memory of Black abolitionists in Philadelphia. We had so many stories to tell. My mother used to walk us to school. When my father bought our house in 1945, there were a lot of Jewish and Irish people living in the area. There were only two white families left on our block when we lived there in a corner house.

What's fascinating is what Philadelphia was like then: it was church-going, it was a community, it was a lot of celebration. I grew up in a house where my mother had a beauty shop. Images were also a part of my life stories. My father was a policeman and was very active. He was interested in making sure that we were looking fine and that people would not mistake us for having any problems. He was protecting us in many ways. He also owned a tailor shop, so he was always looking at dress and fashion. Another thing I think about from my experience growing up in Philadelphia and going to elementary school is lunchtime. My mom would wait for us outside at lunch and walk us back home. The "stories," as they were called—soap operas—were on for like fifteen minutes at the time. My mom wanted to make sure we'd get back so she could look at her stories [*laughs*], fix us lunch, and then take us back to school. It was fascinating, the multi-experiences that we had, the sensory experience.

I grew up with thirteen aunts. They were always very fashionable and theatrical because they loved to sing, dance, and party. We had visual moments from fashion shows that, of course, we went to. We grew up with the Ebony Fashion Fair and other fashion shows that would come to Philadelphia. The church groups would also try to emulate the Ebony Fashion Fair after it left the city. Their fashion shows acted as fundraisers to support scholarships for kids who were going to historically Black colleges and universities or trade schools. So that was that range. I also loved listening to R & B and dancing to it, jumping rope to it, hopscotching to it. We grew up with all that sonic girl sound and it was really fun.

KB: Let's talk a little bit about how you got the camera and how you developed your eye and vision, documenting things around you as you grew up in this post–World War II period [fig. 2.1]. How did your practice as a photographer and your use of the camera move with you as you got older and as the 1960s started to take shape? How did it affect the way that you were approaching photography and maybe even the way you thought of yourself as a photographer at that point?

DW: We always had chores. I don't know why we always had to do so much work at the house. But we also had to go to the library every week to pick a book, which we had to read. The first book I picked up when I was seven or eight was *The Sweet Flypaper of Life* [1955] by Langston Hughes and illustrated by Roy DeCarava. I always loved Hughes because my father read his work all the time. I couldn't read the text, but I could look at the photographs that had so much life in them. It was about Harlem, and I used to go to Harlem with my parents often to visit family. My father loved Harlem and visiting friends and relatives there. Having that book at that age and seeing how DeCarava was able to capture light with a single bulb, as well as shapes, women's bodies, and pictures of extended families, including grandmothers, made me want

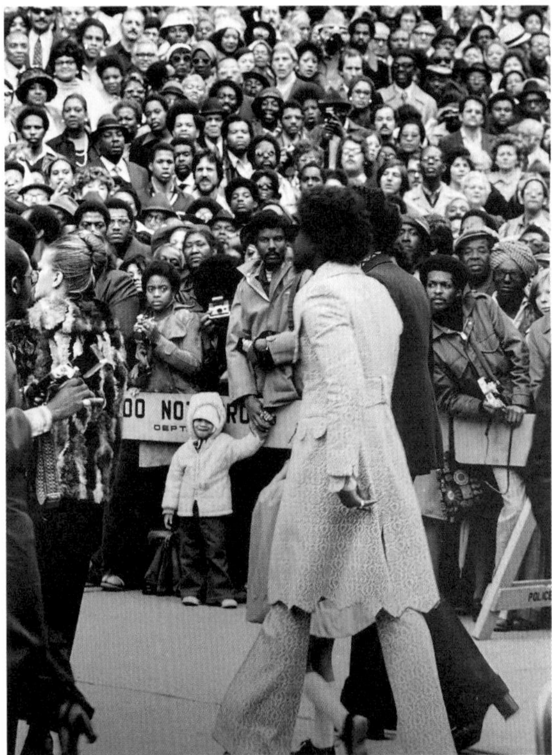

Fig. 2.1 Richard Presha (American, b. 1943). *Guests Arriving at Duke Ellington's Funeral, Cathedral of St. John the Divine, New York,* black-and-white photograph, 20.32 × 30.48 cm, 1974. Deborah Willis is pictured with her camera in the front row.

to tell this story. I loved reading it over and over.

We also had magazines in my mom's beauty shop. We had *Ebony* magazine, which was a Black magazine produced by the Johnson Publishing Company. They had other spin-offs like *Jet, Sepia, Tan,* and *Bronze,* magazines titled after the range of Black skin tones dealing with a plethora of stories celebrating Blackness. Some of them had cheesy images on the cover of girls desiring a love life and different things like that. But we also had *Life, Look,* and *National Geographic* magazines. These are things that my father would collect and have in the beauty shop after he read them. I was also looking at the images. I was constantly looking at different stories, and by the time I was twelve or thirteen, I knew that I wanted to become a photographer. By then, I was looking at Gordon Parks, whose photos were in *Life* [fig. 2.2]. One image that transformed my life, when I was around eight or so, was the image of Emmett Till in *Jet* magazine. I was horrified. I remember I was in my mom's shop. I used to love sitting on the floor and listening to the women talk about their lives—sometimes I had to sweep the floor, but I loved listening.

Seeing that image of Emmett Till in *Jet,* I was horrified. I didn't understand it or his death, but it was constantly discussed on the news. That's what said I needed to become a photographer. I really wanted to become a photographer to tell stories. It really helped shape me. As early as junior high school, teachers and guidance counselors did not support people like me who thought outside the box. They thought I should do other work. One counselor said I would be a great bedpan nurse.

KB: Oh my.

DW: In 1969, I moved to New York to study photography at the Germain School of Photography and build my portfolio. I took classes in commercial photography, scientific photography, and art photography. They were six-week-long classes. I took classes from January to June. There was the worst snowstorm in New York that winter. I was living in Brooklyn and no one could travel. I couldn't get to class, couldn't do anything. Once I was able to get to class, it was the most amazing

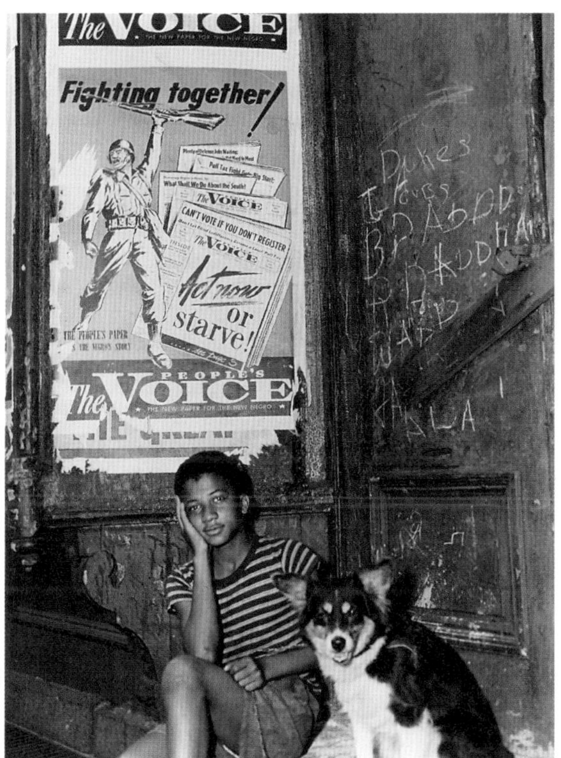

Fig. 2.2 Gordon Parks (American, 1912–2006). *The People's Voice, Harlem, New York, August 1943,* gelatin silver print, 1943. Photograph shown in *Gordon Parks: A Retrospective,* curated by Deborah Willis, New York Public Library, New York, 14 February–28 March 1987.

experience of my life. I made portraits. I used the large-format camera. I used a 35mm camera my father bought me before I left for New York. During that time, I also taught photography at the High School of Fashion Industries in Manhattan and to senior citizens at the Jamaica Arts Center in Queens. In 1969, I was all around the city, teaching photography to a range of people and learning about the communities I photographed. And I loved it. I also began to exhibit, printing and showing my work in different small galleries. I went to see the *Harlem on My Mind: The Cultural Capital of Black America, 1900–1968* exhibition in 1969 at the Metropolitan Museum of Art, which blew my mind.

I know that it was controversial at the time because people didn't see photography as an art form. They saw it as a social document. There were people protesting the exhibition. I, of course, went past the protest line. I'm just this kid coming in from Philadelphia, feeling like I wanted to see this show. I understood that Black artists felt that they were not part of the conversation and the making of *Harlem on My Mind,* but I couldn't pass up the opportunity to see large-scale photography, which was like the IMAX of the time—this was a blockbuster. There was an audio component to the show, so I was hearing the voices of people like Marcus Garvey and jazz music in the museum space. It was all new. There were photographs that were framed traditionally and photographs reproduced on board and not in frames. I was wowed by the experience of walking through this maze of beautiful photographs that ranged from social documentary to portraits. I knew then that I wanted to be a photographer. I was determined to photograph in Harlem, determined to find a way into that world of making images and preserving images.

KB: There's so much in what you described about being a young art student moving to a new city, which many young artists and curators moving to New York can relate to. You moved there in 1969, with everything that was happening not only in the United States but around the world—social justice movements, political unrest, and political upheaval. And you talked about the way you were actively learning about your surroundings through teaching.

You mentioned that just a few years earlier, there wasn't much opportunity for you to study photography in an arts setting and become a maker. Not just study, but to learn how to become a photographer and improve your practice. You moved back to Philadelphia after a year in New York to attend Philadelphia College of Art [1971–75]. Then you're in the school of your dreams. What was that environment like?

DW: Oh, it was glorious. It was the residency for life. There were kilns, glassblowing classes, printmaking classes, and fiber experiences. And then there were the darkrooms. I love working in the darkroom. I had professors, like Ray Metzker, who transformed my life in photography. He was known for being a part of the Chicago School and focusing on street photography, graphic black-and-white images—really amazing work. He knew how to read an image. He would always say, "Look what's in your foreground, look what's in the middle ground, look what's in the background. You want to tell a complete story." And that's how I began to look at images. Then I had Anne Tucker who was my history professor. At the time, we talked only about white photographers, and she had just finished a book on women photographers called *The Woman's Eye* [1973]. I said to her, "I really want to include some Black photographers. Where are the Black photographers in the book, in our books?" She gave me some names of contemporary Black photographers I should look up. I knew of historical photographers like James Van Der Zee because of the *Harlem on My Mind* exhibition. I began to collect more names, and Tucker said, "Talk to the department chair about doing an independent study so that you can just work on this as an art history class project." And I did that.

KB: That set the course for the rest of your career.

DW: I began to connect with other photographic groups. I joined the College Art Association [CAA] as an undergraduate student. I joined the Society for Photographic Education [SPE]. I really wanted to be in the community of photographers and artists to make it happen—to make that world happen. When I graduated, I thought I was going to be a photojournalist and I took my portfolio to *Newsweek* and *Time.* I was going to all these different places and it didn't happen because they were not looking at the work. They would say, "Oh, bring it back in three weeks." But I knew some male photographers who were dropping off their portfolios and getting assignments. That was really a difficult situation.

KB: Did you attribute that to race and gender? Were you conscious or thinking that the reason you weren't getting those assignments was because you were a Black woman?

DW: Yes. I knew they felt I was limited in vision because I only showed images of Black communities. My images did not have a sense of suffering or hopelessness. The images I made depicted, for example, someone washing a window. Just imagine walking down the street and you see an arm hanging, leaning out of a window, and then wiping the window with a white rag. Beautiful. One of the things that struck me really hard was when I was objectified as a student, when a professor said to me, "Oh, you're just taking up a good man's space, all you're going to do is get pregnant and have a baby and a good man could have been in that seat." One of my friends, Steven Fiorella, sat next to me and calmed me down. He touched my hand and said, "Just calm down, don't let it bother you."

KB: I want to pick back up on *Harlem on My Mind.* To me, that's a pivotal moment, especially considering where you were in your career as a student entering into the controversy of that exhibition. But also that exhibition was incredibly impactful for you in terms of thinking about photography as an art form and seeing it show up in an exhibition space. Can you speak more to that experience?

DW: As a young person, walking into a space like the Met and seeing Black faces was pretty amazing. It was shocking. But it also offered me an opportunity to reconsider exhibition design. I'm thinking about some of the signs the protesters outside were carrying, such as "Whitey has Harlem on his mind, we have Africa on our mind." All this was circulating as I was walking through, but, in the exhibit, there were also banners and protest placards in the photographs, with phrases like "The new Negro has no fear." I was looking at the Garvey stories in the exhibit through that aspect of it. Activism was inside and outside, happening at the same time, not necessarily clashing. I was embracing both because, visually, I got really excited about seeing Harlem through this lens of photojournalism. Then when I went to the Schomburg Center for Research in Black Culture to do research, they had photographs in cases so you could look closely at them and but not touch them. They also weren't framed. Those were two different ways of looking at photographs, and I began to consider different ways of looking at images.

KB: I hadn't until now, as I was listening to you, thought about how the Met exhibition was informative in that way, like a technological breakthrough.

DW: If you think about curatorial experiences that can blow you away, you may think about the Tutankhamun's tomb exhibition. But a photographic exhibit can also introduce you to a new narrative about life in New York in 1969, specifically Harlem, through sound, music, and large-scale photographs.

KB: It's such a unique perspective to be an artist and also a curator. There's something extra special about that nuance, which is something I've always learned from you. Since we're talking about *Harlem on My Mind,* can you speak about your experience as a curator and the juxtaposition or intersection of being both an artist and curator, when you knew that you wanted to also incorporate this perspective into your creative practice?

DW: I think it was by default. I didn't know that I wanted to be a curator. I only knew that I wanted to tell visual stories. I had the honor of seeing *Two Centuries of Black American Art* [1976–77] through the lens of David Driskell when it was on view at the Brooklyn Museum. Having the catalog was extremely helpful. When I first met Dr. David Driskell, he was a professor at Fisk University, and I said to him, "I want to do what you do. I want to curate and make art." He said, "You can do both. But you'll be told that you can't because you have to make a difference in one field or the other."

KB: As soon as you got into the Schomburg Center and were uncovering dusty boxes of masterpieces—like those of Gordon Parks in 1980, who was then already a master at his craft—you immediately started curating. What is that impulse to say, "Oh, I've found this and I need to show it to people"? Did you already have in mind that there would be an audience that needed to know about this thing?

DW: I didn't know there was an audience, but I knew I needed to share this story. I needed to have this story shared throughout the community. Some older photographers as well as those first audiences for my curatorial work called me "Debbie Schomburg" because I was always looking to find ways to tell their stories. I was putting together these moments in these cases at the Schomburg Center [fig. 2.3]. But in putting those moments together, I realized that people really wanted to know more about the lives of the individuals who had passed on. When I decided to curate my first show at the Schomburg Center, I wanted to find a way to share these moments with other people in the community, not just with students but with others who had the opportunity to see what it meant to have a space and look at work.

The first exhibition I curated at the Schomburg Center was in 1981 *Photographs by Doris Ulmann: The Gullah People.* I was always curious about the Sea Islands off the coast South Carolina and Georgia. It was an amazing opportunity to see Doris Ulmann's photography at the Schomburg Center and touch these photographs for the first time, some were photogravures, some were photographs she printed.

KB: What did you think about the reception you received? When you produced the publication and exhibition, it generated a massive response. What do you remember about that?

DW: I knew the Sea Islands firsthand, and I knew Jeanne Moutoussamy-Ashe had photographed at one of them, Daufuskie Island, South Carolina. I knew there were people interested in that area, people who migrated from South Carolina to the north. I knew there was

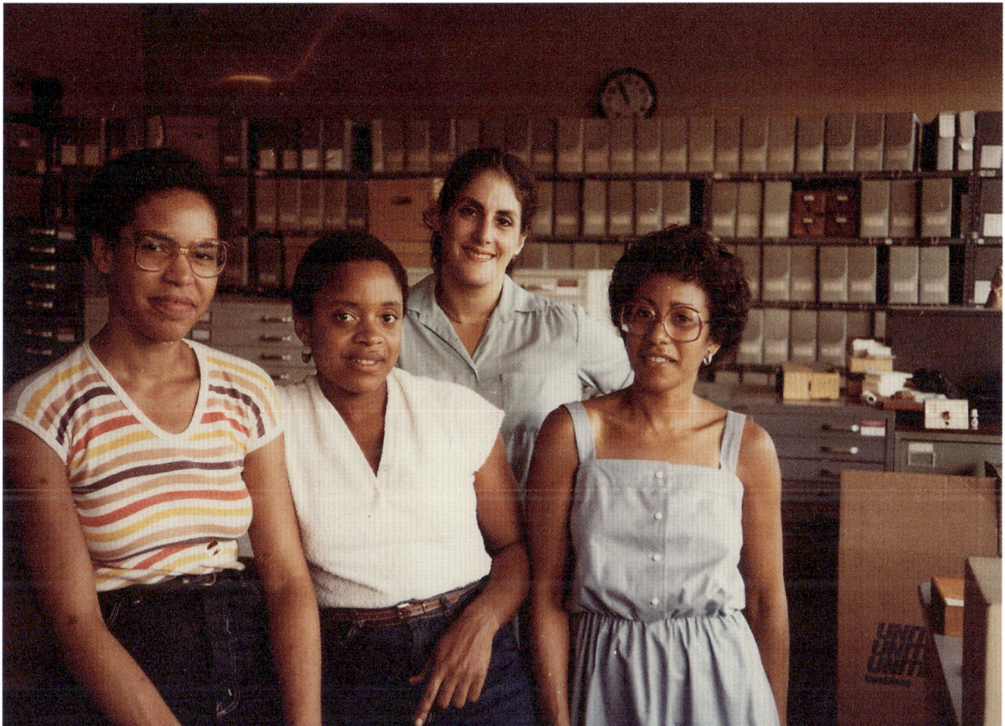

Fig. 2.3 *Left to right:* Deborah Payne, Deborah Willis, Susan Davis, and Diana Lachatanere, Schomburg Center for Research in Black Culture, New York, ca. 1980–89.

a community of people who would appreciate looking back at these images that were created in the 1920s and 1930s. I had to research more to create labels. As I didn't have any training as a curator, I looked to examples at the New York Historical Society and the Met to see how labels were created. The Smithsonian Institution had a project called Exhibit This or something like that and had workshops on how to curate shows. I was a part of that early training. When I opened the door to Ulmann, a white photographer photographing a Black community, I felt joy in sharing this story and learning more about the Gullah Geechee people in South Carolina. So, I enhanced the exhibition by having programs. We had performances and I knew I wanted to have people talk about the photographs. Ulmann was able to find beauty in this culture and in these people who survived slavery, abuse, and degradation, and preserve it all in photographs.

KB: I'm glad you brought up the word *beauty* in the way you did just now. I'd like to hear what beauty means to you. You mentioned it with your mother—my grandmother—having a beauty shop, and how beauty and the way one presents themselves was an early part of your growing up. But you also mentioned it in terms of your own practice in making photographs, reading

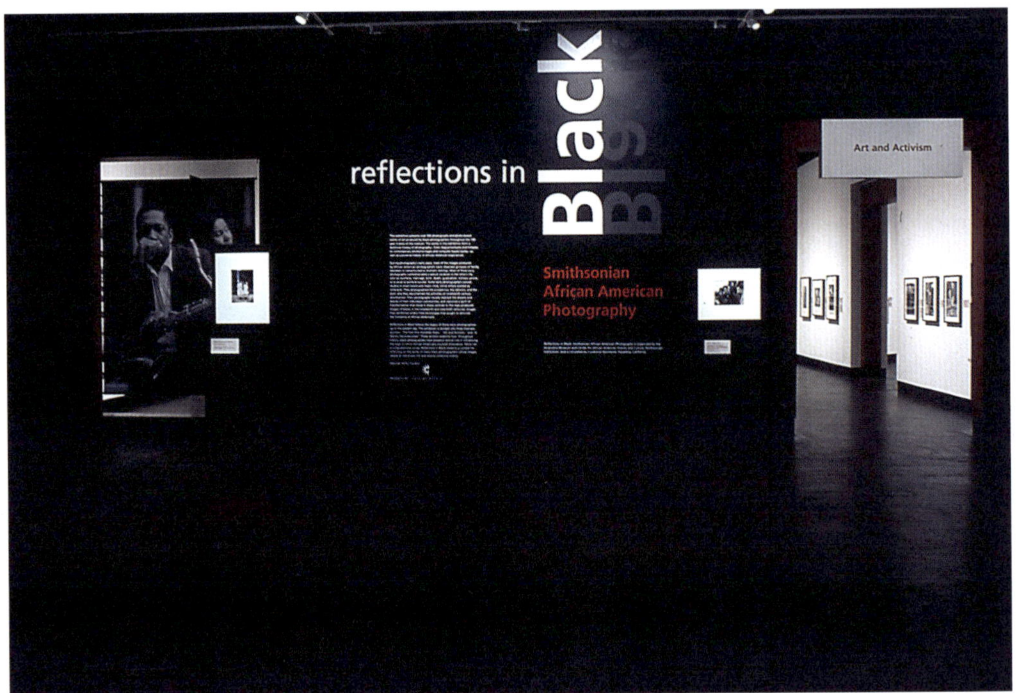

Fig. 2.4 Installation view of *Reflections in Black: A History of Black Photographers, 1840s to the Present,* curated by Deborah Willis, Center for African American History and Culture, Smithsonian Institution, Washington, DC, 4 February–16 July 2000.

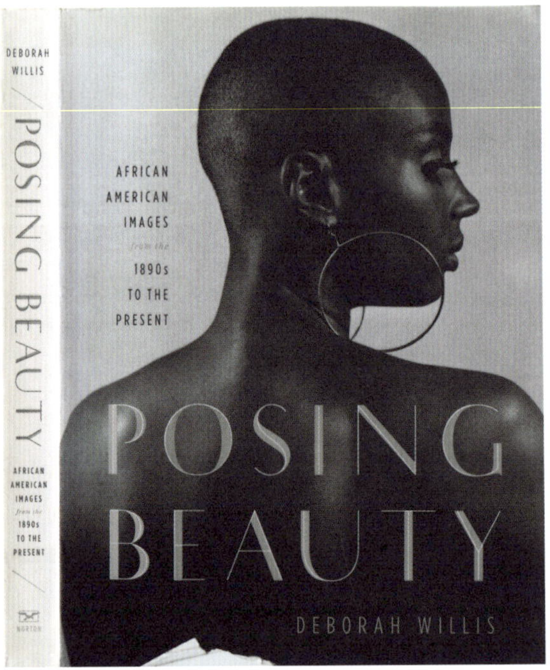

Fig. 2.5 Cover of Deborah Willis, *Posing Beauty: African American Images from the 1890s to the Present* (W. W. Norton, 2009).

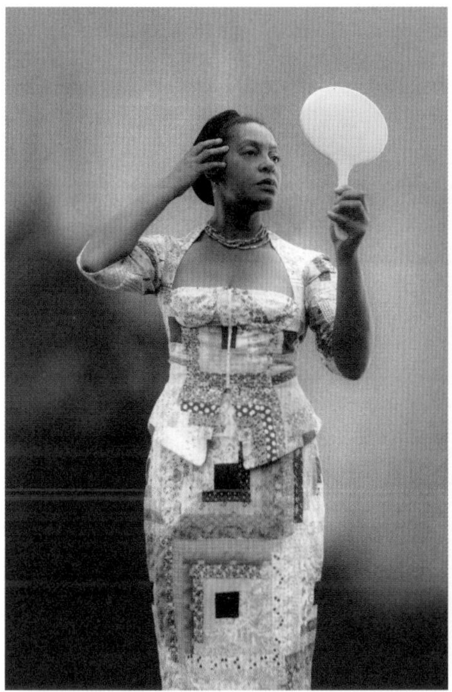
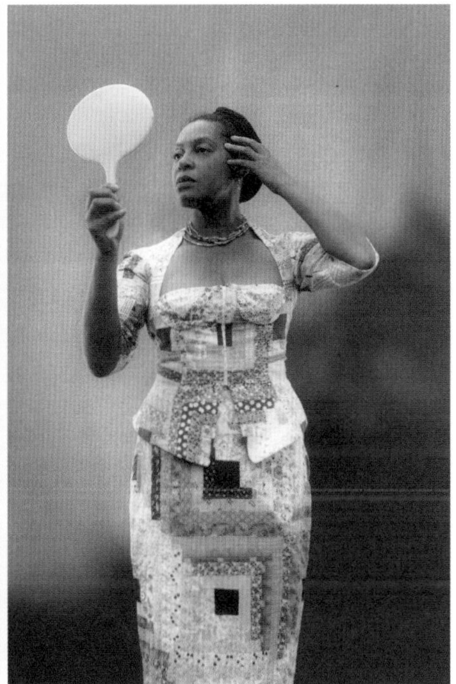

Fig. 2.6 Carrie Mae Weems (American, b. 1953). *I Looked and Looked and Failed to See What so Terrified You,* digital print (diptych), overall 94.5 × 127.6 cm, 2006. Photograph shown in *Posing Beauty: African American Images from the 1890s to the Present,* curated by Deborah Willis, Tisch School of the Arts, New York University, New York, 2009.

beauty in images, as well as in researching photographers. Can you speak about what beauty means to you as a curator and artist?

DW: This is another fraught subject because another missing connector to Black people was beauty. We never talked about Black beauty when I was a student or making images. I thought about the power that beauty had in different communities. Within the setting of the beauty shop, that could mean how people were transformed by what it meant to feel beautiful. Beauty for me was something that challenged negative stereotypes. I wanted to create a way to represent beauty that enhances a sense of humanism and constructs the self in a different way. How do we contextualize beauty? I think it's hard to say, "This is beautiful," or point to something and say, "This is about beauty." But what I felt in my way of thinking was that I wanted to tell stories that made one feel human, made one feel sensitive to the plight of people who were denied a discussion about being human. So those are some of the ways I framed beauty in my work [figs. 2.4–2.6].

KB: It also makes me think about your early witnessing of the Emmett Till image in *Jet* magazine, the kind of shock that that instilled in you, and how you think about this pursuit of beauty as an image-maker. Within the context of everything else going on in the world—to Black people, to women, and to others—that are oftentimes painful and fraught—how do you find beauty in those spaces?

DW: I'm glad you asked because people thought I meant "pretty" when I would talk about beauty. They'd say, "Oh, this is a topic that's so frivolous." When I was an undergraduate, we couldn't even say anything was beautiful. You had to unpack beauty by saying some horrific things and words you couldn't even understand. All you're trying to say is "beautiful." [*Laughs.*] We were denied the opportunity to talk about beauty because it felt frivolous or simplistic. But we knew when we felt good, how else do you define it? You only define it one way. That's that visceral experience one could have, making sure that this is an opportunity to represent a story that enhanced a life about survival. And survival is often a beautiful moment as well.

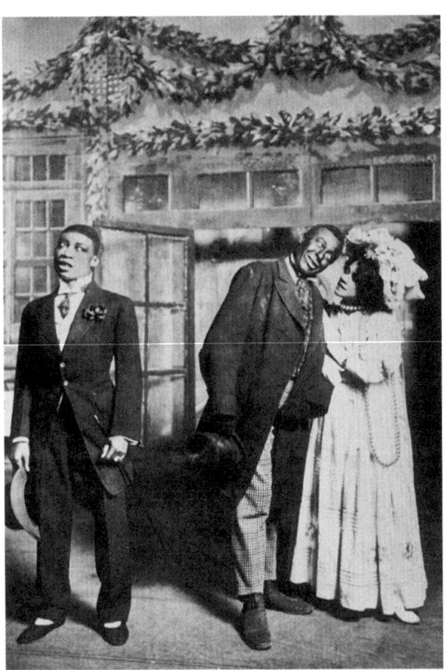

Fig. 2.7 Vaudeville comedians and singers George Walker (*left*) and Bert Williams (*center*), with Walker's wife, the dancer and choreographer Aida Overton Walker (*right*), in *Bandana Land*, 1908. Photograph shown in *Scenes from the 20th-Century Stage: Black Theatre in Photographs*, curated by Deborah Willis, Schomburg Center for Research in Black Culture, New York, 1983.

Becoming a curator was a "desire," but only because I knew I needed a new way of telling stories. I began working at the Schomburg Center in 1980 as curator of prints and photographs. Some of my early exhibitions there were drawn from the Black theater and Black dance collections there [*Scenes from the 20th-Century Stage: Black Theatre in Photographs* (1983) and *Black Dance in Photographs: Images from the 19th Century to the Present* (1982)] [fig. 2.7].

People around the country learned about my exhibitions and began asking me to curate shows, so I started creating other shows. Mary Schmidt Campbell, the director at the Studio Museum in Harlem asked me to curate shows because she knew of my interest in photography. My first show there, *Harlem Heyday: The Photography of James Van Der Zee* [1982], opened at their new building on 125th Street. To backtrack, when I was teaching in New York in 1969, I also took classes in filmmaking at the Studio Museum. I was trying to get as much as I could in the field of art and framing art stories.

As Dr. Driskell predicted, early in my time at the Schomburg Center, the then-director Wendell L. Wray told me "I just want to warn you, you're the only game in town, so you need to be careful about how you work through all of these photographers, because you can't do it all."

KB: What was the difference between curating at the Schomburg Center and doing your first show somewhere else?

DW: It was really exciting to work in a museum setting and with colleagues, like Dr. Mary Schmidt Campbell who invited me to think about the Studio Museum's collections. The photographs of James Van Der Zee were exciting to me because of my experience with *Harlem on My Mind.* I worked with Danny [Charles Daniel] Dawson, the curator of photography at the Studio Museum then. I had the opportunity to look at Van Der Zee 's early images as well as meet him. I also took my son to meet him. For this first research project, I worked with the collections to look for a narrative about Harlem in its heyday. There were multiple themes I wanted the show to address. I wanted to look at migration. I also wanted to think about dress, desire, pleasure, and beauty as well as the aspect of entertainment. I looked for ways to talk about Van Der Zee's photographs and the streets of Harlem, which was pretty exciting to experience.

KB: Did you find that those narratives were already being discussed or were you charting new territory with those particular themes?

DW: Some narratives were already discussing beauty in other ways, but this was an opportunity to look at Black fashion in Harlem. We're thinking about Harlem. We're thinking about fifty years after emancipation, thinking about how we tell this multifaceted history of Black life. I don't think that story has been opened up enough for me. I felt it necessary to open up a different dialogue about Harlem and photography. Photography was also not necessarily talked about as an art form. So talking about that in relation with Van Der Zee's Harlem-heyday photographs in 1982 was central.

As I mentioned, I did the Ulmann show in 1981. So, I'm looking at Black life in different ways. I curated a show at the Schomburg Center called *Art Against Apartheid: A Photographic Exhibition* in 1984. I wanted to use the work of Moutoussamy-Ashe, Peter Magubane, Ernest Cole, and others to look at how artists and photographers were documenting and reflecting on apartheid. In 1985, I curated *New World Africans: 19th-Century Images of Blacks in South America and the Caribbean* at the Schomburg Center. Specifically, I acquired a collection from a collector named Hack [Haskel] Hoffenberg. He had images of Brazilian tobacco, coffee, and sugar plantations. It was just amazing to look at not only because these were Black workers but also because of the way the photographs were made—it was difficult to know that some of these people were still enslaved. These Black Brazilians maintained their connections to their African roots through hairstyles, dress, head wraps, and their methods of work.

KB: That's a lot. In those first years, you were curating simultaneous exhibitions and having at least one exhibition up every year from 1981 to 1984/85. I wanted to ask you to talk a little bit more about navigating difficult situations because I think that's a question a lot of curators have, especially beginning curators or young curators working with living artists. How do you navigate those challenging situations? What was your experience like and what would you impart?

DW: Well, you know, I liked the dance. It's truly a dance. When you said "navigating," I think of a moment in the sea, where we're navigating those ups and downs, those waves. It was and is a treacherous experience for a young curator because you're opening up your heart. For those young curators who are interested, I recommend exploring new terrain. Some encounters will be difficult, but most people will be excited and interested to work with you. For instance, during my first years as a curator, I met a lot of Black photographers who were working as journalists at the Apollo Theater. Garland Anderson was one who was so excited about my interest in his work. He photographed the stage performers in Harlem.

In terms of navigating, don't let one person hold you back because of their pain. There was a lot of pain among photographers in not being at the table or invited into collections that many desired to be in, such as at the Museum of Modern Art [MoMA]. They felt that places like MoMA would help set off their careers and showcase their fantastic works. Finding a mentor was also really important. Gordon Parks was my mentor. I reached out to Gordon and David Driskell early on to ask how they managed. They said the exact same thing.

KB: All this curatorial work you're doing in the 1980s; the comments that you're the only show in town focusing on African American and African diasporic photography; and your experience with *Harlem on My Mind* and the controversy that photography isn't art—how did you think about all this in relation to your practice as a curator? I'm wondering where as a curator you intervened in these conversations. Do you see the work that you were doing as bringing photography into the vernacular of contemporary art?

DW: In the late 1970s, I got my MFA from the Pratt Institute; several years later, in the 1980s, I went to City University of New York for a MA in museum studies. With my experience and credentials, I was invited to be on panels and present lectures. I sat on panels for the New York State Council on the Arts [NYSCA], the New York Council for the Humanities, and the Kentucky Arts Council, among others. I talked about the importance of preservation and seeing photography as an art form. And that happened on the state level. But then I visited museums and gave talks—I sat on panels at CAA, SPE, the Association of African American Museums, and the American Association of Museums. I had those venues where I could open up and talk about photography. Then I started talking about the art form of photography based on my studies of photography and the works of Berenice Abbott, Ulmann, and Dorothea Lange. I aimed to create a way to align the trajectory of images by white photographers and women photographers with those that were created by Black photographers. So when I was invited for public programming, I had the opportunity to do that.

KB: One of the things that I learned from you is the importance of writing as a curator. Given how writing has become such a prolific aspect of your work, what do you see as your responsibility to the subject matter you care so much about?

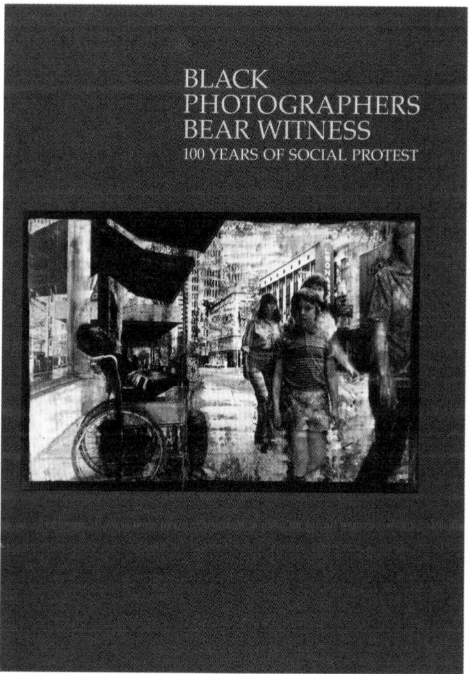

Fig. 2.8 Cover of Deborah Willis and Howard Dodson, *Black Photographers Bear Witness: 100 Years of Social Protest*, exh. cat. (Williams College Museum of Art, 1989).

DW: I curated a show called *Black Photographers Bear Witness: 100 Years of Social Protest* in 1989 for the Williams College Museum of Art [fig. 2.8]. It was an opportunity to look at civil rights photography from the early nineteenth century and how Black photographers were bearing witness to injustice. How do you write about that? How do you think about that? I started reading W. E. B. Du Bois again and how we thought about images at that time. I did not know that Frederick Douglass wrote about photography, but I knew one curator at Howard University, Donna Wells, who was writing her dissertation on his writings. I loved her. She would smile because it was such a big secret. She didn't want anyone to know about it. But she found his writings on photography and talked to me about some of the things he shared. Allan Sekula also wrote about the shadow archive. He gave me an article about Douglass and photography. That's when I began to rethink about how, in the nineteenth century, Black people were also writing about their images.

KB: Do you find that writing—your own writing but also your exposure to other writing, like Douglass's on photography—shifted the way you approach curatorial work, curating photography? It also goes vice versa, right? How has your curatorial practice shifted the way you write about art and photography, but also your receptivity to the way you read about that subject as well?

DW: Yes, it all shifted because I had an opportunity to understand the importance of language as well as its absence. When I think about the way that Black people were described by white curators and historians at the time, they were not seen as human beings. I remember reading an article and people were talking about "the subaltern," you know? [*Laughs.*] I was like, how are Black people seen as subaltern? The other part is the people who picked cotton were described as stoop labor. They were not described as people, individuals, men, women, or children who worked in cotton fields to survive during and after slavery. So, I wanted to find a new language, new ways to depict Black people, but to see them as human and describe what they're doing. Yes, it is stoop labor, but they are people who are bending down, picking cotton in the field. I wanted to try to give them a sentence as opposed to a one-word depiction of their duties and work.

KB: You've written over twenty publications to date. Do you find that each time you approach a writing project, it is an endeavor to find a new language?

DW: Yes. [*Laughs.*] I'm smiling because I remember working on—I can't remember what project it was—but I could find so many beautiful photographs of Black people. I was like, "Wow, these photographs are beautiful." When I traveled to different collections, I would think, somebody needs to write a book about beauty, talk about beauty, and think about the experience because I'm not only looking at art, I'm looking at how images were constructed in popular culture.

After a dozen years at the Schomburg Center, I moved to Washington, DC, to take a position as associate director for Research and Collections and exhibitions curator at the Smithsonian Institution's Center for African American History and Culture. This was the precursor to the current National Museum of African American History and Culture. I created shows there such as *Life on the Road: The Photography of Milt Hinton* [1997], a photographer who was also a musician. I began to think about the search for a beautiful experience during a difficult time when Black musicians traveled and how they survived on the road. They had to live but couldn't go downtown. They had to survive in rooming houses and sometimes in the pleasure and discomfort of families who lived in the towns they played in.

I really appreciated reading broadly across fields. I had been thinking about going back to school for a doctorate and was looking for the right program. I felt that art history and American studies were not suited for me. I loved the writings of Stuart Hall. I started reading Hall, thinking about how to talk about culture and embrace cultural studies, which helped me rethink and write much more broadly about images and the history of art. I'm looking not only at photography but also at the culture of photography, the culture of Black studies, and the culture of whiteness. All of that was going on as I was finding my voice in photography and curating at the same time. Eventually, I settled on a doctoral program in cultural studies at George Mason University where Jeffrey Stewart was a professor. There, I felt I could merge the language of cultural studies, art history, and bring in discussions of beauty. I wanted to explore how we complicate the term *beauty* going all the way back to Van Der Zee's photographs. Certainly, he recognized that Black people were denied this broad history of photography.

When I met Carla Williams, around this time in the 1990s, she was a graduate student and photographing her own body. We decided to collaborate on a book of photography and the Black female body, connecting it all the way back to Saartjie [Sarah] Baartman, also known as the Hottentot Venus. We wanted to think about Black women, their bodies and body shapes, and how they have been historically and publicly perceived as both grotesque and beautiful. The denial of desire and denial of beauty was something I wanted to explore.

KB: I think what you just said is tremendous. *The Black Female Body: A Photographic History* [2002] is one of my favorite books of all time; I love it and always go back to it—it's such an important piece of writing and editing. For many students, and even for others who aren't art students, you gave them the language, a context for what it is they're doing. It must have been incredibly liberating for people who felt isolated or like they were working in a vacuum on this topic until you came along and pointed out that there's this long history and we need to think about how we are acculturated to either see or not see Black women in popular culture. I think that's an incredible contribution and, as Black cultural producers, we're still seeking opportunities like that.

DW: Thank you for making those connections because women curators at the time were also looking for different narratives, like different artists at work. Some artists as well as curators were using the quilt form as a way to create a new encounter with art, outside of the rubric of folk art. Folk art has always been a part of the history, but there was a moment when women curators invited contemporary artists who were looking at quilting and creating textile work to be more integrated into contemporary art dialogues. I think that's another important intervention that happened during the 1980s–1990s.

KB: Is that how would you describe it? If you could describe the approach for artists and curators at this time, particularly Black artists, Black women, and curators of color, would you call it interventionist?

DW: We had to disrupt and find a new language. I know in the South, many of the women felt they needed to use the word *griot,* which was focused on the oral traditions of African cultures that were mainly male. But women started memorializing their histories and stories, and I think that was an intervention in this history [fig. 2.9].

KB: You mentioned navigating Black culture, which is an important point to talk about because, as you stated, you take a

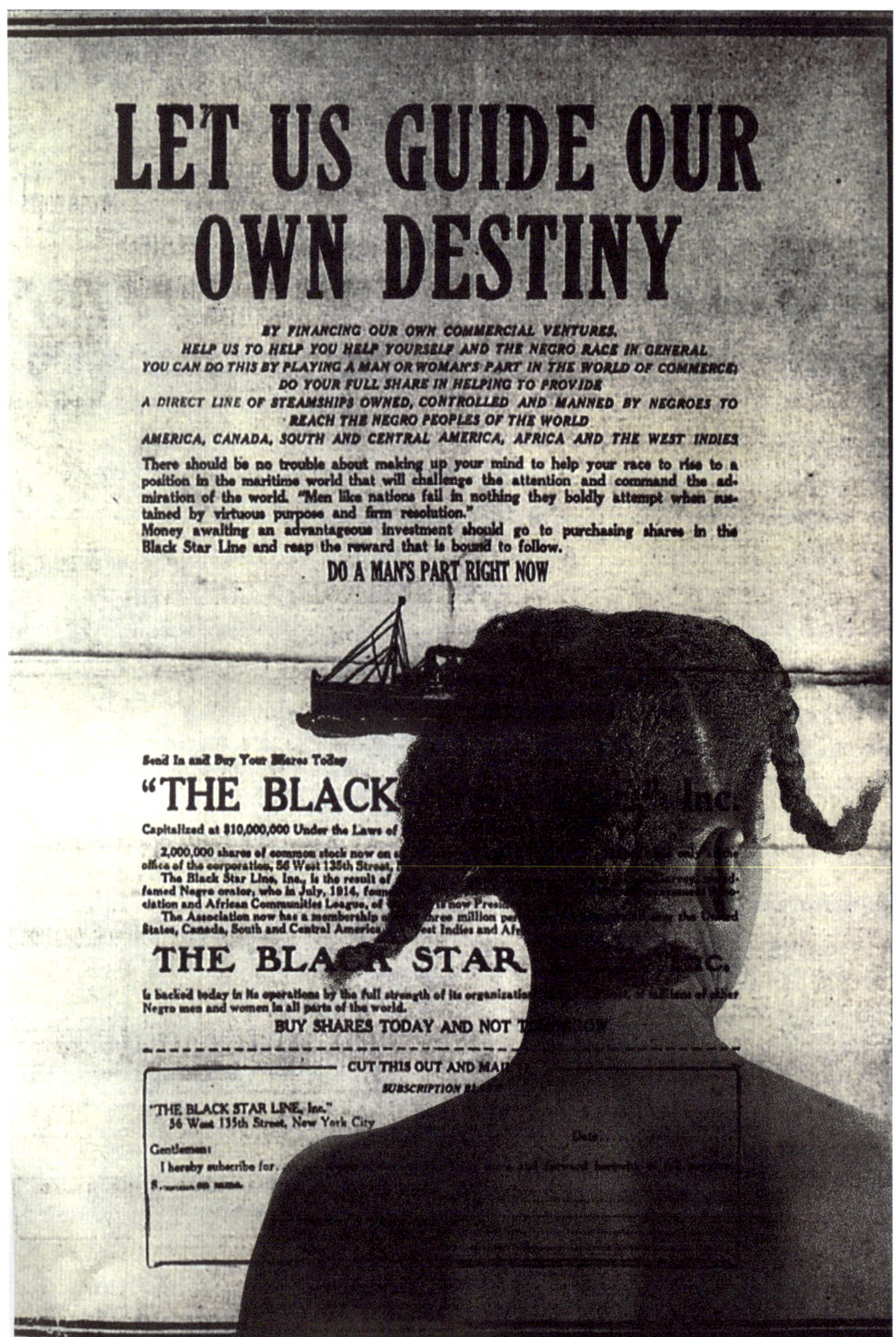

Fig. 2.9 Adama Delphine Fawundu (American, b. 1971). *Let Us Guide Our Own Destiny,* archival pigment on cotton paper, 55.88 × 76.2 cm, 2018. Artwork shown in *100 Years | 100 Women,* curated by Deborah Willis, virtual exhibition, 2020.

position about identification and the radicality that is part of the ability to claim one's subjecthood. I can relate a lot of that to the writings of Stuart Hall. Talk to me a little bit more about that because identification in Black cultural production is a long, fraught subject. How have you positioned yourself within this framework as a curator and photographer?

DW: First, as a curator, I'm always looking for righting and rewriting stories—righting as in R-I-G-H-T and writing as in W-R-I-T-E—to create this way to tell the story from the curatorial side. The curatorial side, for me, is finding artists who are interested in the shows I'm curating or the themes I'm considering for programming.

For instance, I organized a conference with a colleague at New York University [NYU], Manthia Diawara, for the *Black Portraiture[s]* series in Paris in 2013 ["The Black Body in the West/Représentation du corps noir en occident"]. My interest was to look at the experience of Black life globally, to think about the global South, and to consider artists and writers who are multilingual, which I am not. But in my mind's eye, I am. I love to think about words and pictures, and how some of these experiences have broadened my understanding of life, and Black life in particular.

KB: I remember that 2013 conference. It was a phenomenal experience. You would see the same people coming back because there was just such a curiosity and desire to contribute to the dialogue. And that has been true in many ways in the years—more than a decade—the *Black Portraiture[s]* conference has taken place. I wonder what you learned about this qualifier of Blackness in the different contexts it shows up because it shifts as you go to different places. What have you learned through that shifting?

DW: To finish answering your earlier question about how I've positioned myself as a photographer in comparison to my side as a curator and programmer, I've learned that the civil rights movement has been essential for rights movements worldwide. I've learned that the legacy of the civil rights movement has opened opportunities for people in other countries to restate their goals and identify their works. When we think about Lorraine Hansberry and her work on the movement, and connect it to the movements worldwide, we're all remixing these stories. As a photographer, that's something I wanted to visualize when I traveled and made images. I wanted to show different generations of people from the nineteenth to the twentieth centuries and find ways to tell their stories. Think about Zora Neale Hurston, her writings, and what she was trying to do with Black life as an anthropologist in the 1930s. These are my ways of connecting my visual experience as a photographer and my curatorial experience as a visual person. I love the work that I do because it has this multipronged experience. I like the touch of culture; I want to feel it everywhere I go, from tasting foods, to listening to music, to having visual experiences.

KB: In our last session, you discussed the importance of women in the maturation of your career and mentorship. You mentioned several women who were significant in guiding and encouraging you. Can you talk about that experience? Did you recognize it while it was happening, or did you identify it retrospectively?

DW: It happened early on. As I mention often, growing up in a beauty shop, I learned a lot from women and listening to women. As a young churchgoer, my first job was as the church secretary. Miss Mae Rhea was my boss. She was smart and forceful. She was a secretary for public housing in Germantown, but I didn't know that at the time. She guided me in how to become a professional. I was responsible for making sure that church members paid their dues. During high school, I worked at Shapiro's Shoes on Fifty-Second Street in West Philadelphia; Ms. Cookie, one of the owners, was my supervisor. Also, during my early days in Philadelphia, I worked for Linda Clark, who directed the Center for Community Studies at Temple University. At the Schomburg Center, I had the opportunity to work with Ruth Ann Stewart who served as associate director and Jean Blackwell Hutson, the director. All these were women who were guiding me and from whom I learned how to guide others.

When I was working with Mary Schmidt Campbell, I met Kellie Jones as a curator at the Studio Museum. Kellie and I became good friends. We spent time working together, curating shows, talking about our curatorial practice and art history, and looking at contemporary art. For me, women became not only collaborators but also mentors.

KB: How has mentorship from both men and women affected how you show up as a professional in this field?

DW: It's really important to be a mentor. Just recently in Miami, I met Tamary Kudita, a photographer from Zimbabwe who lives in Cape Town. She said, "I'm just honored to meet you. You are a hero for us in South Africa. We read your writings. We follow your books. We follow your exhibitions." She didn't even know that we were in South Africa a few years ago.

I found it fascinating that we can bring communities together, but we never know who's listening or when they're listening, which affects how we reshape our stories over time. With regard to my mentoring, I have a number of students whom I spend time with. I believe in what they want to do with their futures and I want to be there for them. I do that for men and women across the board, so there is an opportunity to support their dreams.

Sometimes being a mentor is hard because you have to tell real stories of how it's not going to be easy. Some people may see you and think that because there are Black people in certain spaces that they can also step into those shoes without paying any dues. And paying dues is really just the structure of hard work. It's like when you're constantly asked to write a blurb for someone's book, somebody you don't even know but they contact you because they've read something you wrote. You can't do it all.

Mentoring is multifaceted. A mentor could also be someone from my generation, like Leslie King-Hammond. I've seen her mentor a number of people, but she's also mentored me. She tells people that I've mentored her by putting her work in some of my exhibitions. That's where mentorship is multilayered.

KB: You're also a mentor in your position as a professor. You've been teaching in the Department of Photography and Imaging at NYU's Tisch School of the Arts since 2001. You are a university professor there. You work with students every year, a new group of students to follow over the course of four years. How has finding your way into the right program and taking pieces from other disciplines to help shape who you are and what you do affected your approach in leading an academic department?

DW: As I mention often, I do this by being a close listener and listening for what's missing. I find it important to create a space for my students to go to exhibitions and put different venues and artists on their radar. This is so they become engaged in the experience of going into a gallery and not feeling that tension of where's my space, where's my place, and am I allowed to go into these museum spaces? It would always bother me when I'd hear people say, "Well, I didn't feel welcome to go onto the steps of the Met or to a gallery in Chelsea."

I'm saying, you don't need to feel welcomed. If you want to go in because you want to learn about the poetics and aesthetics of art and you want to see what art someone has made, then you should go in. Just because someone's at the door wearing very expensive clothes doesn't mean you can't go in, you know? Just because the guard is looking at you in a dismissive way does not mean you know what he's thinking, nor does he know what you're thinking. I push my students to reimagine their experiences and walk into spaces that are broader than the spaces they know, not only on campus but in their own communities. Going to exhibitions is a required part of my syllabus, a required activity that cannot be overlooked. They must write a paragraph reflecting on their memories, encounters, or experiences with the exhibition. Also, I think it's important to go into the archives. I think it's really important for artists to use and understand the importance of archival research and how to incorporate new stories that give you a sense of joy, give you a sense of disgust, give you a sense of pleasure.

So that's why I try to create an open syllabus centered around experience. When students talk to me about belonging and longing, and I say, "What do you mean by you don't belong in certain spaces, but you long to be in these spaces?" I often tell them, "Well, let's create a space that you want to be a part of, and in doing so, make it work."

KB: Creating space for oneself is, to me, an essential characteristic of curatorial practice. As a curator, you fundamentally are creating space—that is what you're doing—and finding a space to show what it is that you are keen to show. This is, as you put it, a tremendous learning experience for how you show up in the world. I wonder if photography is a useful tool to break down those barriers because it gives the audience an opportunity to see themselves in an exhibition space.

DW: That's great. Photography is performative. I believe that oftentimes people can find a voice through this notion of photography as performance, that they can feel a sense of privilege to have access to a space and memory. I think that's really an important part of the educational space when we think about the plight of young students or migrants who move to this country, or someone who decides to leave their home country because they see no future there. But there's a sense of believing there's a future in crossing those waters and borders, which are sometimes violent and really intimidating. I believe that creates a space when we see narratives in images that are sometimes difficult but give a sense of hope.

KB: That's right because the photograph is a space in and of itself, in addition to its context within a larger exhibition. That's really wonderful. I have a bigger question that I think is a good way to round out our conversation: How would you describe your contribution to the curatorial field?

DW: This is like when someone asked me, "So what do you think your legacy is?" And I was like, "Oh my God."

I've been a witness. My contribution has been mainly to cross the border as a witness. By that I mean to create a voice for artists, for viewers, for the community, and for the institution; to find a way to open up this privileged art space; and to fuse and merge my own personal experiences that were sometimes difficult as a curator but also sometimes rewarding. Because I had opportunities to go into archives or into museum spaces that many people have not been invited to, I was able to unpack different stories. People always carry cultural baggage whenever they enter new spaces, but the opportunity to open up sometimes treasured, sometimes difficult images was a chance for me, as a curator, to be not just a witness and mediator but also a voice for many experiences. When I think about encountering difficult things—curating images that objectify the Black body or that explore lynching or death—it gives me an opportunity to shift narratives and to translate them through my voice and vision, providing a different way of thinking about the notion of curatorial practice.

KB: Thank you for that. Are there any curatorial projects that you're working on presently?

DW: I'm considering working on an exhibition on the Black Civil War soldier and the book I published this year, *The Black Civil War Soldier: A Visual History of Conflict and Citizenship* [2021]. One of the struggles and triumphs of being a curator is thinking about how to title an exhibition or book. The title needs to invite people into a space with a curiosity. When I wanted to do a book on the Black Civil War soldier, I wanted to call it "Conflict and Citizenship." Even though these men were not citizens, they stood in front of American flags in countless portrait studios. They saw themselves as citizens.

KB: I think that's an affirming place to end our interview, letting the public know that there's so much more to do. Thank you very much for taking the time. Yours is a tremendous contribution to the *Black Curators Matter* project.

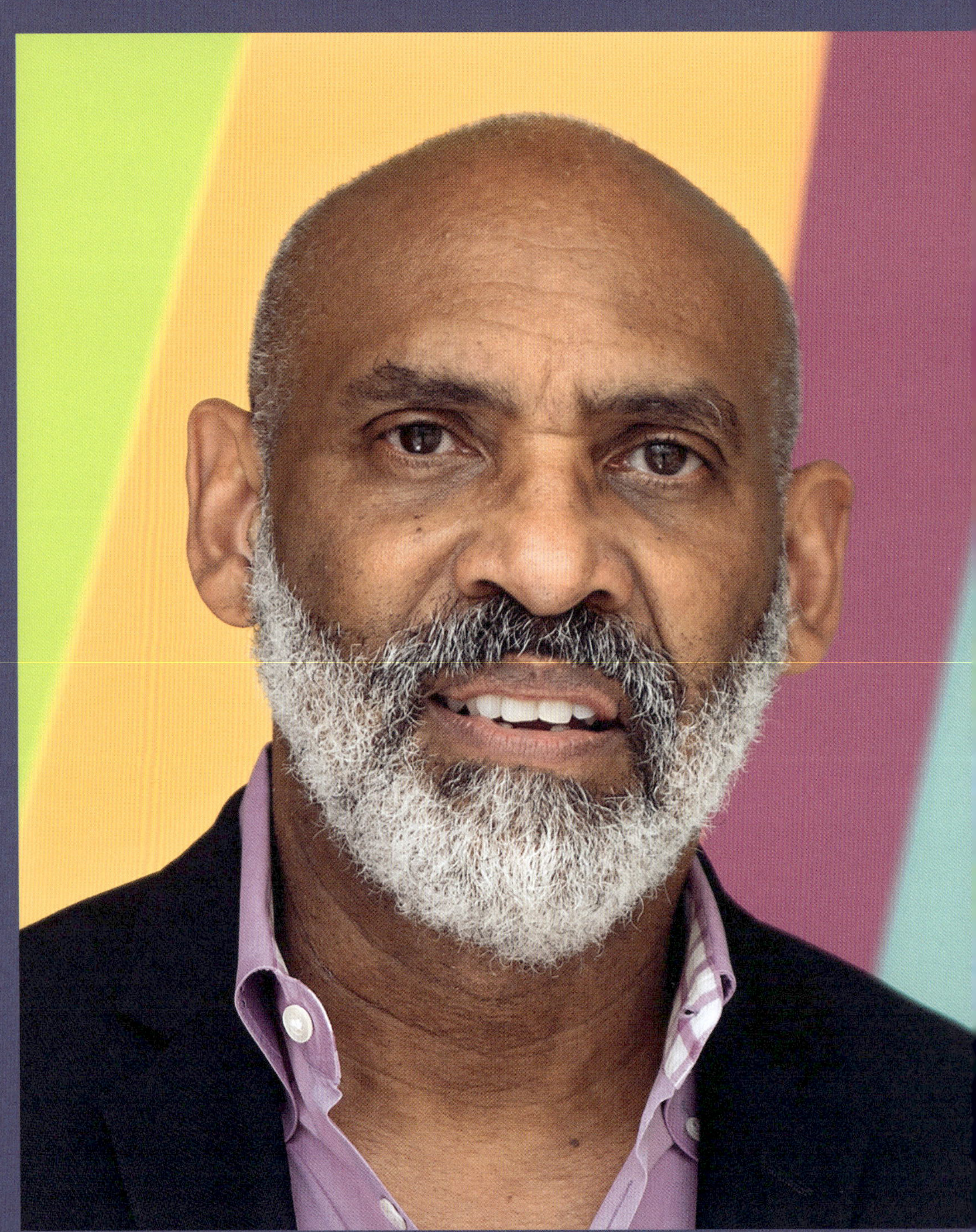

Richard J. Powell

INTERVIEWED BY AARON BRYANT
13 and 30 April 2022

AARON BRYANT (AB): My name is Aaron Bryant. I'm a curator of photography and visual culture at the National Museum of African American History and Culture. If you don't mind, Dr. Powell, I'd like to go ahead and jump in. I'm wondering if you could tell us about where you were born and raised.

RICHARD J. POWELL (RJP): I was born and raised in Chicago, Illinois. Given my age, I have some memories of the 1950s, but I have more vivid memories of the 1960s and 1970s. I attended Morehouse College for my undergraduate education. I left Chicago for Atlanta in 1971.

AB: We'll talk more about that because Chicago during the 1950s and 1960s was incredibly active in terms of the art and culture scene for African Americans. Could you talk about your parents? What were their names and where were they from?

RJP: My father was Louis Colonel Powell. He was born in Oglethorpe, Georgia. He died in 1987. He worked as a waiter at the Palmer House in Chicago. My mother was Eliza Hughes Powell. She was born in Mullins, South Carolina, and was an elementary school teacher. I am one of those first-generation Northerners.

AB: What part of Chicago did you grow up in?

RJP: I grew up at 727 East Sixtieth Street, which is on the corner of Cottage Grove Avenue and Sixtieth Street. It's on the edge of the Midway Plaisance Park right across from Lorado Taft's sculpture *Fountain of Time* [1922]. This is walking distance from the University of Chicago. Woodlawn was my neighborhood and the neighborhood of Hyde Park was nearby.

AB: What was it like for you growing up?

RJP: We lived in a seventeen-story apartment building that had just been built a couple of months before my family and I moved in. It was one of those projects that had been green-lighted by Mayor Richard J. Daley for middle-income urban living. There were lots of interesting people living in my building. I've recently had some conversations about that time with Gayle Wald, a professor at George Washington University who's writing a biography of the folksinger Ella Jenkins, who lived in my building. I was one of the children who studied music, culture, rhythm, and dance with her. As a young person, I attended the Hyde Park Art

Center and also took classes at the University of Chicago's Laboratory School. My parents encouraged my brother and me to explore Chicago's art venues and cultural offerings. I have fond memories of ice skating on the Midway Plaisance and going to the Griffin Museum of Science and Industry, the Art Institute of Chicago, and the Field Museum.

I attended the Austin O. Sexton Elementary School. What was important about that school is that the teachers lived in the neighborhood and there was a real sense of connection between teachers, children, and their families. Since my brother was several years older than me, the teachers I ended up working with were teachers he had also studied with, so there was a connection there. This was before integration and there was a real sense of community, connectedness, and constantly being encouraged to do whatever it was you wanted to do.

AB: What are some joyous memories you have of this period? And what were the challenges, whether in school or as you were navigating the city? What did it mean to be African American, and particularly an African American male growing up in Chicago during such a time of change between the 1950s and 1970s?

RJP: The other part of growing up in Chicago is what it means to live in the city, to have your wits about yourself as you navigate the streets, and to be attuned to all the things around you in terms of dangers and bad influences. Sadly, I must confess that growing up during that period, there were many young people I hung out with who are not here today. Some of my friends did not survive the ravages of living in the city: drugs, gangs, and the like. It's sobering, but it's also life. In retrospect, I'm so grateful for having had an opportunity to walk through the streets and test my skills and abilities to navigate that space. Thankfully I survived. As I said, some of my friends and colleagues did not survive.

What was crucial for me was, after graduating from a public elementary school, I attended an all-boys Catholic high school. I remember talking to some friends at Yale University years later and they called those schools "poor people's preps," [*laughs*] in the sense that you paid tuition to the Catholic archdiocese of the school. The teachers were priests and laypeople. They were tough-on-tough kids. That was really important for me to survive that period. It paid off having some discipline and sense of direction instilled in me.

AB: Looking back now, was there a teacher in elementary school that stood out that you think might have influenced you? And in high school, were there people you interacted with who might have influenced you and your decision to become an art historian?

RJP: Thinking back to elementary school, it was probably my kindergarten teacher who was very encouraging of the scribbles I was making and gave me praise. It could also be that my teacher, Miss Fleming, was looking at my scribbles and noticing that I had good attention to detail;

I made sure the hands, heads, fingers, eyeballs, and ears were all there. High school was also quite special. I was very involved with the arts in high school. I was especially involved in theater, and one of the priests who I worked closely with in theater was Father Barry Schneider.

I was in several interesting theatrical productions in those years. We did an African version of *Hamlet* where we changed the names of all the Shakespearean characters to African names. It was also interesting in those years that some of the field trips we took were eye-opening and informative for me. One of those field trips was to see the sculptor Richard Hunt, whom I had read about.

There were other memorable field trips in Chicago. One production that stood out for me was Les Ballets Africains, the wonderful dance troupe from Guinea. We also went to hear Oscar Brown Jr. and Jean Pace, these two extraordinary cabaret performers, and a Brazilian accordionist named Sivuca [Severino Dias de Oliveira]. They did a show that was called *Joy* [1970]. It was basically songs and dance. Brown was fair-skinned with curly hair and an expressive face. Pace was brown with this big afro and dangling earrings. And Sivuca was albino, a little cross-eyed, and played the accordion in a way I had never heard or imagined. I remember seeing that concert and saying to myself, "There is an art world out there. There are creative people who make music, speak different languages, and look fabulous." All of that stuck in my head. It was this early seed of encouragement and creativity that stuck with me.

AB: It sounds like you were engaged with art, but at that point were you thinking about becoming an artist or were you already one?

RJP: I was definitely making drawings and paintings during this time. I would attend the 57th Street Art Fair and the street fairs in Hyde Park every summer, where artists lined up their works on sidewalks so you could look at them. I would go to the DuSable Museum of African American History and had interactions with its founder Margaret Burroughs. So, yes, I fancied myself an artist. But I was also writing. I was thinking visually, but I was also thinking with words and I had opportunities to perform. All those things mattered tremendously as I moved forward.

AB: It's interesting—as you were talking, all this started to make more sense when I think about your body of work and how it is so interdisciplinary. Not just interdisciplinary in terms of art but the idea of art representing something, representing a voice or an experience, and how those experiences translate across different forms of art and history. I think that pretty much sums up your work when you read your scholarship. It's not just about the art, but the way that you're able to talk about, for example, the blues aesthetic. There is this connection between different art forms that manifest through sound, movement, and gesture, as well as visually.

RJP: I wanted to take it all in during those years. I wanted to read. I wanted to see. And there might've been a little desire to branch out beyond Chicago as a result of watching television. These were the years when public television was beginning to feature Black people on shows like *Soul!* with Ellis Haizlip. I watched those shows assiduously. I looked at all those poets and writers, and said, "Oh wow, I want to be with them." I'm also thinking about Maya Angelou's public television show *Blacks, Blues, Black!* that came out of San Francisco. I was mesmerized by this stunning, articulate African American woman talking to B. B. King, talking about the blues, talking about language, food, et cetera. Those little moments sitting at home watching TV were the things that made me say, "I'm having a great time in Chicago, but I've got to get out of here to do something else and meet somebody else."

AB: It sounds like you were discovering early on that there was a broader world outside of Chicago and television. For me, PBS was really important. I could be a rambunctious kid until a documentary came on, a photograph popped up on the screen, and someone started reading a letter. I was just mesmerized. Or the sound of my father listening to Jr. Walker & the All Stars and I was just staring at the album covers. I could see the music through the colors and forms moving across the album covers, and we take that for granted.

In Chicago, there was so much happening around that time. In large cities, in general, there were tribes of African American artists who were coming together. We're familiar with what was happening in New York, with the Spiral artist collective and Kamoinge Workshop during the 1960s, and the Black arts movement with Amiri Baraka, Woodie King Jr., and others. In Chicago, did you have a similar tribe of young adults who were also into the arts? Did you all create a network?

RJP: I really didn't. I was on the sidelines. I knew of the Organization of Black American Culture, the writers' workshops with Hoyt W. Fuller and Don L. Lee [Haki R. Madhubuti]. But I was never part of any of that. Of course, I knew of the African Commune of Bad Relevant Artists [AfriCOBRA] and their mural. But I never was part of that either. While I was in high school, this must've been 1969, I went to the University of Chicago for the screening of the Jean-Luc Godard film, *Sympathy for the Devil* [1968] with Mick Jagger. This was during the Democratic National Convention, so it was really crazy in Chicago. There were all these political people, all these radicals in the audience. I remember going to see the screening of this film and Abbie Hoffman, the great political figure, was there. Jean Genet, the great poet and radical from France, was also there. He was very involved with the Black Panthers. So, I would occasionally get out. I also remember going to the University of Chicago for a concert with the Art Ensemble of Chicago, which was totally bizarre with costumes and sounds that were all over the place. Those were the few moments of me really breaking out. My folks kept a close leash on me [*laughs*]. Despite all the things I'm telling you, I was pretty much at home all that time and only got to venture out with school events. I was aware of things, but I wasn't directly engaged in any of that.

AB: You're talking about writing, performing in theater, as well as performance art, visual art, and music. How vivid these memories are for you is really something. Art has always been a part of you, and Chicago helped expose and open you up to it. What is it about art and creative expression that is so important to you or was important to you then? What's the connection?

RJP: This may not be a good answer, but I'll give it anyway. It has to be part of your constitution [*laughs*]. What I mean by that is, if you are not disposed to creativity, it's really, really difficult to embrace that world, to think about it as something you want to pursue. I've always had this imaginative, creative part of me. When it came time to declare a major and pursue a profession, I knew it would have to be involved in some aspect of the arts. Education was also important.

Because my mother was an elementary school teacher, I was exposed to important teachers throughout my life. There was value in being an educator—in being an arts educator—and in transmitting ideas about the arts to others as people had done for me. Being creative was just in me, and there was no other way I could function and move through the world.

It was also important to have family and parents who did not put me on the "doctor track," "business track," or "lawyer track." They were just happy I was getting an education. They were happy I had found something I was interested in and wanted to pursue. It was helpful, too, to not have the pressure to think, "Okay, how am I going to feed myself?" [*Laughs.*] Maybe that was there, but it wasn't explicit. I'm sure I'm ventriloquizing them when I say, "He'll be alright because he's going to follow his path and that's going to help him land on his feet."

AB: In the early twentieth century, Chicago emerged as a center of African American culture and history. We often think of New York in the 1960s and 1970s as the place where Blackness was unapologetic and where a lot of art and culture was happening. But, in the national imagination, so much of that era's Black cultural expression is connected to Chicago, regardless of one's educational background. We all grew up talking about *Cooley High* [1974], for example [*laughs*], or watching *Good Times* [1974–79]. So much Blackness was coming out into the world from Chicago. Why do you think that is? What was it about Chicago in particular? Even thinking about the mural *Wall of Respect* [1967] created by the collective AfriCOBRA and how that mural created a movement in Black communities all over the country. What was it about Chicago?

RJP: Now that I'm an art historian, I understand why the 1960s and 1970s were so important, and that there was a precedent for this in earlier decades. There was always a strong Black cultural component to the city. Going back to the Harlem Renaissance era, we have people like Richmond Barthé, who first came to Chicago before going to New York, and Archibald Motley who was doing incredible paintings in Chicago. As I'm thinking about Black art and artists in Chicago, it was almost as if they started in Chicago and then moved to New York. I'm also thinking about Richard Wright and the famous painter Eldzier Cortor. Gordon Parks also made the move from the Midwest to the East Coast. Katherine Dunham first made her mark as a dancer in Chicago on the South Side and, eventually, took her whole troupe and interests in Black dance to the Caribbean, New York, and Hollywood. There's always been a Black artistic energy in Chicago. I would also add that Chicago is one step removed from Mississippi, Tennessee, Louisiana, and deep Delta Black culture.

The blues musicians who came up in the 1940s, like B. B. King and Howlin' Wolf, made their mark in Chicago after having worked in the cotton fields in the Deep South. Chicago has always had its connections to what I would call root Black culture in ways we don't necessarily find on the East Coast. Chicago has always held tight to a fundamental cultural Blackness that, when the 1960s and 1970s arrived, manifested itself in AfriCOBRA, in the poetry of Don L. Lee, et cetera. I was fortunate to have grown up in the middle of that.

AB: This is the first time that I thought about all this. Of course, particularly in classes on African American culture, we talk about Chicago culture and the Chicago blues being very different from blues in, say, Kansas City, or even jazz. It's really fascinating to talk about this idea of root Black culture and how it might be very different in a place like Chicago than in New York, and maybe something to explore.

RJP: The other part of it has to do with economics and sociology. Chicago is a place where working-class people live their lives as laborers. It's no surprise in the 1930s and 1940s that artists like Charles White, Elizabeth Catlett, and others understood their respective art as linked to the folk, common laborers, and the struggles of working-class Black people [fig. 3.1]. Of course, Black people are working-class all over the world, in Harlem as well as in Chicago. But there's a particular kind of industrial life for Black people in the Midwest that's very different from the service-based labor we find in other places. I think that character really shapes what we see.

I have to add I grew up listening to the radio. Radio in Chicago—and I'm sure Baltimore was very similar—was incredibly rich with gospel music, jazz, and R & B. This is the moment of the rise of Motown, great gospel singers, jazz musicians, and the like. This soundtrack has never left me, and in many respects, I see it as a theoretical and philosophical influence on my engagement with the visual arts.

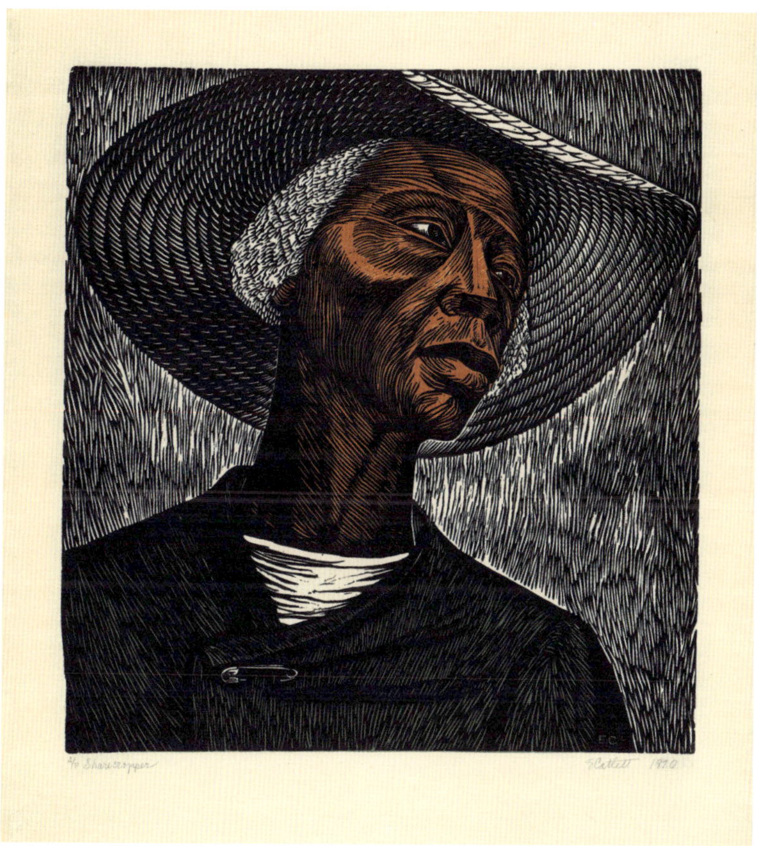

Fig. 3.1 Elizabeth Catlett (American, 1915–2002). *Sharecropper,* color linocut on cream Japanese paper, image: 45 × 43.1 cm, sheet: 55.7 × 51.5 cm, 1952 (printed 1970). Chicago, Art Institute of Chicago, 1992.182. Artwork shown in *African-American Artists, 1880–1987: Selections from the Evans-Tibbs Collection,* curated by Richard J. Powell, Guy. C. McElory, Sharon Patton, and David Driskell, traveling exhibition, 1989.

AB: Yes, and that goes back to my earlier question about interdisciplinarity. You bring in multiple perspectives. It's like a full experience in your understanding and interpretation of art, so it's not just through the lens of a particular discipline or field. You must bring the entire person and all their experiences to making meaning out of visual culture, as it's an expression of so many different things. Are there other scholars who do that kind of work?

Particularly for African Americans, we might use multiple lenses, but I'm thinking of the way you talk about theater and how people may not necessarily see the connections between theater, particularly Black theater, and the visual arts. They're the same thing. When you're curating, it's creating a stage and creating drama, shock, awe, and wonderment, which is what you do in theater. Do you think it's common for people to bring so many perspectives into the interpretation of a single thing, painting, or photograph?

RJP: It wasn't until later that I realized how valuable it was to have grown up when I did and where I did. When I got to Yale for graduate school in 1980, I began to be in conversation with John Blassingame, Bob [Robert] Stepto, Skip [Henry Louis] Gates Jr., Sylvia Ardyn Boone, and Robert Farris Thompson. They were talking about Black culture as a discipline, and I realized I grew up with that discipline. I experienced all of it, not just the visual culture, but the literary, performative, political, and economic culture.

At Yale, I initially was in the Department of African American Studies. I didn't join Yale's Department of the History of Art until 1982. I stress this because my formative years in African American studies underscored the importance of having a broad understanding of culture, which kept me in good stead as I narrowed my studies down to a scholarly subdiscipline and topics within art history. What was also valuable was understanding that the life that I've led greatly informs that scholarship.

AB: So, you're coming to this understanding while at Morehouse College, where you are really involved in the arts scene and receive a BA in art in 1975. You announced yourself as an artist, which takes you through an MFA in printmaking at Howard University [1977]. How did you decide to go from Morehouse to Howard? What was that transition like?

RJP: I was on a track to be an artist. At the same time, I had been educated to understand that to be an artist, I needed to know something. I needed to have seen something. I needed a big world from which to pull ideas to create things. It wasn't just about the skills of making. It was an attempt to understand and absorb the world. I was also very lucky to make a trip to Nigeria in 1974 because that trip began to open my mind to the idea of a Black diaspora. The word *diaspora* didn't exist for me at that time.

Increasingly, I began to understand that Black people didn't just come from Chicago or Atlanta. Black people came from all over the world and spoke different languages. They were not a monolith and, to me, that was exciting. I was beginning to understand the metaphor "shades of Blackness" that people often use. These nuances, versions, and dimensions of Blackness didn't go against the Black arts movement per se, but they complicated it and made it something that was perhaps even more of a delightful challenge to try to make sense of.

AB: When did you become more intentional about how you use all this knowledge to create a distinct voice? Or did you ever become intentional about it?

RJP: I was intentional in being an artist, making art, and exhibiting work. I did one show in Atlanta at a coffeehouse toward the end of my stay, and then, in 1977, I did my MFA thesis show in the galleries at Howard.

My intention was to continue to be an artist. Failure is really important too. I remember applying to several programs to deepen my work as an artist and was rejected from all of them. I was disheartened by that. There was a moment where I just said, "Oh well, maybe I'll leave the country and try to pursue being an artist outside of the country." I was thinking about all the Black artists I was familiar with who realized that they couldn't get anywhere in the United States, so they decided to leave.

Interestingly, Winnie Owens-Hart, the ceramics teacher at Howard, encouraged me to go to an artists' colony in the summer of 1977 in Deer Isle, Maine, which I did and got a lot out of it. She also encouraged me to apply for a fellowship at the Metropolitan Museum of Art called the Rockefeller Foundation Fellowship in Museum Education. I was at my wits' end because I thought I was going to do all these other things and I said, "Well, I'll apply for this." You had to submit your application to a Met curator. I sent my application to Colta Feller Ives, who was the curator of prints and drawings. I am who I am, so I wrote Colta a long letter in addition to submitting my application. I even sent her some of my prints. I remember saying, "This is what I do as an artist, but I'd like to do this fellowship." I got the fellowship.

On my way up to Maine, I stopped in New Haven because I had heard Robert Farris Thompson lecture that spring in Washington, DC, and I said to myself, "I've got to show this guy my art." I knocked on his door and he didn't know who I was. I said, "I heard you speak in DC. I really thought your work was impressive. I want to show you my prints about Richard Wright." He said, "Well, I'm getting ready to go to Paris, but I want to introduce you to some other people here at Yale before I leave." He took me to the African American Studies Department where they were having a conference, and I met Gates and Stepto. Bob [Robert] O'Meally, whom I had met at Howard, was also at this conference. Eleanor Traylor, whom I also knew from Washington, DC, was also there. That was my first introduction to Yale. I kept that experience in my mind, but by the end of the summer I moved to New York and was working at the Met. That's a long way of answering your question about when I began to think about museums. What I began to do at that time—I wouldn't even call it curating or curation—was simply studying artists who nobody else was interested in.

I met Lowery Stokes Sims, who was a curator at the Met working with Henry Geldzhaler. Around the same time, I met Linda Goode Bryant who was running the Just Above Midtown gallery. I enjoyed hanging out with her and I met David Hammons. I'm encountering interesting artists, writers, and theater people because by this point LaTanya Richardson [Jackson] and Sam [Samuel] L. Jackson are in New York—this whole group of people who would be making names for themselves in film very soon. I knew them both from Atlanta. Sam went to Morehouse. LaTanya went to Spelman College and we actually took a few classes together. We reconnected in New York. I remember going to see Ntozake Shange's *Spell #7* [1979] at the Public Theater with them and running into Denzel Washington. They were just off-Broadway

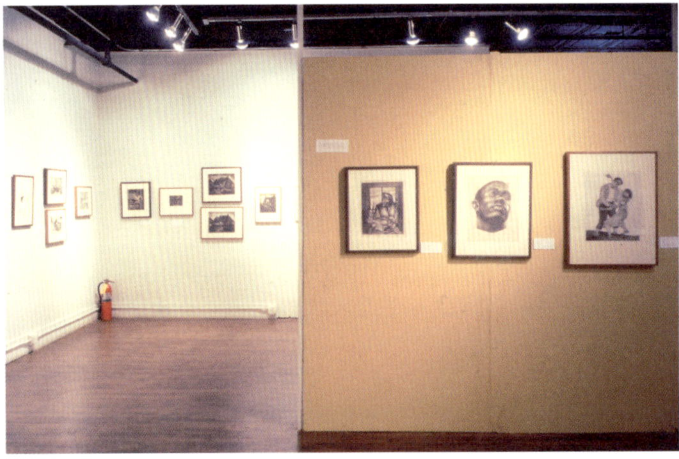

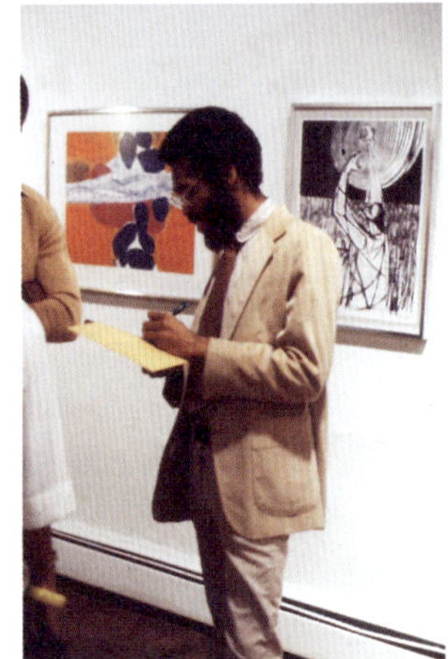

Fig. 3.2 Installation view of *Impressions/Expressions: Black American Graphics,* curated by Richard J. Powell, Studio Museum in Harlem, New York, 7 October 1979–6 January 1980.

Fig. 3.3 Richard J. Powell at the opening of *Impressions/Expressions: Black American Graphics* with Robert Blackburn's *Blue Things* (1963–70) and Samella Lewis's *Field* (1968), Studio Museum in Harlem, New York, 1979.

theater people at the time. I also connected with poets such as Jessica Hagedorn and Patricia Spears Jones.

I also met Mary Schmidt Campbell who had just been brought on as director of the Studio Museum in Harlem. I was having conversations with the Studio Museum's contract photographer, fellow Chicagoan Frank Stewart, and all sorts of interesting people, artists, and photographers. I was working on a project at the Met on Black printmakers, which was what I ended up working on during my Rockefeller Foundation Fellowship. As part of my fellowship, I traveled to San Francisco to interview the renowned printmaker Margo Humphrey. The Met fellowship also took me to Los Angeles to interview Samella Lewis. That was a wonderful year. I took an idea from my Met fellowship to Mary and said, "I'd like to do a show about Black printmakers," and she said yes.

I'd never curated a show before, but I had done enough homework on this for Mary to feel like, "Okay, maybe something will come to fruition from this." So, it was my time at the Met and in New York that really got me thinking about museums. That's how I ended up doing my first exhibition, *Impressions/Expressions: Black American Graphics* [figs. 3.2, 3.3]. It opened in 1979 at the Studio Museum and traveled through the Smithsonian Institution Traveling Exhibition Service [SITES]. It opened just before I started my MA work at Yale in 1980. It was the beginning of something that might be called curating for me. At that moment, I said, "I'm an artist but I'm also a scholar now. But I'm not just an artist and a scholar, I'm thinking about pulling works of art together and telling a story with them."

I always had it in the back of my mind that I had to learn something. You learn from other people, you learn from reading, you learn from travel. The trip to Nigeria was 1974 and starting at Yale was 1980. In those six years, I got this incredible education, globally and intellectually, and in terms of my craft as an artist. I also got to meet some interesting people that helped me figure out what I'm doing now.

AB: Your experiences between 1974 and 1980 really taught you to experience Blackness and all kinds of Blackness, not just study it. That's an important point. It brings it home that I've got a lot of work to do [*laughter*].

RJP: Well, I'm continuing to learn. You don't stop learning because every day is a revelation, and it hopefully helps you better navigate the next day.

AB: We're going to focus on your career and how that all fits within the context of your life history. When I look back at what I learned from our last conversation, it became apparent to me that you were part of this renaissance of artists and intellectuals informed by the 1960s. You graduated from Morehouse College and Howard University in the 1970s, an important transitionary period for both artists and intellectuals coming out of the Black intellectual and arts movement of the 1960s, and then you were at Yale University during the 1980s. That was also a renaissance period for universities across the board, particularly at Yale, with all these stellar alumni and people who would've been a part of your cohort. You were at Yale around the same time as actors who came out of Yale's David Geffen School of Drama, like Charles Dutton, Angela Bassett, and Courtney Vance. There was something in the air and I want to talk about that. But before I get to that, can we talk about your first curatorial project?

RJP: I'm an art historian, so I put a lot of things into a historical context. I came of age curatorially when the renowned artist/scholar/curator David Driskell did some amazing exhibitions culminating with the *Two Centuries of Black American Art* show that opened in 1976 at the Los Angeles County Museum of Art, and later traveled to the Brooklyn Museum. I was present for the Brooklyn show. I had just moved to New York. There was, in the air, this interest and excitement around the idea of organizing shows that dealt with African American art or what was then called Afro-American art.

I was a printmaker myself. I was doing research about African American printmakers and thought this topic might yield an interesting art exhibition. I am always beholden to Mary Schmidt Campbell for giving me an opportunity to organize *Impressions/Expressions: Black American Graphics.* The show opened in October 1979. I organized the exhibition while teaching art and printmaking at Norfolk State University. I was planning on leaving Norfolk State University and starting my MA program in African American studies at Yale. I have fond memories of working with Mary Schmidt Campbell and Frank Stewart.

AB: Your first exhibition turned into a major traveling exhibition. Since SITES took it and traveled it for a number of years, then can we assume it was groundbreaking in some way? Why did you think it was important to do that exhibition? Why were so many people supportive of it? What was happening at that time?

RJP: I was in New York when I first conceived this idea. I was at the Met, working in the Department of Drawings and Prints. I was also making prints. I was working with Bob [Robert] Blackburn at the Printmaking Workshop on West Seventeenth Street, so I was spending a lot of time with artists like Bob. I remember Romare Bearden coming in and getting prints made. I was hanging out with lots of young artists then, but I was also doing research at the Met.

I was also looking at people from the 1920s, 1930s, and 1940s, like Elizabeth Catlett, but also at individuals who really weren't that well-known, like Raymond Steth and other amazing printmakers like Dox Thrash who were working in Philadelphia. I took my research into the 1950s and 1960s, with artists like Norma Morgan and Mildred Thompson. People didn't know that Thompson was a printmaker before she became a painter. Sam Middleton, who was living in Europe, was also a part of my project.

I thought I did a good job, but not everybody thought so. I remember getting a review in the *New York Times* that said something like, "Well, this exhibition is very incomplete. Where is this artist, and where is that artist? Why aren't we seeing this, and why aren't we seeing that?" I was heartbroken. I thought I had done something no one else had even attempted before. I was talking to a good friend of mine, the poet Jessica Hagedorn, with whom I had collaborated years earlier. And she said, "Well, did they spell your name right?" I said, "Yes." She said, "That's fine. Move on. You're good."

Something as simple as that stuck with me. Basically, Jessica was saying you made your mark and no one can take that away from you, and you will continue to make marks. It was a project that seemed to catch on and the confirmation, as you've said, was that SITES saw viability in this exhibition. They viewed the show as a medium-risk exhibition since it was a print show. It could be packed and shipped nicely. I had done all this documentation, so we had beautiful photographs of all the printmakers. So, it was quite successful. I think it was traveling with SITES at least well into the middle of the 1980s.

Luckily, I was able to transition from Howard to New York following graduation. It was a wonderful time to be in Washington, DC. The poet E. Ethelbert Miller was an incredible interlocutor. I remember the Second National Conference of Afro-American Writers, for which I also designed the poster. It was titled "Beyond Survival: Two Centuries of Black Literature, 1776–1976" [22–24 April 1976] and organized by Stephen Henderson, a professor of African American studies and English and director of Howard's Institute for the Arts and the Humanities. There, I met the playwright and performer Ntozake Shange, the novelist Alice Walker, the novelist and essayist James Baldwin, and the who's who of Black literature at the time. Howard was a very important place for me to understand my place within the art world.

AB: Wow. Did it feel like a historical moment? Did it feel like a renaissance was happening? Did you sense something special?

RJP: I sensed that all of this was special, but I would be insincere if I said I understood the historical ramifications of that moment. It wasn't until later when I discussed the 1970s with colleagues that I realized I was living history during that period, that I was seeing creative people coming into fruition as artists, and that Washington, DC, was becoming an important spot in the Black art world. Jeff Donaldson, a founder of Chicago's AfriCOBRA and then professor of art at Howard, was working on Festac [Second World Black and African Festival of Arts and Culture] at the time, which ultimately happened in 1977. I ended up not going back to Nigeria, but he brought an amazing array of Black cultural luminaries to Howard.

I remember going to a party at Jeff's house where I met Jean Pace, who I had seen in Chicago as a high school student. I also met Nina Simone at Jeff's house. Just being in the room with these larger-than-life figures was extraordinary. Another person I remember meeting during this period was Toni Cade Bambara, who came to that 1976 Black writers conference at Howard and ended up being somebody with whom I was in regular communication through the late 1970s and early 1980s. Howard University and Washington, DC, were meccas for Black culture. Jeff was very instrumental in bringing all these interesting people together. Washington, DC, was the Black diaspora personified, even in a bigger way than Atlanta. I was meeting people from Africa, the Caribbean, and from all over the Black world. I remember having conversations with Léon-Gontran Damas, the famous Guianese poet who had been very involved with the Negritude movement in Paris in the 1930s. He was teaching at Howard, which reminds me that I worked hard on my French while attending Howard. I ended up taking classes with professors who, while having nothing to do with my art, facilitated my interest in perfecting my French language skills. Another great professor at Howard was Françoise Pfaff who had conducted a lot of pioneering scholarship on Ousmane Sembène, the legendary Senegalese filmmaker. My world in Washington, DC, was a Black diasporic one that stuck with me and reminded me of the enormity of my artistic projects.

AB: I wanted to talk to you about your global perspective on art. I'm always amazed at, when listening to your interviews or when you're on a panel, your understanding of artists from around the world and their connections. Can you talk about some of the work you've done that's more global in scope and why you thought that work was important?

RJP: If I had to think about important global projects, the first one would be my dissertation that was turned into a book and became the impetus for a major art exhibition. People often think that my book,

Homecoming: The Art and Life of William H. Johnson [1991], is an exhibition catalog but it's not. It was simply a book that accompanied the Smithsonian American Art Museum exhibition that I curated called *Homecoming: William H. Johnson and Afro-America, 1938–1946* [1991–92] [fig. 3.4]. Studying Johnson's life and work was my first inkling that African American art was a global affair. It was something produced by people of color and, specifically, people of African ancestry born in the United States. But William H. Johnson, like so many creative Black Americans before and after him, discovered that he could not realize his full potential in the United States, so he had to go abroad.

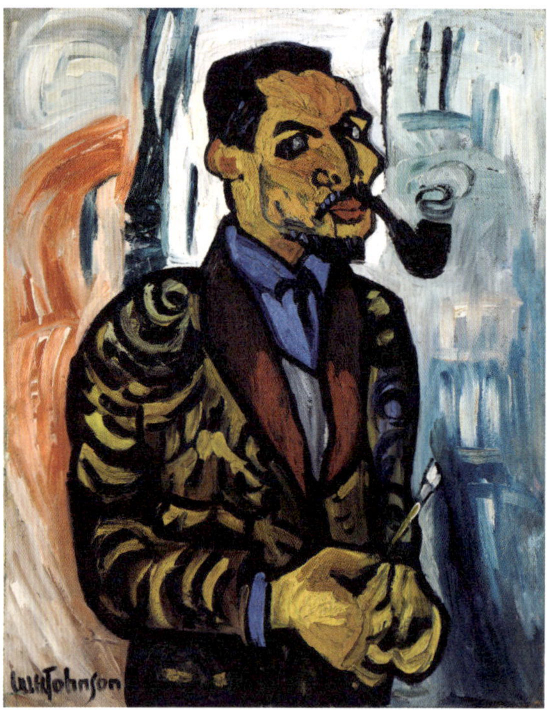

Fig. 3.4 William H. Johnson (American, 1901–70). *Self-Portrait with Pipe,* oil on canvas, 88.9 × 71.1 cm, ca. 1937. Washington, DC, Smithsonian American Art Museum, 1967.59.913. Artwork shown in *Homecoming: William H. Johnson and Afro-America, 1938–1946,* curated by Richard J. Powell, Smithsonian American Art Museum, Washington, DC, 13 September 1991–1 March 1992.

Having been a student of the Harlem Renaissance, I already knew that long list of African American artists who made that trek abroad, mostly to France and particularly Paris. Johnson began his sojourn in Paris but then moved to the South of France and ended up in Scandinavia. While in Scandinavia, he visited North Africa. His beginnings in South Carolina and his seeing the world helped me realize that to understand the totality of African American art, one has to both acknowledge its genesis and dispersal, how it comes into being in different places.

Also important were my conversations with the painter Lois Mailou Jones, who taught at Howard from 1930 to 1977, about her time in Paris and conversations in Atlanta with the scholar Richard Long about his engagements with French culture and his relationships with Baldwin and Beauford Delaney. It was clear that France was one of those places you could not ignore if you really wanted to think about yourself as an educated person around Black culture. That's what kept me interested. The Johnson project, interestingly, didn't just include France but also Scandinavia. I was lucky enough in the mid-1980s to get a Fulbright fellowship that took me to Copenhagen, where I was based for an academic year and ended up traveling all throughout Europe. I traveled to Norway and Sweden. I followed Johnson's path and also spent time in France.

I've often included and been involved with artists who are global and international. There's an excitement and energy when working with these artists, but also a hybridity of imagination when engaging with multiple cultures and languages— all while doing it through an African American lens.

AB: As you were talking, I was thinking there seems to be a curiosity about artistic processes. You have a curiosity as an artist, but also as an intellectual and philosopher. Do you see your work as both a scholar and artist? How does this perspective inform your work as a curator and philosopher about history and art?

RJP: How does it do it [*laughs*]?

AB: It's a tough question. I'm asking because not everyone has your background. How many curators today are interested in literature, theater, and music? How many of them have your background in all that, as well as in visual arts, while having this natural philosophical—existential almost—curiosity? You seem to combine all of that somehow.

RJP: I should separate out curation because curation is the public face of all the things that were talked about, in terms of one's scholarship, one's theoretical philosophical interests, and even one's artistic or inner life. When a curator chooses to make these ideas palpable in the context of an exhibition in a gallery within a museum, they have to make a particular leap. Starting with the *Impressions/Expressions* exhibition, I began to realize that it's not enough to simply transfer your intellectual excitement or curiosity to a curatorial project. You have a responsibility to present the ideas and images in a way that will be coherent, captivating, and that, hopefully, tells a story to the public.

I can't say that in all my curatorial projects I've succeeded in doing this. A curator certainly wants to pull from their background and knowledge, but they also have a responsibility to make something in the public sphere that will connect. Part of the challenge of that—and you know this as well as any curator—is that it's not just *your* show. You're working with an institution and a budget. You're navigating loans that you know will make your show perfect, but the owner of the work may not necessarily agree with you or even want to lend to you.

One of the challenges of curation is that you have to work with a community of individuals and institutions to make things happen. Sometimes it's serendipity and things come together. Sometimes things don't happen the way you want but happen the way they're going to happen, and you have to work with that. There is an improvisational quality to the curatorial project; you have to work with whatever contingencies you're dealing with.

Why I've been able to do what I've done is that I did it at a moment when there was space for me to do it. Many of my projects were realized in the 1990s, a few in the late 1980s, and a few in the early twenty-first century. Those were moments when I filled a niche. To be absolutely honest with you, we're in a very different world now. The early 2020s is a world where there are lots of curators, especially lots of curators of color, and lots of institutions that are interested in doing various projects. You would think that that would be an opportunity, but it's also a challenge because how do you get your foot in the door to make things happen when there are so many other people wanting to put their feet in the door [*laughs*] to make things happen?

What you see when you look at my career was a moment when there was still space for someone like me to come up with an Archibald Motley show [*Archibald Motley: Jazz Age Modernist* (2014)], a Beauford Delaney show using the color yellow as its theme [*The Color Yellow: Beauford Delaney* (2002)], or a show on the Black arts movement like *Back to Black: Art, Cinema, and the Racial Imaginary* [2005] for the Whitechapel Gallery in London. Those were projects that had their moment. Another was my exhibition with Jock Reynolds, *To Conserve a Legacy: American Art from Historically Black Colleges and Universities* [1999]. So, a lot of it is serendipity.

AB: Especially working today, we tend to think of things in terms of isolated moments. Getting back to the idea of serendipity, we don't think about these trajectories and connections—like what you do today can affect what you do ten or twenty years from now. We're a generation, like the iPad generation or smartphone generation, where we think, "I just need it now and I want to get through it now." We're not thinking about how something sets the stage for something else down the road. That is an important lesson for curators.

RJP: I'm also talking about people who open doors. Doors have to be opened for things to happen. You know as well as I do that the museum world has lots of gatekeepers and people who decide on something happening or not. For all the projects I've been involved with, I've been very lucky to have people who have opened the door and said, "We want you to do this exhibition." It's often been museum directors who understood what it was that I was after in terms of exhibition ideas. I'm always beholden to those individuals who enabled me to realize these projects, which goes all the way back to Mary Schmidt Campbell at the Studio Museum with my first exhibition.

AB: We talked about your transition from high school to Morehouse and Howard, and how the environments at Morehouse and Howard were more nurturing. There was a real sense of community. I think that was part of the period but also part of what historically Black colleges and universities [HBCUs] were and are in a very real sense. Do you think there's a sense of community today? Does it feel smaller in some way? How does one access a community like that today?

RJP: That's a very good question. You could say that, in the atmosphere we are currently in, there is a proliferation of work by artists of African descent that is accessible via social media but also available in person, in the analog way. That analog engagement is unusual in the sense that it's not just HBCUs or museums anymore. Now, we have galleries, especially major blue-chip galleries, that have made major investments in works by artists of color, particularly artists of African descent. So, there's a really big community out there.

But community is more than just a critical mass. Community requires the ability to communicate, share, give and take, and feed and foster our talents amongst ourselves. I don't know if the proliferation of what we have now matches up with what one would want to glean from this explosion. In other words, I've often thought that with the proliferation of images, we would have access that we hadn't had before. But one could argue that with the proliferation of images, there's a myopia that transpires. You can't see because there's so *much* to see and you have to work really hard to absorb all the things that are available.

I'm just giving a cautionary note that, in the moment we're in now, there is an abundance and surfeit of art, Black curators, and institutions that seem to be committed to presenting this material. But even in the midst of that, there's still the feeling that something is missing, that there is not the ability to do things in a very intellectually solid way. One challenge now is that things happen so fast that art is presented rather quickly and you don't have time to think about the ideas the work generates. You need time to think about some of these projects to make them happen successfully. But that doesn't mean that great things can't happen now.

It often boils down to the synergies and abilities of individuals to put their resources together. I know we're having this conversation about Black curators, but the reality is that African American art now is something that the mainstream art world has finally come to realize has value and that they want to be a part of. It's no surprise that one of the biggest projects of recent years, this incredible exhibit of Simone Leigh representing the United States at the 2022 Venice Biennale, was organized not by a historically Black institution but by a historically white institution, the Institute of Contemporary Art in Boston.

And, yes, there are important Black minds working with Simone Leigh. I'm thinking of Tina Campt, Saidiya Hartman, and Rashida Bumbray. But this is a very different kind of art scene and there's lots of money available for Leigh to realize her wildest imagination. It's a very different moment we're in. We have different players, different gatekeepers, as well as different door openers, and so you work with the program you have.

AB: Within museums, things have become very different in terms of the curatorial process becoming much more administrative—I would even say bureaucratic to a certain degree. Curating was something that could be intellectual. I see curating as both art and science where there's a creative process and you're dealing with creatives. There's an organic process in creating a show that's artistic, like putting together a symphony, band [*laughs*], or a theater production. But that's no longer the case. It is very much like we're trying to create templates and models for how to put together or organize a very successful show. And that makes it even more difficult sometimes to create what you've done.

RJP: Yes, there's a big difference between working with art that's created now versus art that was created in the past. Clearly, much of my work has been looking at art of the past. Ironically, it's a challenge to work with art from the past. You would think that it's tough to work with living artists, and it is [*laughs*]. But it's very different because it's engaging with art as it's being made and with the minds that are creating it, so there's a negotiation.

Whereas with historical material, you are at the mercy of what you can find and what you can pay to bring into view, and that's not always possible. So there's a real challenge there. But if you are able to raise money and work with administrators who believe in your vision, it can be quite fulfilling. I've been very lucky with many of my past projects in navigating budgets and administrative hurdles to do things that largely approximate the original vision. That's been quite fulfilling.

AB: We talked a bit about challenges and failures. What were some of the more joyous experiences you've had curating? Could you also talk about some of the projects that presented challenges but were really important for your evolution as a curator, artist, and scholar?

RJP: I have a reputation in my family of turning lemons into lemonade [*laughs*]. I have been an optimist for the longest time. That doesn't mean I'm not a realist, but it means I know tough situations are going to hit me [*laughter*]. So I get armored for that. When a mess happens, I work hard to acknowledge and deal with it, but then I try to move on. For many projects I've been involved with, the thing that has been most disappointing for me has been not getting all the objects I wanted to include in a show, which often has to do with logistics. Part of my problem is that I know my field and know what's out there. And if it's out there, I want it [*laughs*], particularly if it's canonical and significant.

When we were doing *Rhapsodies in Black: Art of the Harlem Renaissance* [1997] in London, I definitely wanted this amazing Miguel Covarrubias painting that was in Mexico City called *Rapsodia en azul* [*Rhapsody in Blue*] [figs. 3.5, 3.6]. It was done by Covarrubias in 1927 and was in a private collection in Mexico. My vision was to bring this piece out as it had not been shown publicly in years. But I failed. I was not able to get it out of Mexico City. It was administrative. It was financial. It was a diplomatic gauntlet, and so it didn't happen. The show still turned out to be quite nice [*laughs*] and successful in its own way. I ended up including the work in the catalog, although we never borrowed it.

I'm not the only person that this has happened to. There have been many incredible exhibitions in which curators couldn't get all the works they thought they would be able to because of financial or logistical reasons, or because of lenders who were leery. And yet, you find a way to make it work and succeed. It didn't just happen with *Rhapsodies in Black,* it happened with other projects as well. But that is kind of the

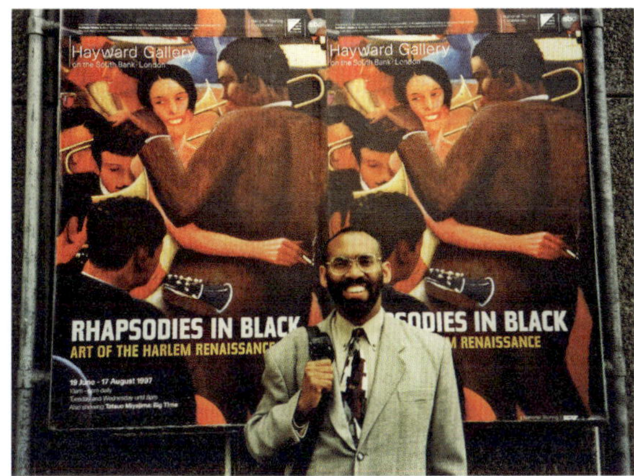

Fig. 3.5 Richard J. Powell in the front of poster for *Rhapsodies in Black: Art of the Harlem Renaissance,* Hayward Gallery, London, 1997.

thing that's always gnawed on me, that I've not been at a place like the Met or the Museum of Modern Art where they can just say, "I want it," and it comes [*laughter*]. They have the money and diplomatic cache to make it happen.

The reality is there are few institutions in the world that can do that, and I've learned that. The sad part is when we do exhibits that deal with the Black diaspora, we simply haven't had the kind of clout that those institutions have to do things in the big, full-blown way that I've envisioned them happening. That's the downside. But the fun side is that the Archibald Motley show was beautiful, and I loved it. The way that it was presented at the Nasher Museum of Art at Duke University, my home institution, was perfect. I loved that we got all the works we wanted to get, most of them anyway [*laughs*]. I loved how I worked with great preparators in placing things the way I wanted them placed.

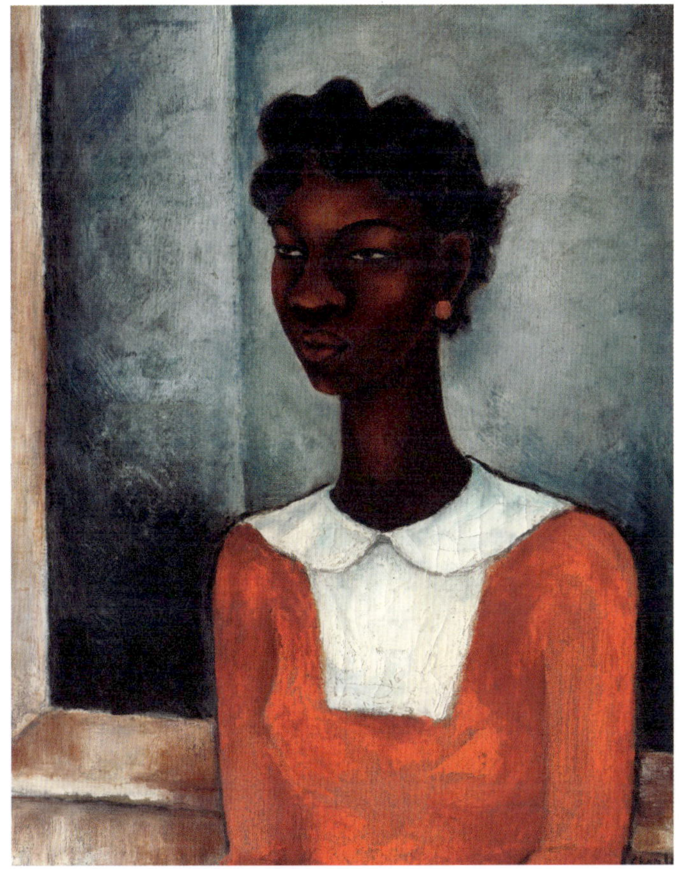

Fig. 3.6 Charles Henry Alston (American, 1907–77). *Girl in a Red Dress,* oil on canvas, 71.1 × 55.9 cm, 1934. New York, Metropolitan Museum of Art, 2021.25. Artwork shown in *Rhapsodies in Black: Art of the Harlem Renaissance,* curated by Richard J. Powell and David A. Bailey, Hayward Gallery, London, 19 June–17 August 1997.

AB: As you were talking, I was thinking about a couple of things. One, *To Conserve a Legacy,* why was that important? I thought that was an incredible catalog [fig. 3.7]. I didn't get a chance to see the show, but you worked with Jock Reynolds on that one. His name has come up in so many conversations I've had here in Baltimore. He's a good friend with Doreen Bolger, who was at the Baltimore Museum of Art. Could you talk about that?

RJP: I met Jock upon coming back to the US from Copenhagen. I got a fellowship at the Smithsonian to work on William H. Johnson and was living in Washington, DC. He called me and introduced himself. We struck up a friendship and he was interested in doing an exhibit on James Lesesne Wells for the Washington Project for the Arts [WPA], an alternative art space in Washington, DC where he was director. He needed help with it, so he said, "Would you be willing to co-curate this show with me?" And I said, "I'd be delighted." We did that show, *James Lesesne Wells: Sixty Years in Art* [1986–87], and it was a big success. Mr. Wells was delighted because he was getting attention after many, many years of neglect [fig. 3.8].

Following that project, Jock asked me to be the director of programs for the WPA. In the two years I was director of programs, I had a chance to organize some incredible exhibits. One show was *From the Potomac to the Anacostia: Art and Ideology in the Washington Area* [1989], which looked at contemporary art in Washington, DC. It was a blast. My fondest memory of that show was collaborating with the poet and activist Essex Hemphill to do this incredible performance piece in the galleries called "From the Anacostia to the Potomac." It was wonderful.

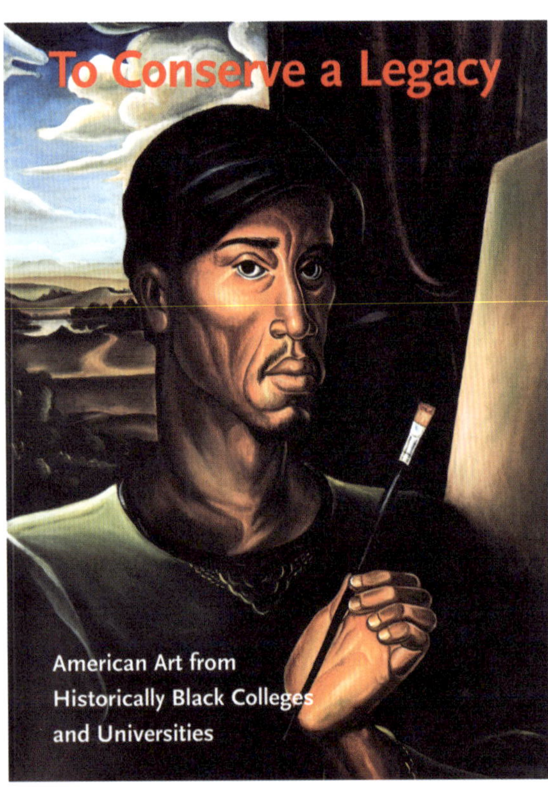

Fig. 3.7 Cover of Richard J. Powell and Jock Reynolds, *To Conserve a Legacy: American Art from Historically Black Colleges and Universities*, exh. cat. (Addison Gallery of American Art and Studio Museum in Harlem, 1999).

Afterwards, I did a show called *The Blues Aesthetic: Black Culture and Modernism* [1989], which started at WPA and then traveled throughout the United States [fig. 3.9]. The most infamous part of that exhibit was the installation by David Hammons of *How Ya Like Me Now?* [1989] on the corner of Seventh and G Streets where it was knocked down by a group of disgruntled bystanders. But the show was wonderful, and it gave me a chance to stretch out and think.

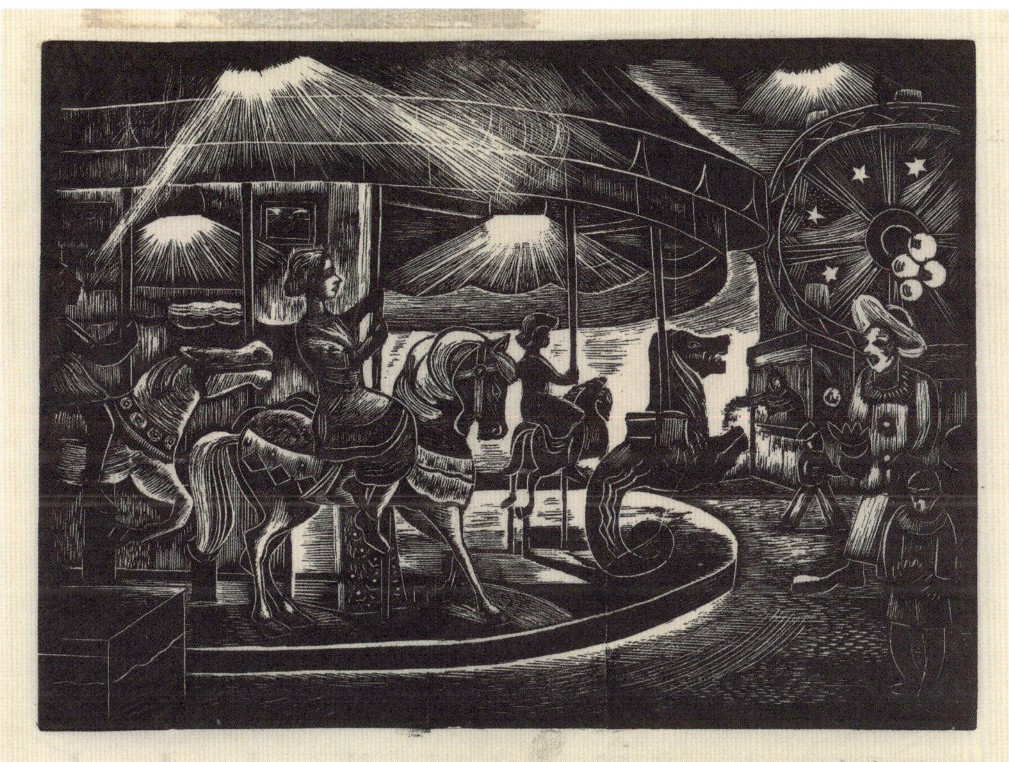

Fig. 3.8 James Lesesne Wells (American, 1902–93). *Untitled (Carrousel),* ca. 1949, wood engraving on Japanese paper, 35.8 × 43.3 cm. New York, Metropolitan Museum of Art, 1999.529.174. Artwork shown in *James Lesesne Wells: Sixty Years in Art,* curated by Richard J. Powell and Jock Reynolds, Washington Project for the Arts, Washington, DC, 4 December 1986–24 January 1987.

Again, it always pays to have a director who will say, "I believe in what you're doing."

After that, I moved to Duke and Jock moved to the Phillips Academy in Andover, Massachusetts. He then reached out to me again and he said, "You know, when we did that show on James Lesesne Wells, I was blown away by all the amazing work at HBCUs. Has there ever been a show?" I said, "Actually, there were shows done on HBCUs back in the 1970s with people like Edmund Barry Gaither [director and curator of the Museum of the National Center of Afro-American Artists], but they were relatively small projects." And he said, "Well, I've been talking to the folks at the Knight Foundation and the Williamstown Art Conservation Center. They like the idea of doing a show from these collections but also tying in conservation and preservation."

Jock and I put our heads together and came up with *To Conserve a Legacy* [fig. 3.10]. So, we put a little twist on it for the public. We're announcing that these Black institutions are collecting the American art legacy. I think that exhibition was a real contribution to the American art story.

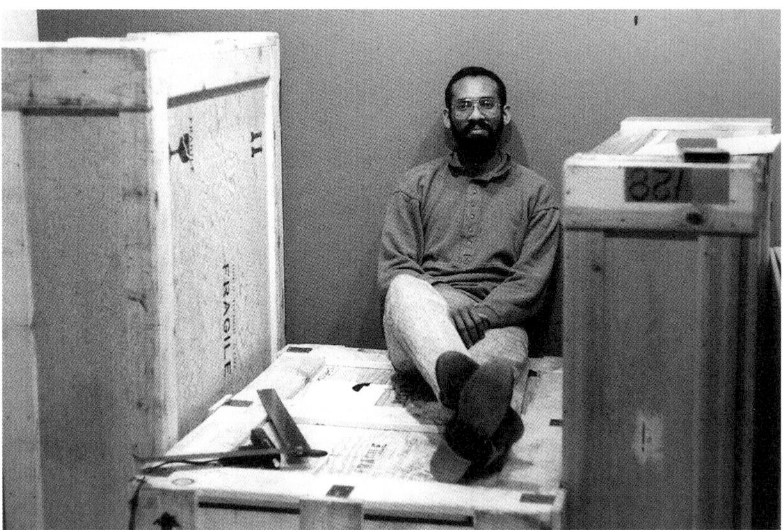

Fig. 3.9 Richard J. Powell during the installation of *The Blues Aesthetic: Black Culture and Modernism,* Washington Project for the Arts, Washington, DC, 1989.

AB: If we look at what's happened between then and today, how might we talk about Black artists, artists as curators, and the history of Black art in the context of Sam Gilliam, Melvin Edwards, William T. Williams, that generation, and Black artists who are working today?

RJP: With regards to Williams, Gilliam, Richard Hunt, Mel Edwards, and other abstract artists like Howardena Pindell, I'm thinking about the tensions between what was then called the Black art survey versus the thematic exhibition. I was a witness to the moment when there was this whole succession of survey exhibitions done in the 1960s and early 1970s, which culminated in *Two Centuries of Black American Art* fulfilling a historical space and need to provide this big overarching history.

Many artists understood the value of that. At the same time, many felt that it either wasn't inclusive of them as contemporary practitioners or it was too much of a survey and didn't take on any ideas that might bring works together in a meaningful way. What we have, beginning in the late 1970s and into the 1980s, is this corrective. I'm thinking, for example, of Lowery Stokes Sims and Leslie King-Hammond's *Art as a Verb: The Evolving Continuum* exhibition [1988–89], which was an important group exhibit around the idea of action and art as a verb or as something produced and enacted, as opposed to operating in a static place.

I'm also thinking about all the great monographic exhibitions that were beginning to happen, particularly in the late 1980s and early 1990s. My William H. Johnson show was one of those pioneering exhibitions that looked at one artist and what that career yielded. There were a whole set of other focused exhibitions, such as the Jacob Lawrence and

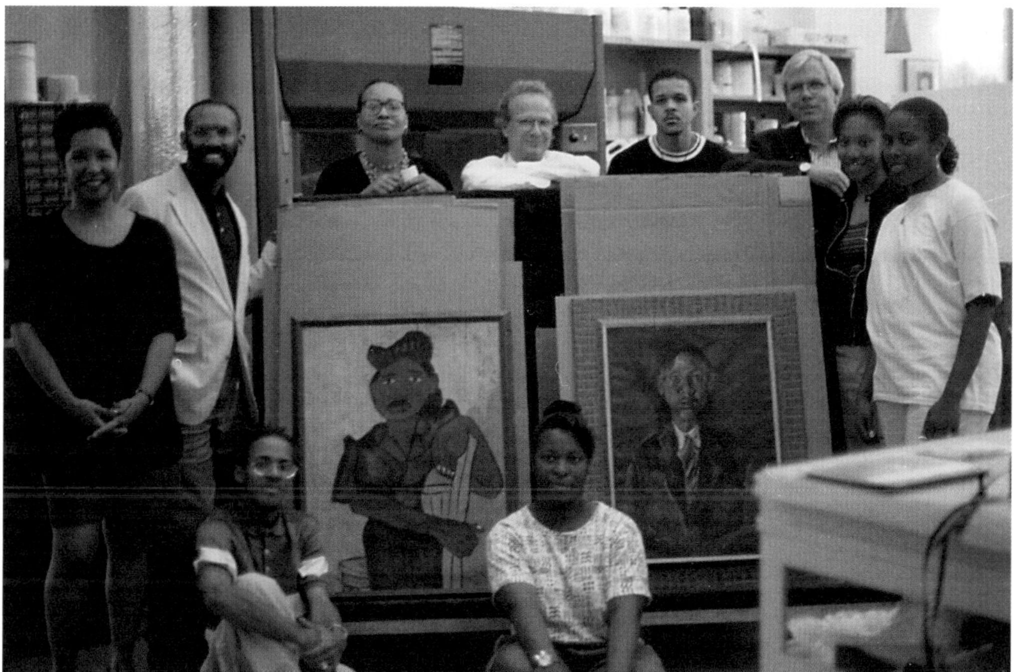

Fig. 3.10 Student interns, conservators, and curators at the Williamstown Art Conservation Center in preparation for *To Conserve a Legacy: American Art from Historically Black Colleges and Universities*, summer 1997.

Alma Thomas shows a few years later. From a curatorial perspective, there are multiple ways that we can address African American art.

Then there's the case of artists who don't necessarily fit into an obvious narrative—and one could say that abstract art doesn't fit into a narrative unless you're talking about Black abstraction. Focusing on artists' careers and the different aspects of their works has proven to be useful for the public, and it has been helpful for artists to see their work in this broader, more comprehensive way.

AB: Do you have a preference when it comes to curatorial work, whether it's more like a survey—you also do a pretty good job at focusing on artists—or focused studies of artists?

RJP: What's nice about focusing on an individual artist is there's a built-in logic [*laughs*] for the public, which has proven to be successful. I've done theme shows like *Rhapsodies in Black* and *To Conserve a Legacy;* those exhibitions seemed to succeed around a particular idea and historical period. I don't have a preference. A lot depends on all the things pertaining to an exhibition falling into place that will allow the institution to buy into an idea.

As you know, Aaron, things happen. Institutions wake up one day and say they want to do this or that—either you're there to make it happen or you're not. I don't have that kind of clout where [*laughs*] I can say, "I shall do this," and it's going to happen. That's why I believe the stars have to align for things to come to full fruition. I'm very attuned to being ready for that moment of everything lining up and getting the call.

AB: We've talked about the challenges within institutions for curating today. What do you think those challenges might be in the future?

RJP: The biggest challenge is vision. Institutions have competing interests connected to them. For art institutions, it takes resources to make things happen. Institutions and art museums in particular have so many challenges. Some of those include conserving works of art, collecting them, and presenting material to the public and addressing their expectations, particularly in an environment fraught with politics and resistance to an intellectual approach. That's why I say the biggest challenge of the future is vision, which includes directors and chief curators being able to rise above what I just described and allowing the work—and the ideas that the work generates—to have the primary place in how things proceed and are experienced in an exhibition context. It's very difficult.

Directors who are successful with this are a rare breed because all those things I described often get in the way. I see the future as being more complicated than our current moment. I don't think it's an impossible goal to let an aesthetic vision rise to the occasion and be the goal for how things get presented in museums. Of course, that's easy for me to say because I'm not in a museum or administrative role that has to deal with all those other complicated things. But I'm still hopeful. I'm still that optimist who believes that interesting things can happen with the right constellation of people.

AB: How do you get so much done? You're not just multitasking, you're multithinking. You're an artist, curator, scholar, educator, and mentor, but you still have a personal life. You're still a husband. You have a life within the community and your own life. You're the guy that sits on the couch and watches television. How do you balance all that and what advice could you give younger curators working today?

RJP: That's a two-pronged question. It's: How do I do what I do and how do I advise people to do what they want to do? [*laughs*]. The answer to the first question is that I'm very lucky to be married to C. T. Woods-Powell, who is very supportive of me and whom I'm very supportive of. We have a home and environment that is both attended to and creates space for us to do what we feel we need to do professionally and personally. I work really hard to create a balance in my life between what I do professionally and in my personal life.

It has allowed me to take on projects that perhaps people think, "Wow, that seems like a lot." I turn down a lot, too. I don't necessarily say yes to everything. What I do say yes to, I have been able to successfully incorporate into my schedule and give it my all. And that's along with all the other things that I do, like teaching, advising students, and the like. All of it seems to work. It's not labor, it's love, and when it's love, you just do it because you're really enthused about it.

To answer your second question, my advice is for people to come to a sense of themselves, decide what matters, and find ways in their professional lives—whether that's in museums or in a freelance capacity—to do what they want to do, but to do it well and find a community. Find a cohort in your profession who believe in you and understand what you're doing. It's a challenge to find the people who speak your language and with whom you can be in conversation. But that's also about give and take, so you're not only talking but also listening to what other people have to say.

AB: Looking back, are there paths you wish you would have taken? That's such a hard question because it's like, what would we do without the work you've done [*laughs*] if you had done something else?

RJP: When I was coming up, I didn't even know what a curator was. I learned what it was through the examples of people like Robert Farris Thompson and David Driskell. If I had to rethink career paths, I might have pursued film. There's a part of me that would've preferred that career track, but I don't know how I would've ended up. I don't know if I would've been as fulfilled as I am with what I've been doing. When I think about the world of cinema, filmmaking, and the art of cinema, I wish I had taken courses in some of that work and engaged with it more.

I also realize that I probably wasn't cut out for that [*Bryant laughs*]. There is such a cutthroat and business part of that profession and a hustling part of filmmaking that's not really part of me. I'm much more of—and I hate to use this French term—an auteur. I'm into images, visions, colors, and mise-en-scène. I'm not into banking, budgets [*laughter*], and negotiating distribution deals like the Spike Lees and Tyler Perrys of the world [*laughs*]. That ain't me. So, I'm even pausing to answer your question. Yes, maybe film, but then maybe not.

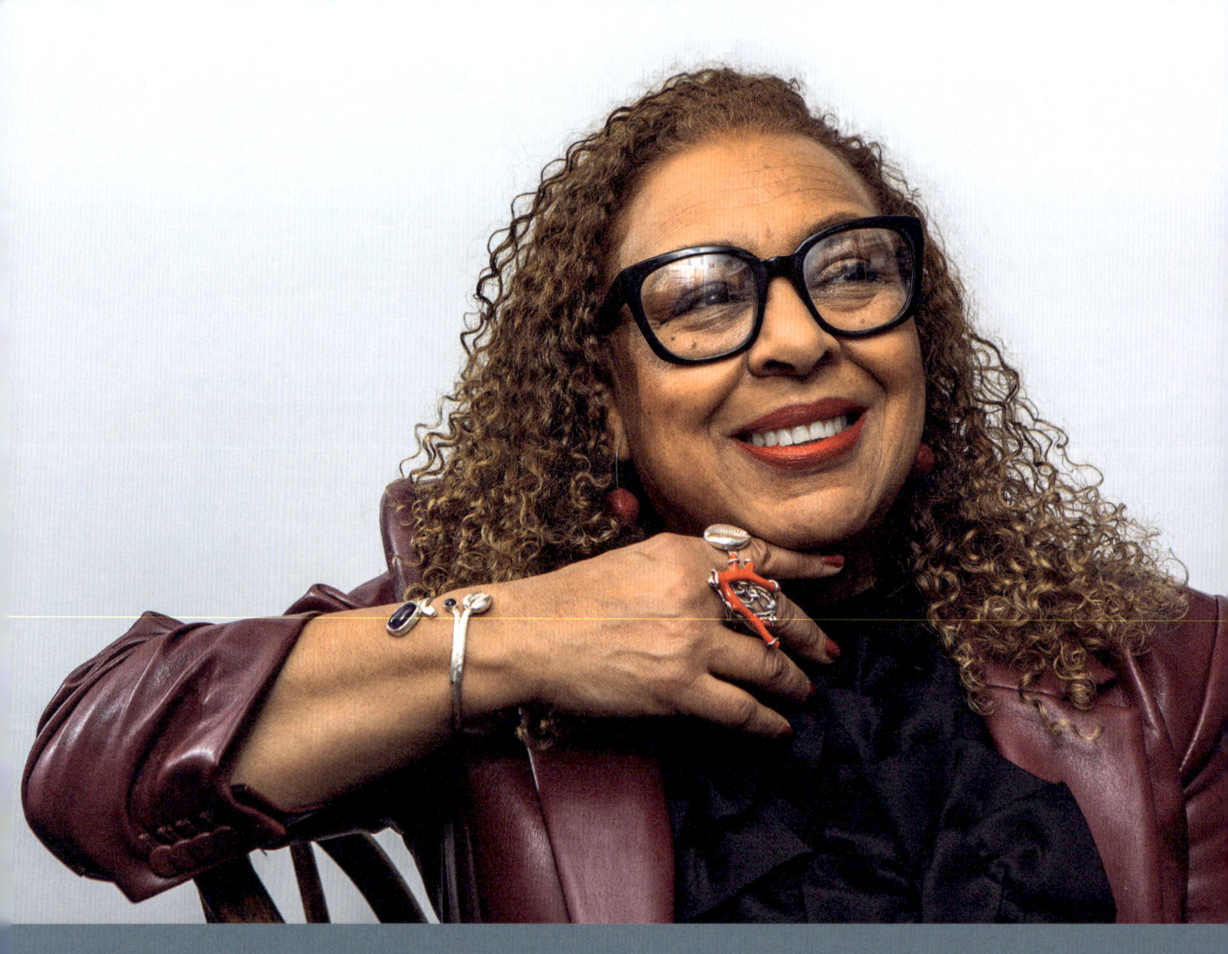

Kellie Jones

INTERVIEWED BY THOMAS JEAN LAX
12 and 13 July 2022

THOMAS JEAN LAX (TJL): In your work, you have generously shared some of your origins, and I wanted to ask you to start with some of your earliest memories of art and artists.

KELLIE JONES (KJ): I put together my book, *EyeMinded: Living and Writing Contemporary Art* [2011], with my mother [Hettie Jones], father [Amiri Baraka], sister [Lisa Jones], and partner [Guthrie Ramsey] as contributors in dialogue throughout the book. Through these dialogues, it chronicles how I came into the art world. I provided context for my work. Some might call it a biography, but biography, as many people know, is like the third rail of art history; you're not supposed to talk about that type of context. But, for me, if one did not provide details of that context—that milieu—you put creators of color at a disadvantage. It only made them equal to what the traditional standards were, which were based largely on what elite white men did. And that's not everybody, that's not how everybody makes art, and that's not how everybody gets to art. *EyeMinded* offered other ways of presenting a discourse on art and art history.

When you ask me about my earliest memories, the main takeaway is that art was always many things. For instance, my parents got divorced when I was about six, and I was back and forth between my dad's home in Newark, New Jersey, and my mom's place on the Lower East Side of New York City. Those places were vibrant spaces for art-making, and they were different.

I recall you asking me, "Do you remember your earliest recollection of something called Black art?" Black art was always with me because Black art was what people did in Newark. That's what it was about. It was about supporting African-descended people through education, performance, making things, poetry, all that stuff. It was different from what people did on the Lower East Side. Some people on the Lower East Side might have done that. There were places that did Black art in New York, such as the Harlem scene. The Lower East Side was much more diverse; it had a different group and type of people. There were still Black people in that scene, but they were going at art from a different perspective.

As a child you say, "Oh, well, some people make art like this, and some people make art like that." That was something I always knew and didn't necessarily judge. One play I remember participating in at my father's Spirit House theater in Newark was *Slave Ship* [1967]. The play opens in a dark theater to smells, sounds, and screams. It's a meditation on the experience of enslaved Africans in the hull of a ship crossing the Middle Passage. As kids, we were part of the soundtrack, screaming offstage. The stage directions for this speaking part note: "Children:

voices and bodies in the slave ship." We were taught the significance and terror of that historical moment. At the same time, it was exciting to participate. It was the one time you were encouraged to scream at the top of your lungs!

Another important memory was growing up on the Lower East Side above the saxophonist Archie Shepp and his family [including his son the photographer Accra Shepp]. Was that Black art? Sometimes it is, but it also has another kind of valence, another kind of affect in the free jazz avant-garde world that may be seen differently. Growing up above avant-garde music, meeting many of the musicians, and hearing that that sound—to this day, that music has a kind of comfort for me. It's the art I grew up on. In fact, on the cover of Archie's album *Attica Blues* [1972] is that studio below our apartment.

I always thought art was just a large thing. You're a kid—you think everybody knows about art. Then as you get older, you realize, one, they don't know about art and, two, they don't know people of color make it—Black people, Latinx people, Asian people, Native Americans. In fact, certainly then, most people didn't even know artists were alive. I knew artists were alive before I knew that most books were about dead ones because I grew up with people like Jack Whitten, Al Loving, William T. Williams, Melvin Edwards, Daniel LaRue Johnson, and Virginia Jaramillo.

I went to what is now the Fiorello H. LaGuardia High School of Music and Art and Performing Arts. It used to be two separate high schools in two different locations. The High School of Music and Art, which I attended in Harlem, abutted the City College of New York's campus. It developed so many people, like Fred Wilson, Whitfield Lovell, Billy Dee Williams, Kurtis Blow, Alva Rogers, and Omar Hakim. Many of these people were around my generation. A few of us won MacArthur genius grants. The other arts high school was the High School of the Performing Arts located near Times Square in the theater district. The critic and curator Hilton Als went there and we knew each other in high school. These were both very diverse public high schools. That says something about the investment in public education that this country has to get back to if we're going to survive.

TJL: It's colorful to hear the texture of what it was to be a part of art-making from such a young age. As you were thinking about moving between these different worlds, where did you find a sense of belonging? Did you sense that Newark, Loisaida [Lower East Side], or what became LaGuardia High School, was a place for you? Or was there a process you went through to claim your own sense of identity in these different locations?

KJ: Being flexible and a shape-shifter was my process because these contexts were all different. There was a flow between the different art contexts in New York City. My sister Lisa and I shared a junior high school with the Wayans family, the large and boisterous comedic family including Kennan, Damon, Kim, Marlon, and others. Going uptown to Harlem for high school was another context for art-making. Being in New York, there was always a sense of creativity that flowed. At the High

School of Music and Art, you had bands, singers, and visual artists, and I was the latter. The High Schools of Music and Art and of the Performing Arts were specialized high schools that drew students from all over the city.

The Newark thing was very different in some ways because it was about Black nationalism. There was a definite goal: there was a way you dressed and spoke, you learned Swahili, and it was very specific. Going in and out of that environment gave me the ability to weigh those things. If I had been solidly in that Black nationalist space, it would have been a different story.

My paternal grandparents, Coyt Leroy Jones and Anna Lois Russ Jones, also lived in Newark. They were migrants from the South, part of the Great Migration, and they went to a Baptist church, which we went to with them. That was another form of culture. I learned so much from those people. Becoming a historian of the African diaspora, I recognize that as part of history. For instance, my grandmother's brother's first name was G. L. When he was born, all they gave him were initials. Why? So you could write it. When he grew up, he called himself George Lewis. This story is really part of the history of slavery. You learn it from these people. You thought it was just everyday fun; however, later you find out the origins of that almost inconsequential detail.

My grandfather always told me this story about arriving in New Jersey from South Carolina. He was on his way to New York, but on the train, they said, "Newark." He thought they said New York, so he got off. This is his story, and I believed it was just his for years. Long after he died, I read the exact same story in Isabel Wilkerson's *The Warmth of Other Suns: The Epic Story of America's Great Migration* [2010]. This was a tale that Black migrants from the South told. So, I'm being exposed to those ideas and language. Growing up with poets, I became very sensitive to language. My father Amiri Baraka is celebrated for a use of language that honors Black people and culture. But the reality is when you hear his family, you can see how he got there. He transformed it into something for his generation and those beyond. His family, in their language and comedy, were pretty amazing. I also got that part of culture from New Jersey, but those two sources were very different on the surface: one was more traditional, of churchgoing migrants, and the other captured the Black nationalist ethos of the 1960s and 1970s.

When I was in college, when I became a curator, and when I became a professor, I encountered academic discourse and theory that didn't at all acknowledge my experience and viewpoint. In my family, you change things. My response to that discourse was, "No, sorry, this is wrong, and we're going to have to tell people our stories because they are unaware." Even in high school, you read all these art history books and you're around all these Black and brown people, but not one of them is in the books unless they're ancient Mayans or Egyptians—they're not even sub-Saharan people. They're either Egyptians or Mayans, and that's it. You think that's just wrong.

TJL: I want to ask you more about Amherst College in a second, but can I ask one more question about your parents?

KJ: Absolutely.

TJL: The influence of Hettie Jones and Amiri Baraka cannot be understated. I'm curious to know when you came to understand that these two people meant something in the world beyond what they meant to your family or even to your immediate community? Were there specific moments when that reality came into focus for you?

KJ: It was early. I always remember having a sense of being in public. Especially, with my dad, part of being in Newark in his space was being in public. You were part of various cultural and political organizations that had a national profile. He was a public figure. There was a sense of how the people and programs in these organizations were also being scrutinized by law enforcement; and you needed to be aware of that. There was a publicness about your life from the beginning.

My mom was always working. When I look back to her resume and what she did to support two kids on the Lower East Side as a writer, I realize she wrote to stay alive, to bring food home. She did it by writing, mostly, and what kind of feat is that for people? It took her all over the world to work with people like Rita Marley. I had a sense of that even before it happened. I had a sense of it from my dad and then it just made sense that my mom's work took her to a lot of places and that people would pay her for that kind of stuff. Especially later, retrospectively, I appreciated it even more when *EyeMinded* came out. My family and I started doing book tours together in groups: me and my mom, me and my dad, and me and my sister. My mom and I did about two or three book events together. The reception she received was wonderful and it's only grown with her work now that it's been translated into French and Spanish.

TJL: When you got to Amherst College, you imagined that you were going to be a diplomat. What took you from that path toward Black studies, Spanish, and fine arts, which you ended up majoring in?

KJ: You go to a school that is historically filled with elite white men and you are neither of those things. From its origins in the nineteenth century, Amherst had been an all-male school. In the 1970s, it became coeducational and I was in the third class of women. The first class in 1975 was composed of transfer students; in 1976, the first class started as freshmen; and I was in the class that started in 1977. So, change was afoot when I arrived. Some of the professors, and I'm sure administrators, were not keen on this change in the status quo. They were not happy for you. Sure, there were women's schools, but let's be frank, most of the people in the class were white men. I had not gone to an elite boarding school, so navigating these things at Amherst also became part of my training. That certainly had an impact on me. It was challenging. However, I never want to say my training was bad because I love where I went to school and would never change it.

As an example, since I wanted to be a diplomat, I started studying French—I had studied Spanish throughout high school and probably junior high. I wanted to learn about the Caribbean and Africa. Those people speak French and I wanted to communicate with them. In classes at Amherst, all they talked about was France. I love Paris, but those aren't the only people speaking French. So, if that was the only way I was going to learn French, I was going to be turned off.

I went back into my art head, but I didn't want to be an artist. Then I said, wait a minute, I can do something else and write about artists and curate. By that time, I had come across David Driskell's *Two Centuries of Black American Art* [1976] and Samella Lewis's, *Art: African American* [1978]. These books changed my life because I saw that there was something else you could do. There were histories and they were exciting. Doug Davidson, who I think was an adjunct professor at Amherst at the time, allowed me to do an independent study with him where I interviewed Jack Whitten, Norman Lewis, and other people I knew. I asked them the question: What is Black art? They all laughed at me. They were like, "We're going to dial you back from this one. Let's talk." They knew me as a little baby and were like, "Okay, she's been reading now and now we have to do something else with her." That was funny. Lewis especially was chuckling away.

I taught myself about African American and Latin American artists because it wasn't necessarily taught at Amherst. The great thing about Amherst was that you could do an interdisciplinary degree and create your own major. That's the beauty of the liberal arts. For people who don't fit into a box and are finding new things that then are going to be in the world, the liberal arts provides a space where they are free to explore. Amherst allowed me to find my own path. Many thanks to Amherst for what it gave me. Not that I didn't have to work for it, but it allowed me the space to explore and find something new.

TJL: Is there anything pedagogically that those classes catalyzed for you? The seminars I've taken with you had an incredible sense of openness, a kind of refusal of hierarchy but also a clarity of direction. You moved us in subtle ways that I only realized, after the fact, were invitations to step into deeper understanding. I'm curious if you have any recollections of how those classes were organized and what you took from them?

KJ: Asa Davis was a professor who taught the history of the African diaspora, which blew me away. I learned about Brazil from him. Andrea Benton Rushing was an English professor and advisor on my senior thesis on African American and Mexican murals in the 1930s. James Maraniss was a professor of Spanish, a famed translator of *Don Quixote,* and my adviser on the Latin American side. Doris Sommer taught advanced Spanish and was a great support—she later went to Harvard University. John Pemberton III was an anthropologist and professor of religion who taught courses on African art.

I took a lot of my art history courses away from campus. I went abroad for a semester my junior year to Colombia where I studied at a satellite campus of the Universidad de Los Andes through the Great Lakes Colleges Association, which was where I got my Latin American art history knowledge. During the spring semester, I ended up studying with Angela Davis when she was teaching at San Francisco State University before she went to the University of California, Santa Cruz. San Francisco State was a commuter school and radically different from Amherst. These were working people. I took a class on Chicano performance and theater with Carlos Barón, who worked with the renowned El Teatro Campesino.

Yes, there was an openness. To roll back a few years, Amherst hired Sonia Sanchez as its first Black female faculty member. It was the 1970s and they're changing things amazingly enough in that Pioneer Valley area of Western Massachusetts. There was also Smith College and Mount Holyoke College and a strong Black lesbian cohort throughout the area. It was a very progressive space. There was also Hampshire College. The Five College Consortium model meant that you could be at Amherst but could take classes at four other schools including the University of Massachusetts, Amherst. They had a free bus that took you to all your classes at these schools.

The other thing that drew me there was Archie Shepp and his family had moved to Amherst, so he was teaching there. You had people teaching at University of Massachusetts, Amherst, musicians like Archie, Max Roach, and Marion Brown. Nelson Stevens, the muralist who was part of AfriCOBRA [African Commune of Bad Relevant Artists], was also up there for a while. It was another space for Black art and avant-garde musicians to have a livelihood.

TJL: When you graduated from Amherst, did you know you were moving back to New York? Did you have a sense that you were going to be working in the arts at that point? How did you go from being immersed in this world and studying it as your scholastic pursuit to pursuing it as a career? What was that transition into a professional person like?

KJ: It made sense for me. Was I excited? Probably. I'm always all-in about everything, but also it needed to be done. This is something that my parents, grandparents, and family did. The world needs changing; we've got to change it and do something. You can't sit around and eat potato chips. The world can change, but you have to be an active part of it. There was—I don't want to say anger, but a certain kind of righteousness. Going through college, I realized how my whole life was basically cut out of history in some ways, especially in the arts. I was uniquely positioned to understand that it could change.

That extends to today. One reason for doing this oral history project is because I really get sick of reading in periodicals, things like "Wow, these are undiscovered artists." These people are not undiscovered. We knew about these people. We knew about them as children, so why is this news? It's not and I'm going to tell you why it's not. Because you can't own that narrative. You can have a narrative, but it's not solely yours. Everybody has a piece, and I think my piece is really valid, so I'm going to tell it to you.

The summer before my senior year in college I interned at the Studio Museum in Harlem. I returned there full-time when I graduated. I served as the caretaker of the Adam Clayton Powell Jr. State Office Building Collection, which was housed across from the Studio Museum. The museum was the caretaker of that collection; now I believe it has been moved upstate. That was some of the work I did while I was at the Studio Museum. The other aspect was assisting in the activities around opening the museum in its new home at 144 West 125th Street in 1982. In particular, I was a curatorial assistant on the exhibition *Ritual and Myth: A Survey of African American Art* [1982] organized by Leslie King-Hammond. Two other shows rounded out the trifecta of opening exhibitions: *Images of Dignity: A Retrospective of the Works of Charles White* [1982] and *Harlem Heyday: The Photography of James Van Der Zee* [1982].

TJL: What was the cultural disposition and differences, if there were any, between your generation and the folks who were ahead of you in terms of your bosses and leadership there?

KJ: Mary Schmidt Campbell and Kinshasha Holman Conwill were the director and deputy director, respectively, when I worked at the Studio Museum. They both had advanced degrees. Mary, as director, was quite young to take over and really pushed the institution to the next phase. The differences that I might note are not so much within the Studio Museum but in broader generational changes.

Writing for your exhibition catalog on the Just Above Midtown [JAM] gallery helped me clarify these things. For instance, it clarified how strong the relationship between the Studio Museum and JAM was and how the Studio Museum trained so many of us over the years, including Linda Goode Bryant, the founder of JAM. For me, the generational difference marked the transition from the 1970s to the 1980s. In the late 1970s, I was in college. In 1981, I graduated and returned to New York City. I missed some of the battles Linda and others went through, such as the controversy surrounding the 1979 *N***** Drawings* exhibition at the Artists Space gallery when a white artist exhibited abstract works under a racially provocative title, leading to accusations of racism and protests.

Artists Space was a showcase for contemporary artists, and they kept a contemporary archive: Artists dropped off their images and curators could go through that archive to research and select candidates for upcoming shows they were working on. In 1987, I was invited by Susan Wyatt, the director of Artists Space, to curate a version of *Selections from the Artists File,* which was a standing show for the organization. Some folks in the Black art community were aghast due to the history of the space being the site of the *N***** Drawings* controversy. Before committing to my show, I, of course, read up on that incident. I then decided I was going to use that history of Artists Space and address it to some degree in the brochure. Of course, it was a diverse show with

Fred Wilson, Félix González-Torres, Stefani Mar, and Marina Cappelletto, among others. But agreeing to organize a show there despite the prior controversy was crossing a line in some ways, which always happens with different generations, right?

For instance, somebody would say, "Oh, why would T. Lax work at the Museum of Modern Art [MoMA]? MoMA has a history of blah." But you, T., are like, "Why not? Why not be a curator, not the curatorial assistant, but a curator at MoMA? Yes, I'm going to do it." Should Denise Murrell not organize *The Harlem Renaissance and Transatlantic Modernism* [2024] for the Metropolitan Museum of Art because of the problems surrounding *Harlem on My Mind: The Cultural Capital of Black America, 1900–1968* [1969]? Of course not. In fact, these institutions have indeed learned something over time.

There are always those lines in the sand that different generations cross without the same pain as previous generations, and that's what you're supposed to do. One thing I've always thought about, especially when I made my transition to primarily being a professor, was that I want to train more people to participate as curators and art historians to move these narratives forward, so I can retire!

TJL: We were talking about specific cultural organizations in New York when you moved back, and I wanted to ask you about the Jamaica Arts Center [JAC], that other important space—alongside the Studio Museum and JAM—that was a crossroads. For readers who might not know its importance, can you tell us what it was, how you found yourself there, and some of the work you did while you were there?

KJ: I was hired at JAC in 1986. I was working with Bill [William] P. Miller Jr., who sadly passed from AIDS during my tenure there. It points to the significance of losing a generation of cultural workers and how that affects where we are today culturally.

At JAC, I did many shows. The exhibition schedule had a tripartite structure. First, there was a show curated by me, the visual arts director at the time. Then, there was a community gallery where the people from Jamaica, Queens, and its environs got to show their work. Finally, there was a co-op gallery of a group of Queens-based artists who had rotating exhibitions and who, I believe, paid for some of the costs, following the traditional co-op gallery model. One person who was part of the co-op gallery was Ann Tanksley, who had been an early member of the women's art group "Where We At" Black Women Artists. There was also an artist-in-residence program. Lorna Simpson was an artist-in-residence on my watch. We met as interns at the Studio Museum in 1980. Later, Glenn Ligon would intern at Studio Museum as well.

Some of the shows I organized at JAC included: *Artists Installations: Camille Billops, Claudia DeMonte, Yong Soon Min* [1987]; a collaboration with our Queens neighbor the Isamu Noguchi Garden Museum to show some of Noguchi's works [*Works from the Isamu Noguchi Garden Museum,* (1988)]; several shows of abstract painting—one was a pairing

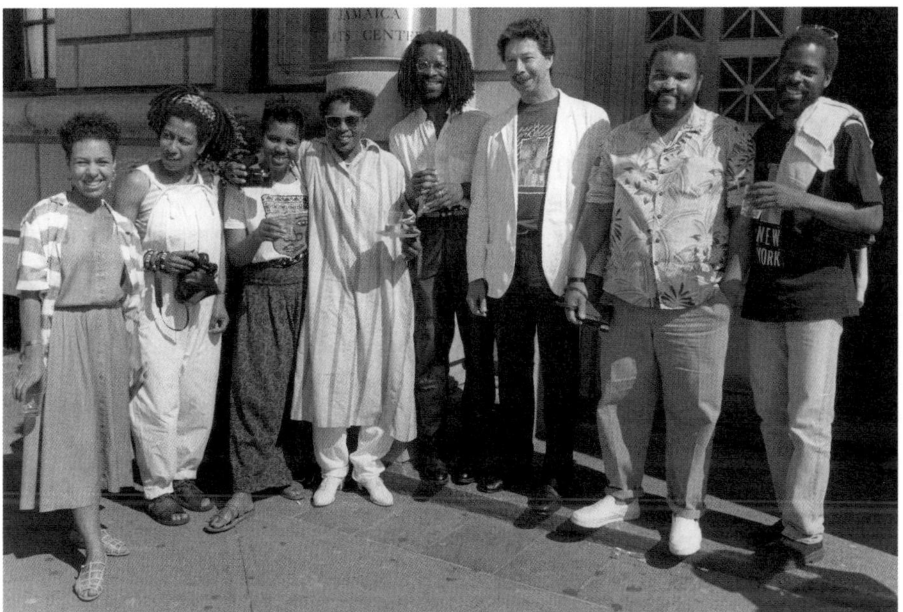

Fig. 4.1 *Left to right:* Kellie Jones, Ingrid Pollard, Maxine Walker, Mikki Ferrill, Rotimi Fani-Kayode, Charles Biasiny-Rivera, Dawoud Bey, and David A. Bailey at the opening of *US/UK Photography Exchange: Transatlantic Dialogues*, curated by Kellie Jones, Jamaica Arts Center, New York, 1989.

of Vivian Browne and William T. Williams featuring a guest essay by Lowery Stokes Sims in the catalog [1988] and another was *Abstract Expressionism: The Missing Link* [1989], which took up the work of people like Ed Clark, John Rhoden, Paul F. Keene Jr., Romare Bearden, and others; and a show focused on graffiti artists and hip-hop, *Stoopid Fresh: Queens and Hip Hop Culture* [1989–90]. We started a video project on this last exhibit and somewhere there are videotapes with LL Cool J and other Queens-based hip-hop artists.

From JAC, I also launched my international profile as a curator. In retrospect, these shows had an important impact on my intellectual career going forward. *US/UK Photography Exchange: Transatlantic Dialogues* [1989] [fig. 4.1], premiered at JAC, traveled to Camerawork Gallery in London, and toured England for eighteen months. This was a group show with Dawoud Bey, Mikki Ferrill, and Charles Biasiny-Rivera from the United States and Rotimi Fani-Kayode, Maxine Walker, and Ingrid Pollard from England. I wrote something for the catalog, as did the British artist/curator David A. Bailey.

It was my sister Lisa who got me started on the international side of things. In 1983, she moved to London for a year to launch her career as a writer. Of course I had to go check her out. She was involved with a lot of feminist writers, such as Jackie Kay and Maud Sulter. From there, I met artists such as Lubaina Himid, Zarina Bhimji, Roshini Kempadoo, Ingrid Pollard, and Sunil Gupta. I got to know Isaac Julien—Sir Isaac!—and the intellectuals Kobena Mercer, Paul Gilroy, and Stuart Hall. I marveled

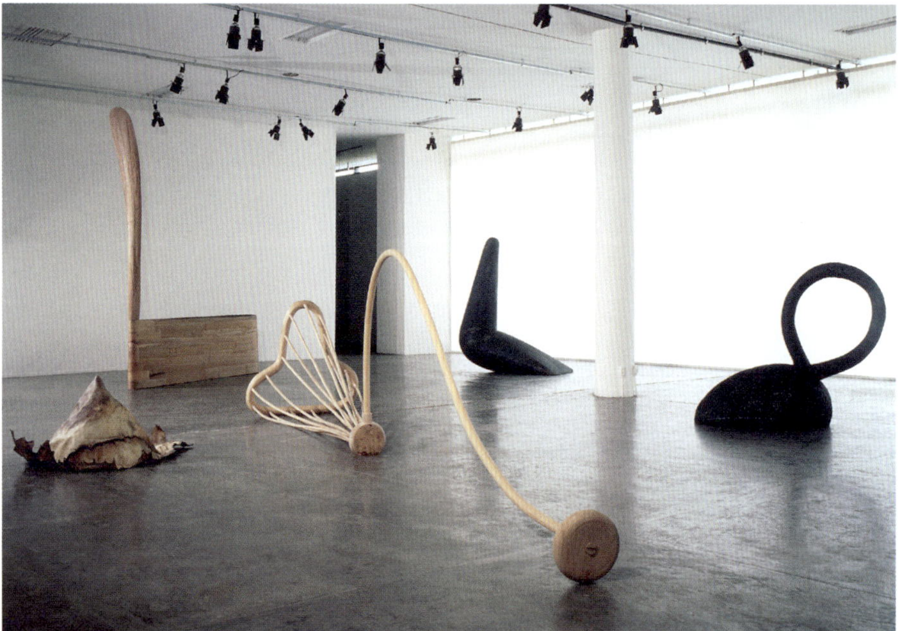

Fig. 4.2 Installation of Martin Puryear's works at the Bienal de São Paulo, curated by Kellie Jones, São Paulo, 1989.

at London's African and Asian diasporas. They were so familiar to my own in New York, but different. Developing exhibitions and collaborations between London and New York in the 1980s often meant bringing a portfolio case full of photographs on the plane in hand luggage. This started a whole connection with the Black British art scene. In 1988, I organized a show of photography at the Camerawork Gallery, *TransAtlantic Traditions: Women Photographers from the USA and Puerto Rico,* as part of the Spectrum Women's Photography Festival. The exhibit included photographs by Nina Kuo, Coreen Simpson, Lorna Simpson, and Frieda Medín from Puerto Rico.

Another international show I launched from JAC was the US participation in the twentieth Bienal de São Paulo presenting the work of Martin Puryear [1989] [fig. 4.2]. Support from the Fund for U.S. Artists at International Festivals and Exhibitions allowed smaller community art centers, like the one I worked for, to compete for such a great opportunity. I applied with Martin's work because I thought it would be excellent in an international setting. I did not know Martin—it was a cold call. I said, "Hey, can I put you in my application?" and he said, "Sure," and it worked. It was great to have the support of the United States government in this instance and to work with E. J. [Evangeline Juliet] Montgomery, also an artist, who was at the United States Information Service sending US art worldwide for many, many years and was a big supporter and mentor in terms of my working internationally.

I was reminded recently about the controversy surrounding our participation in that Bienal. The Brazilian Bienal team was not happy with the US selection, or as Martin recently put it, they were expecting something else. In any event, Martin's show won the grand prize for best individual exhibition that year. That was when I met Kynaston McShine, who was involved with the larger international Bienal committee and helped navigate things behind the scenes. The cover image of *Eyeminded* shows Martin's *Lever #1* [1988–89], which I showed in the Bienal exhibition.

While I was running around the globe in 1989, we hired Thelma Golden to keep things running at JAC and her hometown of Queens. From there, she went to the Whitney Museum of American Art and beyond. What was happening in these community spaces, really from the 1960s onward, really changed the landscape for art in New York in a major way.

Among my last shows for JAC was *Deja Vu: Haitian Influence in Contemporary American Art* [1989], a mix of painting and sculpture by Paul Gardère, Alison Saar, and Ken Tisa. I invited Robert Farris Thompson to be a guest essayist for the brochure—another cold call—and he graciously said yes. The following year I started working with him on my doctorate at Yale University.

While the experience of the liberal arts education at Amherst gave me the space to think in this expansive way, I learned what pedagogy meant and should look like from Robert Farris Thompson. I was his head teaching assistant for all his large lectures for three years. These classes routinely had over one hundred students. He used the Socratic method, calling on people for answers, in a class of that size! There was never a wrong answer in the classroom, just a position that might be shifted with more knowledge, study, and conversation.

Once I entered graduate school in 1990, I would continue to do exhibitions as an independent curator or what I have called a "deinstitutionalized curator." I would do more projects on Black Britain. I co-curated *Interrogating Identity* [1991], with the late Thomas Sokolowski, who was the director of the Grey Art Gallery and Study Center [now the Grey Art Museum] at New York University. That show toured the United States. When Tom approached me to co-organize a show of Black artists, I insisted that it be international. The show ended up including artists from the United States, Canada, and Great Britain and framed Blackness in a more expansive manner after the more politicized, rather than US-identitarian, Black British model of the 1980s. The title was inspired by a Homi Bhabha essay and our guest essayist was Sarat Maharaj. Included in the show were the likes of Yinka Shonibare [Great Britain], Rebecca Belmore [Canada], and Glenn Ligon [United States]. Belmore's *Rising to the Occasion* [1987–91] offers an Indigenous critique of Canada's colonial ties to Britain [fig. 4.3]. Ligon's *Profile* series [1990–91] takes on racial profiling and the Central Park Five case through a series of portrait panels featuring his signature-smeared black-text-on-white canvases. The following year, I organized a solo show of Ingrid Pollard's installations and photographs for *Oceans Apart* [1992] at the Art in General exhibition space in New York, cosponsored by the Bronx-based photographic organization En Foco. Because of the rebellions in Los Angeles following the Rodney King verdict and how many places were even boarded up in New York City because of a fear of a similar backlash, I don't think that Pollard's show received the kind of attention it should have. Eventually, Black Britain, and later Black Europe, would become an important part of my teaching.

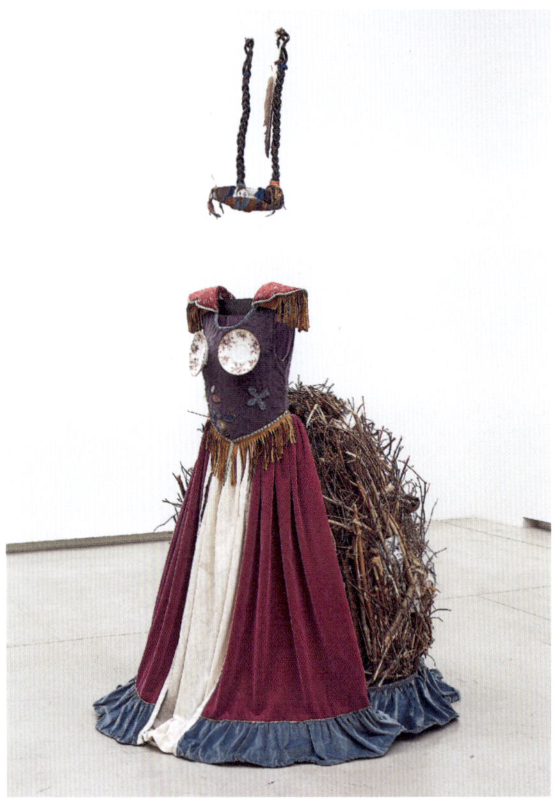

Fig. 4.3 Rebecca Belmore (Canadian Ojibwe, b. 1960). *Rising to the Occasion,* mixed media, 200 × 120 × 100 cm, 1987–91. Toronto, Art Gallery of Ontario. Artwork shown in *Interrogating Identity,* curated by Kellie Jones, Grey Art Gallery and Study Center, New York, 12 March–18 May 1991.

Another thing that came into my practice in the 1990s was that the curatorial act spurred on additional writing projects. Here is where you see curatorial work as part of intellectual and scholarly work. For instance, my article, "In Their Own Image" [1990] on Black women using image/text in the US and Britain appeared in *Artforum;* it was part of the mix and expansion of my intellectual work on Black Britain in that moment. I also published several articles as a companion to or extension of my thinking on South African artists in the wake of my show, *Life's Little Necessities: Installations by Women in the 1990s* [1997].

My international curatorial experience in the 1980s led to my work on the Johannesburg Biennale in 1997. My experience working on the Brazilian Bienal was one reason why Okwui Enwezor tapped me to curate an exhibition for the Johannesburg Biennale. Not working for the US government with translators, cars, and all that and working in the postaparthied moment was a totally different experience. But that's where I met Tumelo Mosaka! The show I organized was *Life's Little Necessities* [figs. 4.4, 4.5]. Thirteen women from across the world got a room of their own—as Virginia Woolf would say—to do their own thing. Lorna Simpson, Zarina Bhimji, Berni Searle from South Africa, María Magdalena Campos-Pons, and Wangechi Mutu were all in it [figs. 4.6, 4.7]. Neither Wangechi nor Magdalena could travel to South Africa due to visa issues. So, they sent the work, and we had to install it based on their instructions. Fatimah Tuggar represented Nigeria. Melanie Smith, a British artist who has been based in Mexico for many years, also participated. Pat Ward Williams was in South Africa on a Fulbright scholarship, so it was great to include her. After my experience in São Paulo, I told them all to bring their own tools and make them cordless. Believe me, the installers, mostly young white art students, were shaken up and totally entranced by these powerful beauties. At the same time, I received a lot of pushback in the press for doing a "women's show." It was passé; we didn't need these

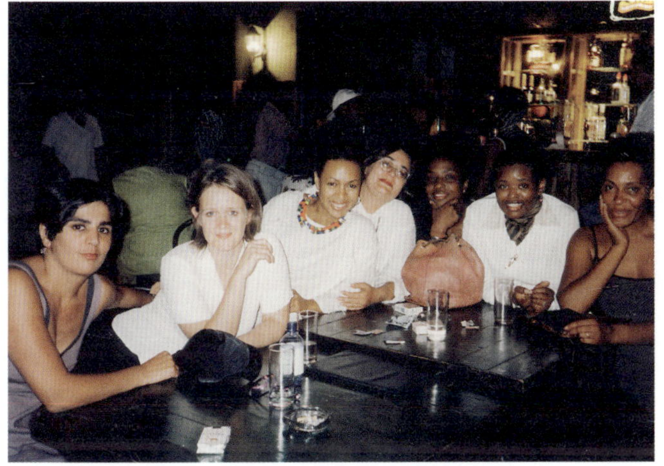

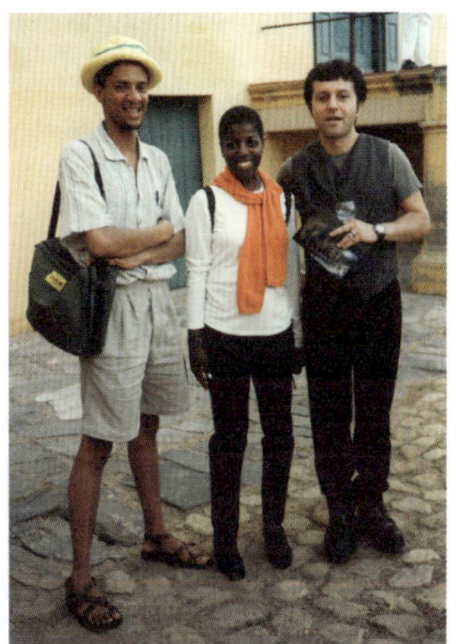

Fig. 4.4 *Left to right:* Zarina Bhimji, Melanie Smith, Kellie Jones, Valeska Soares, Lorna Simpson, Veliswa Gwintsa, and Carrie Mae Weems, Cape Town, 1997.

Fig. 4.5 *Left to right:* Tumelo Mosaka, Thelma Golden, and Octavio Zaya at the opening for *Life's Little Necessities: Installations by Women in the 1990s,* Castle of Good Hope, Cape Town, 1997.

things anymore in 1997. But, as we know, the art world continued to lag in these areas.

The show took place in Cape Town at the Castle of Good Hope, so it was outside the main Johannesburg orbit. As far as I know, it was, and still is, a working fort. So, to do a project there was already intense. I found out a Black woman was buried there, under the building. Krotoa [also known as Eva van Meerhof] was a seventeenth-century Indigenous woman and seen somewhat disparagingly for aiding the Dutch in their quest for colonization of the Cape. Of course, when she was no longer of use, she was thrown in prison. She was one of the first people to be jailed on Robben Island by the colonizers. When she died, she was buried under the fort. That period of the Johannesburg Biennale was also the moment Saartjie [Sarah] Baartman [the Hottentot Venus] returned to the public imagination with the impending return of her remains from being on public display in France. One of the themes across the various articles I would write in this period was about women and the notion of agency and consent throughout history. There were so many things that were so generative about that time in South Africa. Curating that show opened me up to the histories of this place I was walking around. So, once they told me that a woman was buried at the Castle of Good Hope, consecrating the ground, I thought, "Oh, we're good. We have a guardian here." So that was very impactful.

I can say in retrospect that it was one of the hardest shows I've ever done. But then afterwards, I went to Robben Island and saw where Nelson Mandela lived for most of his twenty-seven years of incarceration and said "I didn't do shit" [*laughs*]. You go there and you just say, "Okay, what Nelson Mandela did, *that* was hard." It was a humbling

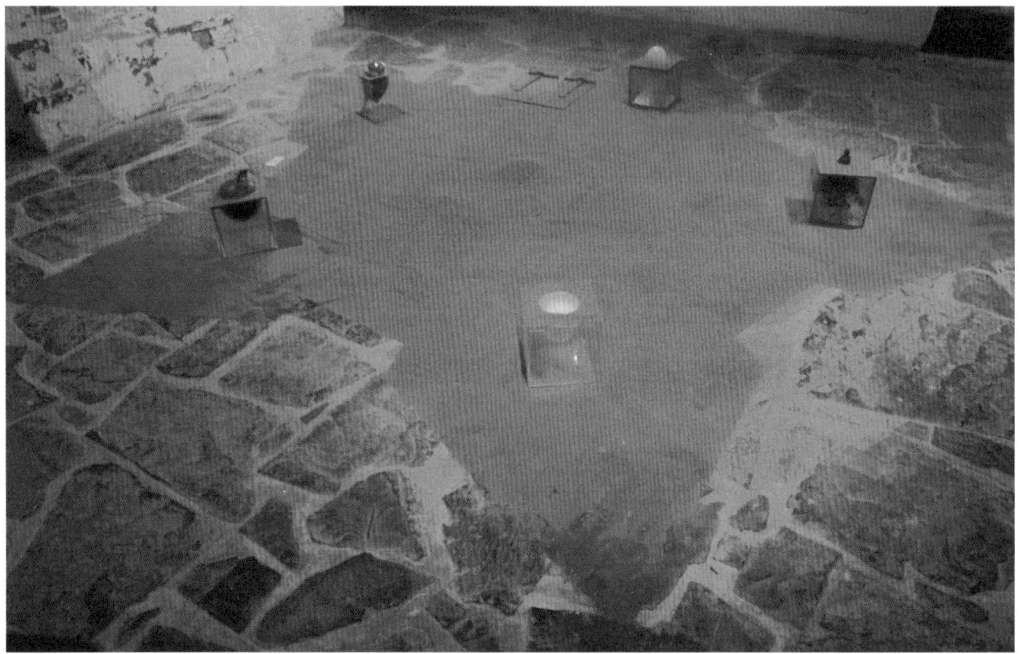

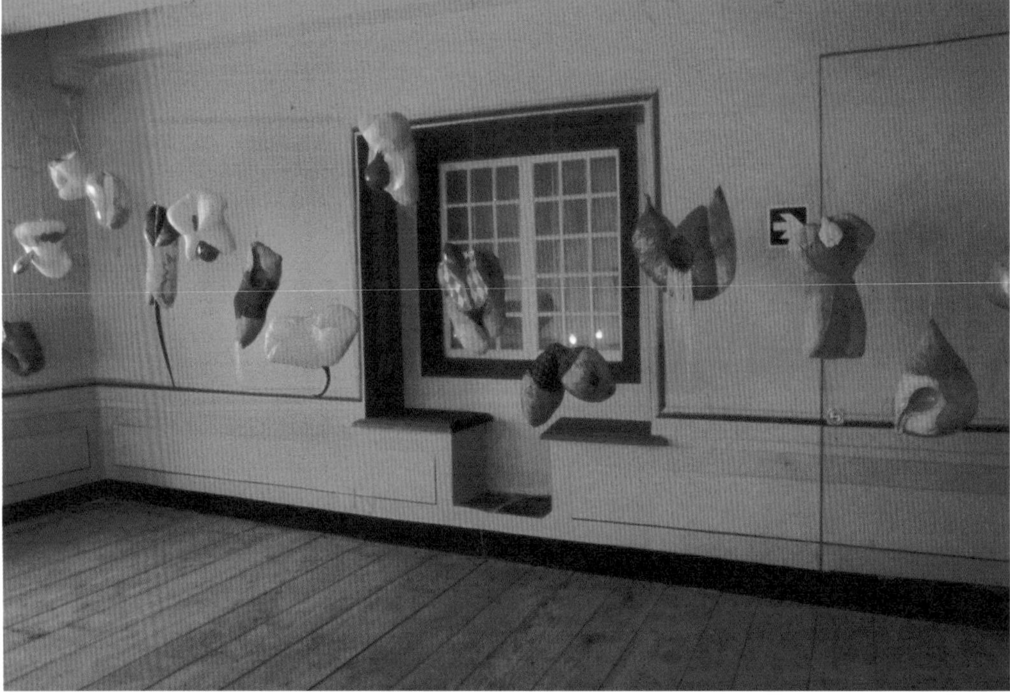

Fig. 4.6 Installation view of Berni Searle's *Com-fort* (1997) in *Life's Little Necessities: Installations by Women in the 1990s,* curated by Kellie Jones, Castle of Good Hope, Cape Town, 1997.

Fig. 4.7 Installation view of Wangechi Mutu's *Four Square Pillahs* (1997) in *Life's Little Necessities: Installations by Women in the 1990s,* curated by Kellie Jones, Castle of Good Hope, Cape Town, 1997.

moment. Yet, for me, as a Black person supervising white people in 1997 who weren't used to it, it was no walk in the park. Because, think about it, in 1997, very few Black people had been given the training to work in the curatorial field, but that was changing.

Yes, it was the hardest show I've ever done, but it was also the most amazing thing I've ever done as a curator. As a kid growing up, you're learning about apartheid and fighting against apartheid. At JAC, we had antiapartheid shows. To go there when apartheid has ended, that's when you realize, "Okay, this is over, but there is still work to do." To be in that mix in some very small way, to contribute to building a new country, was amazing. The pride in that—the inspiration—I'm sure is what led me to produce those other articles at the time. It was great to see that I could still do what I wanted to do as a diplomat: travel the world, speak different languages, add art in, and think that art is still changing people's minds about things.

TJL: So, at this moment, you also decide you're going back to school. What prompts that move? Can you walk us through that early 1990s moment?

KJ: After those international shows in the 1980s, I wanted to know more. That was one thing. The other part was something that is not as true today, which is in order to move up in the museum hierarchy, you had to have some kind of advanced degree because they weren't just letting BIPOC people in to work at MoMA. I can't tell you how many jobs I applied for and was rejected, even though I had a degree from Amherst College, magna cum laude, and had a bunch of experience.

I was either going to get an MBA like Linda Goode Bryant or do a PhD. I realized I was never going to sell anything. At that time, people were getting MBAs to be directors of museums. I said, "I'm not that person, let me think about the PhD." I knew and was working with people who had PhDs, like Lowery Stokes Sims and Richard J. Powell. Arlene Raven, the feminist art historian, was another. She, along with her partner, the artist Nancy Grossman, were also part of my support system.

I decided I would get a PhD, with the thinking that when I got out in six years, I would more easily find a job in a museum and nobody would bug me. I intended to go back to the museum. At the same time, I got this feeling that there was more—it wasn't just about me, there was a history that I wanted to know. I wanted to say intelligent things. I didn't want to say what was off the top of my head, I wanted to have some depth behind that. That was really the motivation.

In the 1990s, I also worked as an adjunct curator with the Walker Art Center in Minneapolis. They took my *Interrogating Identity* show that had been traveling. I developed a show on the braid of history and pop culture there called *Malcolm X: Man, Ideal, Icon* [1992]. The idea had germinated while I was working in Queens, but I was able to realize it at the Walker. Another show I organized during my time in Minneapolis was *Dawoud Bey: Portraits 1975–1995* [1995] [fig. 4.8]. These latter two

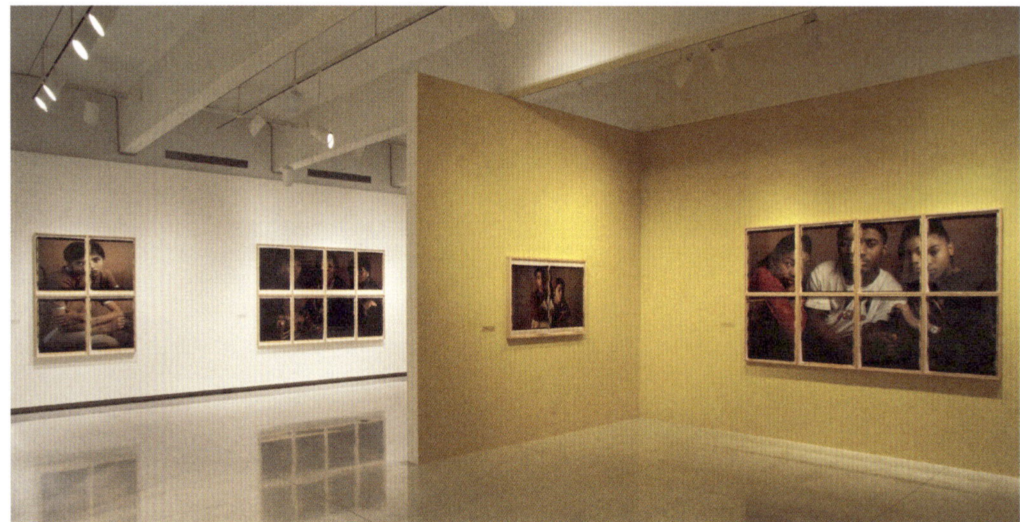

Fig. 4.8 Installation view of *Dawoud Bey: Portraits 1975–1995*, curated by Kellie Jones, Walker Art Center, Minneapolis, 17 September–10 December 1995.

shows traveled widely, and in the case of Dawoud's solo, it also went to London and the Barbican.

TJL: There are so many projects I could talk about. *Art Performs Life: Merce Cunningham, Meredith Monk, Bill T. Jones* [1998] is one. This was the exhibition you organized about Merce Cunningham, Meredith Monk, and Bill T. Jones twenty years before dancing with the art world and the archive became something people were talking about.

KJ: *Art Performs Life* was a co-curated show. Each of us, the curators Siri Engberg and Phillippe Vergne and I, had different people we were working with. I was working with Bill. It was exciting because it was about dance and the archive. The show was the brainchild of the Walker's visionary director Kathy Halbreich. It was phenomenal to work with her to see how she operated and to work with a non-Black person who says, "I see you. I want to work with you." That's Kathy's generation; they've championed people of color for decades now. It's been great to work with and for people who have that vision that allows me to step into my vision. It was so interesting working with dance as an archive. And you've done it beautifully with your exhibition, *Judson Dance Theater: The Work Is Never Done* [2018–19].

During my time working with the Walker, Kathy also supported another idea I had, which was to develop an internship program to increase diversity in the museum sphere. A number of people came through that program and ended up working at the Walker for a time, including Olukemi [Kemi] Ilesanmi, who went on to become the director of the New York's Laundromat Project, and Eungie Joo, who became curator and head of contemporary art at the San Francisco Museum of Modern Art.

TJL: It's wild how deep these threads go. There are questions you ask and are able to offer answers to but then revisit later. Given the time and place, you have the opportunity to explore them anew. I hadn't made the connection between all the ways in which that kind of space, of overlap, has come back again and again. What is it when these things come together?

KJ: I think part of it I got from my family: you pass it on to the next generation and you do all this for somebody else. You see it and say, "I want other people to see it and take this forward. It's not about me."

TJL: As one of those people from the next generation, Kellie, I want to say for the record, thank you because it's an incredible gift. The matter-of-factness with which you say something that could easily not be that way for many others reflects the expansiveness and insistence of your imagination. That it's like, "Yes, this will be our reality." I am indebted to you for that.

KJ: It's something Thelma and I have talked about too. She has that as well—we're of a certain generation. Whatever your gift is, you better do something with it. Don't sit around and watch reruns on television [*laughs*]. You've got to do something with this. What will you do with what you have to offer? That's the question for every single person. The answer is different for everybody and that's the beauty of the world.

Growing up in New York was such a gift because, as you know from living there, you see so much. You see the whole world on a subway car, on a street, and it's just every day. You hear different languages and eat different foods. I feel that that made me a better citizen of the world.

TJL: So far, our conversation has been about the exhibitions you curated in the 1980s and 1990s. I also want to touch briefly on some of your more recent shows that people may be more familiar with because of the impact they've had.

I'm going to start with *Now Dig This! Art and Black Los Angeles, 1960–1980* [2011–12], an exhibition we're still living in the long tale of [fig. 4.9]. Certainly, the *Just Above Midtown: Changing Spaces* show [2022–23], which I'm working on and for which you have written an essay for the catalog, would not have been possible without *Now Dig This!.* I've spoken to many curators who have organized solo shows and group exhibitions. They said that seeing this show at the Hammer Museum and then as it traveled was what made their exhibitions possible. So, regarding *Now Dig This!,* is there a moment that you want to raise up for a textural experience?

KJ: I was already working on my book *South of Pico: African American Artists in Los Angeles in the 1960s and 1970s* [2017]. I had also known some of the artists featured in the show for many years, from the JAM days, especially David Hammons, Senga Nengudi, and Maren Hassinger but I didn't know others. So, I got really interested in that context, started researching, and started going to Los Angeles a lot. L.A. is one of my favorite places, along with London, and I just bumped into an opportunity to do this show. For me, the show offered a chance to give back to artists and provide them with high-resolution images of their work. Some of them didn't even have digital copies of their work. It was also a way for me to expand my own research because if you're working on a show, you can get into MoMA or the Met and walk around in storage and they will pull things out for you. That might not be so easy when working on a book. So, the context of the Hammer Museum and the Getty's Pacific Standard Time initiative, which I participated in, were quite important, both for resources and as a platform to present these artists and their works.

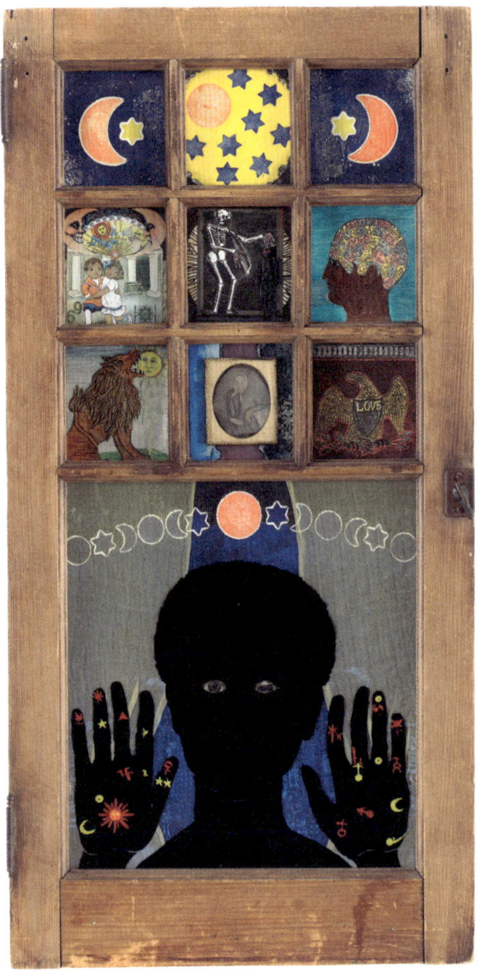

Fig. 4.9 Betye Saar (American, b. 1926). *Black Girl's Window,* wooden window frame with paint, cut-and-pasted printed and painted papers, daguerreotype, lenticular print, and plastic figurine, 90.8 × 45.7 × 3.8 cm, 1969. New York, Museum of Modern Art, 549.2013. Artwork shown in *Now Dig This! Art and Black Los Angeles, 1960–1980,* curated by Kellie Jones, Hammer Museum, Los Angeles, 2 October 2011–8 January 2012.

I was able to expand my book because I was able to see pieces that I'd only seen in black-and-white pictures in books. Noah Purifoy's sculpture, *Untitled* [1970], acquired by the Whitney in 1971, is an example. It may not have been shown in fifty years and wasn't photographed at that time. It's not black and white at all. It's orange and hangs on the wall. For my shows during that 2000s period—*Now Dig This!* and *Energy/Experimentation: Black Artists and Abstraction, 1964–1980* [2006], which we'll talk about a little later—I knew all these works from teaching them and from books, particularly those by David Driskell and Samella Lewis. I finally took those pieces out of the Met, MoMA, the Whitney, and the Los Angeles County Museum of Art [LACMA]. Those institutions had taken great care of these objects, but nobody showed them. They were nicely wrapped and conserved, which was a good thing. The curators at MoMA, the Met, and all these other places appreciated it too because then it gave them a context to show those works within their own collections. So that was another benefit. It delayed my own book a bit, but it was well worth it to have that giveback to the artists, to meet some of these people, to work with them before they passed away, like the late curators Karen Higa and Cecil Fergerson.

I got to work with Naima J. Keith [now the vice president of Education and Public Programs at LACMA]. She was my curatorial assistant. We had a meeting every week for three years either on the phone or in person. I couldn't have done *Now Dig This!* without Naima. She named the show. She was my eyes and ears in L.A. because she's an Angeleno. She told me the meaning of the phrase "South of Pico," which became the title of my book.

A great thing about the show is that the whole catalog and all the programming exists online, thanks to a digitization grant from the Mellon Foundation. You can see all the videos, including the video where they ask me what is Black Los Angeles, and I start cracking up. And I say it's how Black people in Los Angeles affect their city, the country, and the world. For me, Black Los Angeles is an entity that impacts people, right? White people, Black people, Latinx people, Asian American and Pacific Islander folks—all of whom are in the show. L.A. is one place, like New York, where you have a lot of those kinds of collaborations and I wanted to talk about that.

TJL: You've named so many of the conditions and the grace with which you moved through those conditions. It's inspiring to hear all those crossroads. I want to ask you about another important exhibition: *Energy/Experimentation* at the Studio Museum [fig. 4.10]. It's another exhibition you can trace many solo shows and group projects back to. I want to hear some of your pathway and the reverberations of that exhibition as you think about it today.

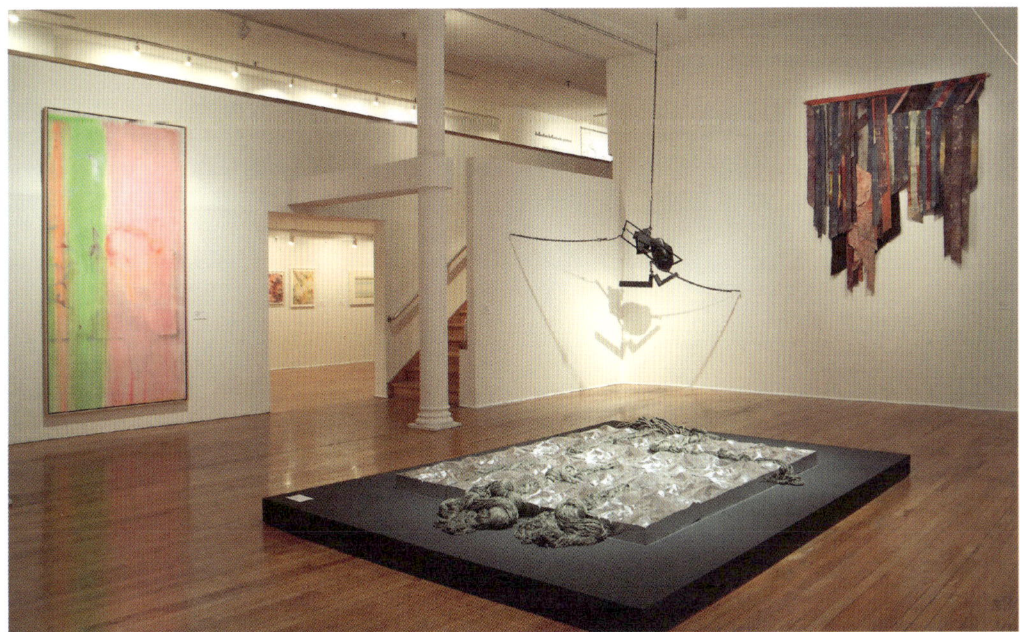

Fig. 4.10 Exhibition view of *Energy/Experimentation: Black Artists and Abstraction, 1964–1980,* curated by Kellie Jones, Studio Museum in Harlem, New York, 5 April–2 July 2006.

KJ: It was great to organize that show for the Studio Museum because that is where my roots are and because of what it stands for, what it is, and what it does. I was so glad to come to work today at Columbia University to see the outline of the museum's new building going up. Lowery Stokes Sims was the director of the museum at the time and invited me to organize the show. The Studio Museum has a long history of showing Black artists working abstractly, a direction pioneered by Mary Schmidt Campbell when she was its director in the 1970s and 1980s. I was following up on that legacy through a group show for a new generation. It also gave me an opportunity to think about the idea of Blackness and abstraction because the narrative then, and perhaps to some degree now, is that abstract art has nothing to do with Black people. I wanted to show how artists like, Ed Clark, Melvin Edwards, Al Loving, Howardena Pindell, Jack Whitten, William T. Williams, and others had been really involved in their own ways with moving the dialogue forward about Blackness and race in this country. Many of them were originally from the South and were as committed to a kind of politics as they were to the fact that they were going to keep making this kind of work. And nobody was going to tell them what to make.

What you see with Black artists in the nineteenth- and early twentieth-century period is that they're getting a hold on the image of Black people. What does a Black person look like? Was that really tied down before? What do Black people think they look like, themselves? How do they represent themselves? The issue of representation is so important. In the United States, you've been enslaved. A dominant white class has been controlling your very existence: how you work, how you look, how many babies you have, what you do. You deal with rape. You are property. So, you're going to claim representation, maybe a small thing in the scheme of things but still important in our field, right? Representation. The idea of the figure is very important. Fundamentally, it signals an autonomy and this approach to the figure broadly characterizes the Harlem Renaissance period. But, after a while, Black artists also don't want to be forced to always have to think about that. They want greater freedom; they want to figure things out another way, for instance, finding another way to get to portraiture, to memorialize without pictorial representation, as in the case of Whitten's *Black Monolith* series [1988–2017].

It was important to make the point that artists making abstractions in the 1960s and 1970s could still be politically active; for instance, fifteen artists withdrew from the *Contemporary Black Artists in America* show [1970] at the Whitney because they didn't like the way the show was coming together. They pulled out as a political act, right? Thinking about their actions in this way comes in addition to thinking about how they were using mediums. For me, the curatorial process is something that has driven my scholarship. It's the way I research and then say, "Hey, I want to know more. I want to write more about this particular person or period." Certainly, *Energy/Experimentation* did that for me.

TJL: Thank you, Kellie. Yes, as Black artists working in figuration are welcomed into a certain market and institutional apparatus, your refusal of the binaries of representation in abstraction—drawing from the history you're describing—makes possible for this tradition to exist in new ways. This is especially important in this moment where certain parts of the practice are valorized over others. What about the blockbuster exhibition *Basquiat* [2005] at the Brooklyn Museum that built off so many of your projects and long-term engagement with an individual person in real life and scholarship?

KJ: I was invited by the then-director of the Brooklyn Museum, Arnold Lehman, to organize the *Basquiat* show. I co-curated the show with three others: Franklin Sirmans—one of the expert voices on Jean-Michel Basquiat—Fred Hoffman, and Marc Mayer. The last weekend of the exhibition, around thirty-five thousand people came through. That's when I realized how important Basquiat was and still is. You can see what's happened with the whole Basquiat craze since then. He will never go away because he is a diasporic subject and speaks to so many people. It was really an honor to learn that from him.

A similar thing happened with *Now Dig This!*. There were lines around the block to get into the show, and people were like, [*gasps*] "For Black artists? Does that happen?" I was not even shocked. It was the same for my show, *Witness: Art and Civil Rights in the Sixties* [2014], which I co-curated with Theresa Carbone, also at the Brooklyn Museum. I was not even shocked. People wanted to see this and guess what? It was not only an audience of Black people. That's the thing, it was like hip-hop, folks. Everyone wanted to know about this. It was new, they don't know about it, and it's exciting. They saw the work and said, "Wow, this is great." *Basquiat* kind of started that off for me—a confidence that an audience could be as excited about these things as I am.

TJL: As you have worked in and between a variety of high-end institutions and culturally specific institutions, do you have hopes or desires for places like MoMA—or where you are now at Columbia University—in terms of what remains to be done around artists of color? Are there specific designs that you would care to offer, or is that not necessarily your concern or work to take on?

KJ: If you think about the protests against museums—such as at the Whitney, MoMA, and the Met in the 1960s and 1970s—the things Black constituencies are fighting for are more Black artists in the collection and more shows by Black artists generally. Those things did occur. But Black people also wanted Black scholarship and Black curators, which was not going to happen to a major extent in the 1960s or 1970s. Lowery Stokes Sims became a curator at the Met in 1975. Kynaston McShine amazingly worked at the Jewish Museum as a curator from 1965 to 1968 before moving on to MoMA. That was it for thirty years until Thelma Golden was hired by the Whitney Museum in 1991. Then the Black Lives Matter movement took hold in the 2000s and more Black curators began to be hired. As a historian, I don't think this is an accident. To many museums' credit, they were going in that direction, but certainly Black Lives Matter made it even more important for many more institutions, not just the Whitneys and the MoMAs of the world, to follow suit. I'd also like to point out that places like the Museum of Fine Arts, Houston, and Contemporary Arts Museum Houston have had Black collections and Black curators, including Alvia Wardlaw and Valerie Cassel Oliver, respectively, because they're in the South and the Museum of Fine Arts, Houston, also collects self-taught "folk" artists. Your beautiful show *When the Stars Begin to Fall: Imagination and the American South* [2014] has given us some new language to appreciate those kinds of relationships as well.

Things will change. I'm always optimistic. I did my part and museums will also do their part because it's also about who's going to come through the doors. Who is the audience? If you're talking about the changing demographics of this country, what are you going to show? I'm always hopeful.

TJL: Let's use the quiet time to talk about quieter things. It's vital that we've heard about the landmark exhibitions you've organized. I want to talk about some of the behind-the-scenes work, commitments, and steadiness it takes to make those things happen. I know about your incredible daily routine and want to know if you'll share some of that with folks who are curious to know how this magic happens. What has been part of your routine that has allowed you to do the many things that you have done?

KJ: As Thelma Golden always jokes, "Do you still get up early?!" Yes, I get up very early. I'm a very early riser and would write before I went to work. It's about the quiet. What part of the day do you find the quiet? The artist Whitfield Lovell finds it in the middle of the night. He's a late-night person. But I'm an early person and if you can touch something every day or most of the week, you can get it done. Because you're always working a job, when do you have time? These shows I mentioned, most were work for hire. They were outside of my job. *Now Dig This!* came out at the same time as *EyeMinded.* I can't even believe that happened—it was the same year. And I have another job, which is working at Columbia. [*Laughs.*]

So that's part of my practice. You have to exercise. You can be writing—even if you have the weekend to write or are writing all day and thinking—but you've got to go out in the street. That's what I love about New York. You can be in your head and then you can just go out in the street, and there's so much happening. You're seeing everybody else go about their day, which for me is always exciting in cities. That's what I like. I'm a city gal. Although I'm getting more interested in plants, trees, and having that experience of astonishment. You need to be astonished out of your own head.

As Thelma and I always talk about, Lowery was the only curator we had ever heard of. Who had ever heard of being a curator? We didn't know Kynaston. Even Thelma met him later. I met him during my time

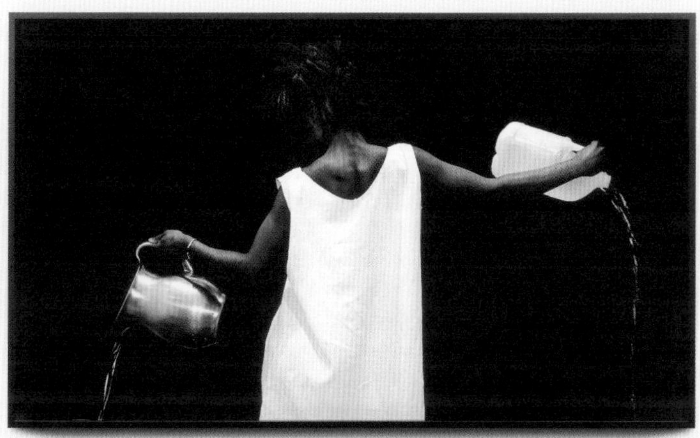

Fig. 4.11 Lorna Simpson (American, b. 1960). *Waterbearer,* gelatin silver print with vinyl lettering, 135.9 × 208.3 × 5.7 cm, 1986. Artwork shown in *In the Tropics,* curated by Kellie Jones, Longwood Arts Project, New York, 22 March–19 April 1986.

working on the Bienal de São Paulo in the late 1980s. We knew Lowery though. Lowery actually worked in the Met! Wow, you could actually do something like that? I want to thank all those people who saw me as part of this tradition. Richard J. Powell, Lowery Stokes Sims, and Deborah Willis who gave me essays and things to do. I want to thank the cohort of curators, which this whole project is about. How did we get there? People like David Driskell, Samella Lewis, and others who had come before us were always so generous. Floyd Coleman is another, as well as people like the painter Elizabeth Murray and Kathy Halbreich, people who put you on for different things. Elizabeth recommended me for my very first guest curatorial job in 1984. She was on the board of a storefront gallery called Small Walls on Chrystie Street. I organized an exhibition called *Speaking in Tongues* [1984] that featured three women sculptors: Jamillah Jennings, Alison Saar, and Linda Whitaker.

The friendship or relationship you have with artists is super important because otherwise you can't get anything done. You could possibly borrow work from a collector, but that loan still might get shut down. In fact, the sculptor Fred Wilson hired me for another early show of mine, *In the Tropics* [1986], which thought about art made in or about the area defined cartographically as tropical—its aesthetics, its engagement with tourism, et cetera [fig. 4.11]. That show took place at the Longwood Arts Project in the Bronx where he was the director. This was where he also launched his critical curatorial and installation practice with the show *Rooms with a View* [1987].

TJL: Thank you, Kellie, for bringing all those people into this space and acknowledging the incredible social technologies that your work comes out of, as well as your personal ability to creatively galvanize those relationships toward a shared vision that reflects you. Awards and getting your flowers are important because they offer a chance to say with all of this possibility, this is what you have done for us, with us, and for yourself. I want to ask how that felt in perhaps the most spectacular moment of getting a MacArthur genius award, to really have the community affirming the specificity of your contribution. What ran through your mind when you got that call?

KJ: It was a shock. It was amazing, but you're right in saying that it was about feeling the community honoring you, honoring this work, seeing your work, saying you have done something to change the field, to impact this field. That was incredible. It really, really was.

TJL: Are there any dream projects you want to speak into existence that are on the immediate horizon, or do you want to use this chance of self-reflection to say, "I'm going to open up that folder again and see what's in there"? What can the MacArthur offer you, not just as a recognition of what you have done but also as a chance to reflect about how the work continues in an open-ended way?

KJ: The one thing about the MacArthur is that it's about celebrating the work you've done but not having to continue to do it. They're very specific about using the award as an opportunity to rethink. So, one of the things that I spoke into existence was to collaborate with younger people and that has happened. I can look into the future with what you all are doing, your generation of people who are really changing the dialogue for us with different languages about gender and the visual field. That's some of the work I've been doing. You can take this same material that you've looked at for decades and think about it through queer theory, art and queer artists, or ideas about gender, and it's a whole different story. It gives you a new way to understand what's going on in the work. You see a different part of an artist's practice. Some of my thinking on this can be seen in my article "Nancy Elizabeth Prophet and Augusta Savage: Sculptural Habits of Black Modernism," in *Black Modernisms in the Transatlantic World,* edited by Steven Nelson and Huey Copeland [2023]. At Columbia, a certain cohort of students that I worked with over the years declared that they were only going to write their dissertations on women artists and most of them did. That got me thinking, What would art history look like if it was narrated through the accomplishments of women?

You have got to make time for life and family too. You can't just be a machine. That's what I've also learned from your generation. This whole idea, maybe it's the post–George Floyd period, post–Black Lives Matter, or Black Lives Matter going into the future. You have to rest. You have to stop. You cannot keep working like a machine that this country makes you work like. You've got to stop or you have to make different choices. You have to make different choices because you also want to think about how all these systems were not set up for you. They were set up for rich white men with wives and girlfriends and boyfriends. They did their thing. Everybody else was doing the work. [*Laughs.*]

TJL: That's so true.

KJ: It wasn't set up for you. You have to recognize that. When people say, "I have imposter syndrome"—you're not an imposter! This wasn't set up for you! It was set up for a whole other thing. You have to take time to remake it. You have to do that. And it's not just about the scholarship. It's also about life and honoring all those people who got you to this spot and honoring all those entities, plants, animals, and oceans too. You have to really give back to that or sit with those things too because they are so generative. Don't rush around from thing to thing to thing. Maybe that's what happens when you get older! But a younger generation brought that up about rest and time and things like that. I'm looking forward to digging more into those things, but also to keep writing. Writing is my happy place. Curating is exciting. My students always ask, "Why would you want to be a teacher when you could go all around the world doing amazing exhibitions? What are you doing sitting here talking to us?" Well, I've done those things. They were great. I can still do them, but this is great too because I learn something. I see the future and get to be a part of it by speaking to people like yourself. You get to see what the future looks like, just a little bit, and be happy for the world that people like yourselves are in and that means we did a good job.

TJL: It's inspiring to hear those changes narrated in the first person, especially when that perspective includes so many beloved ones. I want to say thank you on behalf of everybody who is going to read this. I see, already in your walk to where you are, the character of New York, and you as part of an emerging future, whether it's the rising building that is the Studio Museum and all the things that will happen there, or the figure of this city within your work, specifically the projects you've been working on for so long that are already here in the world. Thank you for allowing us to be entangled and indebted and just finding places to dance together. So, on behalf of so many, Kellie, thank you.

KJ: Thank you for doing this, really. I really couldn't have had a better interlocutor. Thank you so much T.

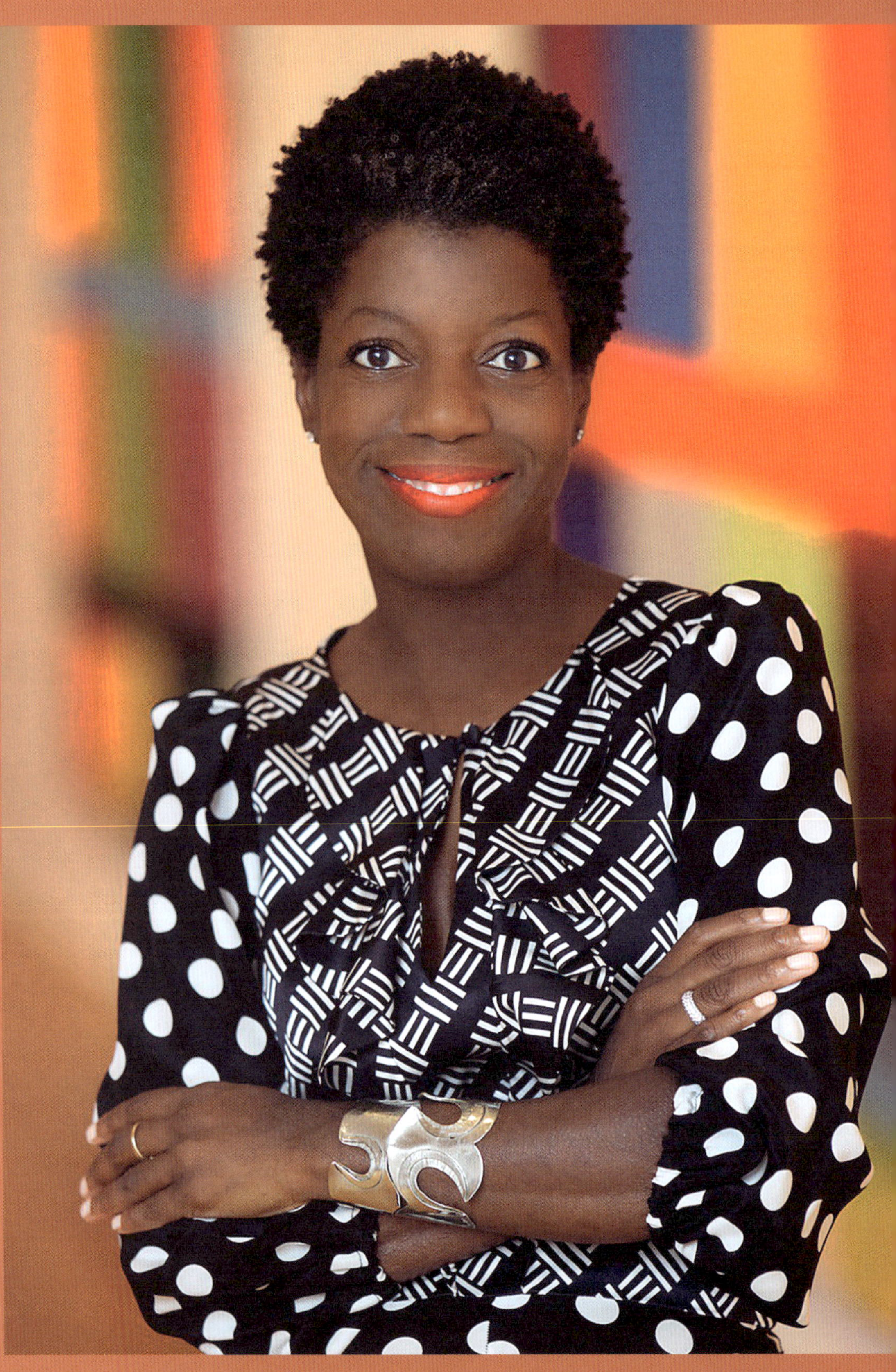

Thelma Golden

INTERVIEWED BY RUJEKO HOCKLEY
22 and 29 March 2023

RUJEKO HOCKLEY (RH): I'm so excited to do this because I've known you for so long. I know so much about you, both from talking to you and knowing you, but also because you're a person in the world who's done interviews. There are so many people we love connected to this project: Kellie Jones, Tumelo Mosaka, and Columbia University, where I completed my undergraduate degree before coming to the Studio Museum in Harlem. I'm going to ask you things that you're going to be like, "Well, she knows the answer to that, but—"

THELMA GOLDEN (TG): Oh, I know.

RH: You know how it goes.

TG: I was born in Queens, New York, at what used to be called Hillcrest General Hospital, which is now part of a bigger hospital system. My father is Arthur Ivanhoe Golden. He was born on 14 January 1926 in Harlem. My mother is Thelma Ometa Eastmond, and she was born on 18 January 1930 in Brooklyn. My mother was raised in Bedford-Stuyvesant, Brooklyn. They married in 1963, moved to Queens, and I was born in Queens and lived there.

RH: What was the world that you were born into? What was the world of your childhood in Queens and the community that your parents and family built around you?

TG: My childhood was defined by the fact that my mother and father were deeply community invested. With my father, it came through his business: a small insurance brokerage firm. He worked on behalf of individuals and small businesses, insuring and doing legal work around their homes, businesses, nonprofit organizations, and churches throughout the five boroughs. My mother was involved in a number of community service organizations. My childhood was defined by a sense of being deeply embedded in community.

RH: Let's talk about the outer boroughs. You were raised in Queens. You were in Harlem, which is not technically a borough but also absolutely is. Then you spent time in Brooklyn. You had family there. How did you think of New York when you were growing up? The city versus where you lived—were those the same things?

TG: They weren't. Manhattan represented something different than Manhattan below 110th Street. I was raised with a deep understanding of the whole city, a lot of which came from my father's business and the nature of his clients. For example, if my father had clients in the Bronx, he had to visit them in the Bronx; for clients in Brooklyn, we went there.

My parents, who were born and raised in the city, saw this city as a place fully open to them. So, we also engaged, particularly, in the culture of Manhattan. I grew up going to Broadway plays, the Lincoln Center for the Performing Arts, Alvin Ailey American Dance Theater, Dance Theatre of Harlem, National Black Theatre, and many of the places in New York that tourists come to visit. But I did so as someone who grew up here.

RH: What were your early thoughts about your future?

TG: I don't know that I had early thoughts about a future that predated my high school thoughts about my future. By the time I was in tenth grade, I knew I wanted to be a curator. There was never really another path. I was interested in museums from the time I was in elementary school, a result of my having gone to an independent school in Long Island called Buckley Country Day School. I got an amazing education at Buckley. The way we were taught opened a lot of space not just for learning but also for discovering.

The advantage of living in New York is that we, like many schools, went on field trips to museums. While at home I'd been deeply exposed to the performing arts—Broadway plays, community theater, and dance—I really discovered the depth of museums through field trips. I became interested and started asking my parents to go to them. I grew up going to—when my brother had hockey—the Queens Museum. I left Buckley and spent one unfortunate year in boarding school, but ended up, for my last three years of high school, on the Upper East Side at the New Lincoln School on Seventy-Seventh Street between Second and Third Avenues. Because New Lincoln was a progressive independent school, we were allowed to take electives. They could be like independent studies in college, but you could also have activities as electives. Because of my deep interest in museums, a teacher at New Lincoln introduced me to the High School Internship Program at the Metropolitan Museum of Art.

I was in the Met's High School Internship Program my junior or senior year. I worked in the American Decorative Arts Department for Alice Cooney Frelinghuysen—who is still a curator of American decorative arts at the Met—when the Frank Lloyd Wright Room was being created, and the American Wing was forming. When I graduated in May 1983, technically that spring, Randy Williams and Rika Burnham offered me a job. The summer before I went to college, I worked for the High School Programs Department, which felt like my first job because I got paid.

I was deeply invested in what it felt like—what I knew intuitively—was this incredible opportunity to be in that museum every day. Even when I was in the High School Internship Program, I treated it like a job.

I just loved it. When Randy asked me to work for them, that was a dream come true.

RH: It feels like not a coincidence that you were at the Met at this formative period as a very enthusiastic person and lover of the arts. Somebody else very special was there at the same time: Lowery Stokes Sims. At that time, Lowery was dropped from the moon to the Met. Did you know Lowery? Did you know of her? What was Lowery's space in that museum like and how did you perceive it?

TG: I knew who Lowery was because I had expressed this interest in pursuing museum work to my parents and they, of course, took it super seriously. At some point, my father showed me an article from a newspaper or magazine that Lowery was in. Once I saw that, I knew who she was. Now, when I was there in those days, I always hoped I'd run into her. That's how I thought that would go down, and for three years I wanted this to happen. As you know well how Lowery is, when I said this to her a few years later when we finally met, she said, "Why didn't you just call or come up?"

But the person who I met in those years and really was an encouragement and mentor was the late Joan Sandler, the former community education director of the Met. Joan worked in the realm of community affairs and education and had a wide berth at the Met and in the arts community broadly. She had this great Black matriarch energy and became a real guide for me, not just in the museum but in the larger cultural world.

RH: And so you went to Smith College following your job at the Met knowing that you wanted to study art history.

TG: Yes, I did. I knew I wanted to be a contemporary art curator and I knew I wanted to major in art history. Smith had a yearlong introductory art history course called Art 100 that all art majors had to take. It was legendary. You took it semester one and semester two, and it took you through the history of art. I took Art 100 the first semester of my first year at Smith with full intention of majoring in art history. I also began to imagine what it would mean to intern during both the January term and summer term.

My first year at Smith I interned at the Terry Dintenfass Gallery. Terry Dintenfass represented Jacob Lawrence, which was the only reason I applied for the internship. That was a January-term internship. My sophomore year I interned at the Studio Museum. I'd already taken a course in African American literature, but in my mind, I was taking it to fill out my interests. But after the internship at the Studio Museum, I came back to Smith and made the decision to double major in both art history and African American studies.

RH: Who was at the Studio Museum during your first official engagement with the institution?

TG: Dr. Mary Schmidt Campbell was director; Kinshasha Holman Conwill was deputy director; Patricia [Pat] Cruz was director of development; Cheryl Lynn Bruce was director of communications; Sharon Patton and Grace Stanislaus were curators; John Hutton was the registrar; Al Cucci was director of graphics; Winston Cherry was head of buildings; and then there was a whole group of program and administrative staff. I can't recall all their names.

RH: This level of recall is very impressive [*laughs*].

TG: During my first internship at the Studio Museum, I did not get into the curatorial department. I did not make the cut. My first internship was in communications, and I was Cheryl's intern. Cheryl had an office that was where the copy machine went. That's how small this room was.

I loved working with Cheryl. She worked closely with Kinshasha, Pat, and Mary. It should not be lost on anyone for what it meant that I had a museum experience where the leaders were Black women. I saw them, literally, run a museum. After that, I had other internships, always with the goal to graduate and work in a museum.

RH: How did your relationship to contemporary artists of your time develop?

TG: I grew up going to museums, but this was early 1980s New York and the gallery world had grown ever-present in SoHo. Like today, galleries were free, so I often went to galleries. During that era—between the Whitney Biennials and going to galleries—I was hyperconscious of the idea that museums were about the past in many ways, but there was also this whole world of living artists. That really, really determined how I understood art. Even more specifically, at the Studio Museum, there were many people working at the museum who were practitioners in some way. So, I also understood the life of artists.

RH: I imagine, outside of the Studio Museum, the art world appeared to be a very white world to you then. Did you see Lowery as an example and say, "And then there's going to be me"?

TG: I didn't think of it as a very white world because I understood, from that early internship, the kind of exclusions that happened. I understood there were many people who had the interest, intellect, and ability, but they were only able to thrive in certain places. At the Studio Museum, that's where, from early in my career, names like David Driskell and Samella Lewis were deeply real to me as people whose work didn't exist in traditional art histories of that moment.

I came to know Driskell's *Two Centuries of Black American Art* [1976–77] as a college student, which opened a whole realm of exhibitions that happened, again, sporadically. I understood there was this wealth of energy and effort, but with the way the traditional art world was structured, it was not as known. I know often when people enter realms where we haven't been, they'll say, "And I didn't know anyone else was there." No. That was not it at all. I knew the opposite.

RH: You knew, yes.

TG: I knew there were plenty of people. By this point, I knew who Kynaston McShine was. I knew he existed in the museum world and art historical world because I saw his name on shows he organized. I came into this with a sense of the people who'd done a lot of work but not been credited. I knew Just Above Midtown existed. I knew Linda Goode Bryant. I didn't get to meet her, but I knew these places were there. There was a whole realm of nonprofits, some which are no longer with us, that were doing exhibitions, programs, and showing artists.

I went and worked for Kellie Jones. I got to know Kellie when I was a student at Smith. Kellie had been at Amherst College a few years before me and majored in art history, African American studies, and Spanish. I think Kellie did a triple major.

RH: [*Laughs.*] Not surprised.

TG: She's a genius. Many of the people who taught me in African American studies at Smith knew Kellie. Then when I did the internship at the Studio Museum, they said, "Oh, Kellie worked there." I'm not sure exactly who introduced us first, but there were multiple points of entry and engagement. I lived and grew up in Jamaica, Queens. The Jamaica Arts Center [JAC] was on Jamaica Avenue. Many of the businesses on Jamaica Avenue were clients of my father's, and JAC came out of a project called the Greater Jamaica Development Corporation that my father was on the board of.

Kellie and I met, and when I came home for vacation, she invited me to JAC. I went and saw the show that was on view. Kellie organized an incredible program. She was curating at the highest level in what had been a bank building turned into a multi-arts center. I always have to separate Kellie and JAC because Kellie was doing amazing work. JAC was not an organization that, at the time, was living up to everyone's aspirations. Kellie carved out an incredibly generative space and did it with very few resources that she had to, in many cases, claim herself.

When I was at the Whitney Museum of American Art, Kellie was named the commissioner for the Bienal de São Paulo and Martin Puryear was going to represent the United States. She wrote that proposal and grant similar to how you would now—an organization had to take this on. JAC, at its scale, required her to staff in a way that could keep things going and replace some of the time that she needed to work on the Bienal. Basically, Kellie hired me as her assistant. In that role, while she was on trips to Brazil with Martin—site visits, et cetera—my role was to assist her.

RH: Keep it going.

TG: She planned it out beautifully and I learned so much from her. By the time the show was over, Kellie had applied to graduate school, something she had wanted to do for some time. When she knew she was leaving, the most generous thing she did was make sure that JAC kept me so I could stay employed. And I did.

RH: Where were you living at this time?

TG: At this time, I still would've been living at home because this would've been 1989, 1990. That's what's so crazy about it. I graduated in 1987. I was at the Studio Museum from 1987 to 1988, the Whitney as a curatorial assistant from 1988 to 1989, and then with Kellie for maybe half of 1989 into 1990. I came back to the Whitney in 1991.

RH: Yes, only four years. That's not that much time.

TG: Yes, exactly. At the time, it felt like twenty years [*Hockley laughs*]. When I look back on it, I'm always like, "Yes, that was only ten months." All those periods felt like a long time. I didn't move out until 1992. I was at the Whitney.

RH: Can you talk a little bit more about the Whitney at the Philip Morris headquarters? I think people don't remember or understand what it meant for there to be branches of the Whitney.

TG: When I went back to the Whitney, I was director of the Whitney at Philip Morris. The Whitney had a very innovative program—it was probably the early 1980s—where they created art spaces in corporate buildings.

In some cases, they were newly built buildings, like the Whitney at Equitable Center, which was run by Adam Weinberg. There was the Whitney downtown branch in what was the old IBM building, which Lisa Phillips ran at one point, and a Whitney branch in Stamford at what was originally the headquarters for Champion International Paper. I was director at the Whitney at Philip Morris. All these spaces were free and open to the public. They were physically smaller, meant to engage a local public, and featured programming that reflected the Whitney's mission.

The Whitney at Philip Morris was in the lobby of Philip Morris' headquarters. It was about a fifteen hundred square-foot space that was adjacent to a big open atrium. The atrium had an amazing performance program that predated my arrival, curated by the fantastic performance art curator Jeanette Vuocolo who really brought the idea of performance into museums. That branch also had an amazing arts program, one of the first that engaged city shelters, created by the artist Hope Sandrow and the late Whitney Museum educator Dina Helal.

RH: Oh, Dina, yes.

TG: When I came to the Whitney it was because David Ross had become director, and he hired me. I proposed that we do a site-specific commissioned-artists program, and David was open to it. That's what my first curatorial life was like.

RH: What did you understand was the Whitney's mission at that time? When you say these branches were charged with extending the Whitney's mission into different localities, what did you understand was your imprimatur as a representative of the Whitney? You had this idea to do a different sort of program, but did you think about it that way, or were you like, "This is my little world"?

TG: No, it's hard for people to remember this, but in the 1980s and 1990s, museums did not do contemporary art in an ongoing way. The Whitney did.

RH: Was this because of the Biennial?

TG: In general. So, this all felt very Whitney—the idea of working with living artists. However, the Whitney was also very collections focused. What perhaps distinguished it was that my own interests made it so that I moved into that program with the thought of working with younger artists.

RH: Yes, your peers.

TG: My peers and artists of color. So that ranged from doing projects with Glenn Ligon, Lorna Simpson, Suzanne McClelland, so many artists [figs. 5.1, 5.2]. We began a brochure project where all those exhibitions were accompanied by free brochures that people could take. From 1991 until 1993, I did that. In 1993, I began working on other kinds of exhibitions.

We moved to two or three of those projects a year. I'd come up with an idea and present it to the larger curatorial group. We'd budget it out and think about the physical conditions of what we could do. Once we figured that out, I was off to the races. The idea for that space was probably equivalent to going to the Studio Museum in those early years. I had what felt like complete and total free rein.

RH: Is that what you remember—doing what you wanted?

TG: Yes. What I thought more about at that time was how it was a way for me to engage with the larger history of the museum. I understood my choices not to be just my own. I understood that the choices I was making were going to live within institutional history and how important it was to think about it in that way.

RH: When you look back, what were the turning points for you in your trajectory before this moment that everybody thinks of?

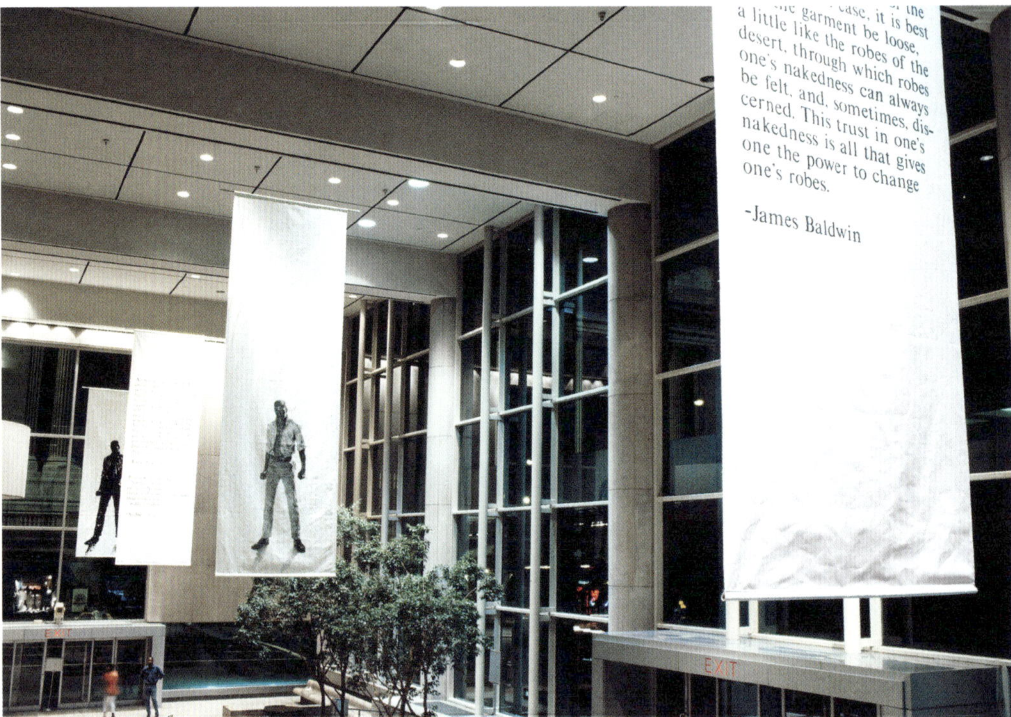

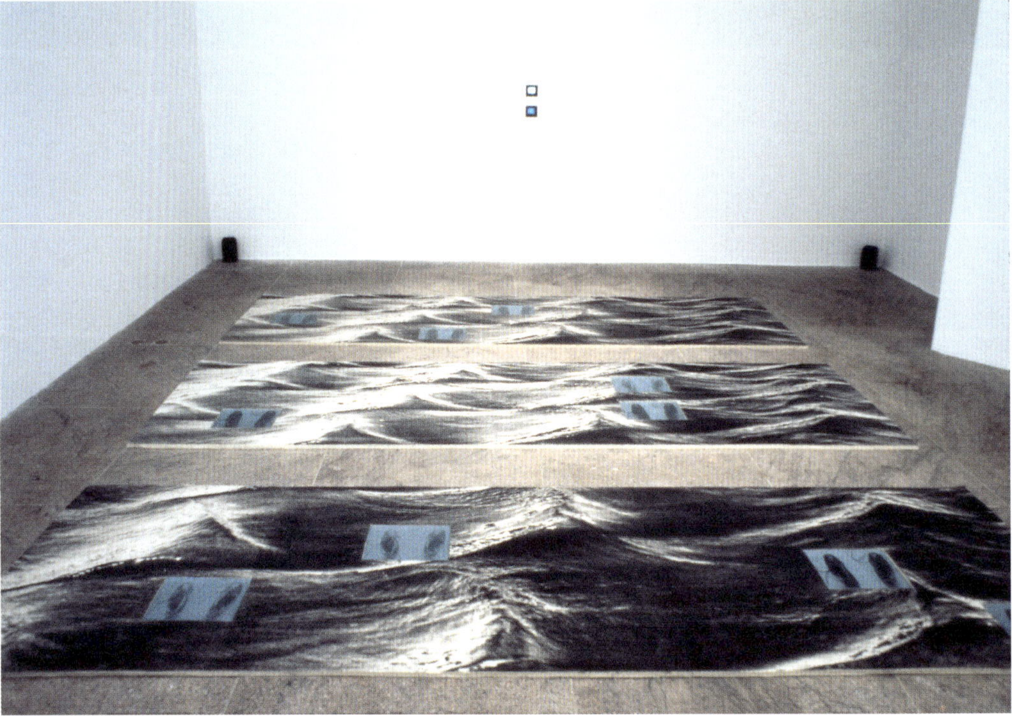

Fig. 5.1 Installation view of *Glenn Ligon: Good Mirrors Are Not Cheap,* curated by Thelma Golden, Whitney Museum of American Art at Philip Morris, New York, 17 July 1992–1 January 1993.

Fig. 5.2 Installation view of *Lorna Simpson: Standing in the Water,* curated by Thelma Golden, Whitney Museum of American Art at Philip Morris, New York, 20 January–25 March 1994.

I'm talking about before the 1993 Whitney Biennial and before you became someone who was no longer living a quieter, more person-to-person life—before it was the kind of life the *New York Times* was talking about.

> **TG:** I don't know if 1993 was the turning point. I even think back to when I became a curatorial assistant at the Whitney because, to everybody's record, that made me the first Black person to have an administrative role at the Whitney. So even when getting that job—

RH: Even to type [*laughs*].

> **TG:** Right. Even the elders of our field were all like, "You know that nobody else has ever worked there." Even in that role, I understood. I felt extremely aware of how much responsibility people were placing on me, even in a role where I did not feel I had that much power. But I understood their sense of what power I did have being inside.
>
> I would say there are many people who made me understand that: Mary, Lowery, and Kynaston. I didn't know Kynaston then, but I felt that there was an expectation, and I had to meet it. Then there were people who made me understand that in a much more specific way, like the late Jeanette Ingberman, who was cofounder with Papo Colo of the nonprofit cultural center Exit Art. Jeanette asked me to join her board in 1992. I was twenty-seven years old. I'd been working for no time at all. That's the part I always have to remember.
>
> When I tell this story, it all feels like me now, but I really want everyone to remember much of this happened before I was thirty. Jeanette was very conscious in a way I wasn't and made me very conscious of this larger sense of responsibility I had because I was on the inside. It was an art world that still was very downtown vs. uptown; multicultural vs. predominantly white; big rich institutions vs. small alternatives. All those things meant something.
>
> She was like, "This is great, but you have to understand that you have access to power and privilege. The only way any of that is okay is if you are using it on behalf of the rest of us." When Jeanette asked me to be on their board, in my mind I was like, "What do I have to bring to this board? I love being here and I'm learning so much." Jeanette was like, "You bring what you know and what you see." Jeanette wasn't the only person who came at me that way. There were many people. But Jeanette did it with so much love—it formed a huge sense of responsibility. Jeanette was the person who made me know this is not about you.

RH: It's so interesting to hear you also talk about your family, your childhood, and the community you were raised in. It was not alien for you to think in that larger community-based—and not even altruistic but really intuitive—way. It's bigger than me. Whatever it is, it's always bigger than me.

You've had a career in institutions, but was there ever a time when you felt you should do something else? The Studio Museum is in the middle. It's both and. Were you like, "Maybe I should go to the nonprofit arts organization Creative Time or I should start another version of Creative Time?" It can be taxing to be on the inside.

TG: No, I never thought that.

RH: No?

TG: No. Because I understood that for me, what felt like the greatest need in that moment was the transformation of the museum space. There were very few of us in museums. Most people doing curatorial work concerned with artists of color were freelancers or working in alternative spaces. I understood the responsibility and the opening I had, so my commitment was to museums in a super specific way.

RH: How were you received by your colleagues as far as this very particular commitment to artists of color?

TG: With an incredible amount of support and enthusiasm. Literally, from day one. Coming back to the Whitney in 1991 at Philip Morris—those projects working with Elisabeth Sussman, who was directing Lisa Phillips, John Hanhardt, and me on the 1993 Biennial—and in my own curatorial efforts presented to my colleagues, I felt 100 percent support. Many people think I say that to promote some narrative of racial harmony. [*Hockley laughs*]. No, it was an absolute truth.

I want people to understand that that's really what it takes for certain kinds of institutional transformation. The reason my own commitment in supporting curators is so deep is because I know, even with all that support, how hard it is to navigate. I know that for most people, that is not their experience in museums.

My first big exhibition was the 1993 Biennial. I was launched into my curatorial career in an exhibition that—no matter what it was—came with a lot of attention, a lot of scrutiny, et cetera. My colleagues were also teaching me. We had an incredibly engaged relationship—one that was a huge part of what made it so I could not just feel the weight of my responsibility but lean into it in ways that made it possible for me to do deeply, deeply engaged work.

RH: I want to talk a little bit about that responsibility and about creativity. At the end of the day, there has to be something else that keeps it engaging. What was it like to be a part of that team for the 1993 Biennial, and what are some of the things that Elisabeth, who's incredibly still at the Whitney, taught you? What are some things you remember from that experience in terms of the creative practice of being a curator?

TG: The thing that really defined my curatorial career at the Whitney was the ability to pursue my interests, which I knew would be where I could do my best work, and match the institution's needs in that moment. I was therefore getting to curate at a very high level.

At the time, Gary Simmons was making work about the lasting symbolism of the Ku Klux Klan. When Gary said, "I want to make a garden out of real azaleas to continue to explore the symbols of white supremacy," I could make that happen. When Sam Gilliam and I had a conversation—the kind I've had with many older artists, who, like Sam, had a whole career trajectory of doing what they were doing—we could meet in the middle and he could say to me, "Okay, here's a project that I'd like to do." He was experimenting with a new surface. It was a fabric like what Handi Wipes are made of, so not canvas but using the same technique he used on canvas. The project we did for the Philip Morris branch was called *Golden Elements Inside Gold* [1994], which he named for me.

It was not just exhibitions. I worked with the designer Bethany Johns, whom I had the privilege of seeing a few weeks ago at the Rhode Island School of Design; Bethany chairs the graphic design department. Back in that moment, Bethany was an active coconspirator in coming up with ways to document all this work. I always understood the creative impulse around my work.

Now, again, because I knew Lowery, I also understood that curatorial work is administrative work, so, I spent as much time on collection work because I knew that's what lasted. I learned deeply from Lowery because of the years of work Lowery did at the Met bringing works into that collection. So, understanding what curatorial practice meant was different; I was formed around not just these outward expressions, which for me were the most creative, but also the inner ones.

RH: What I'm hearing from you, and what I know about you, is how deeply committed you are to the future and to mentorship. What is your vision for this field? Given your thirty-plus years of committed mentorship, which comes out of your own experience of being mentored, what's your hope and aspiration?

TG: My hope and aspiration is for as many Black curators as possible to find their path in this field; to have it be rich, broad, and generative; and to have it exist in institutions that see them as individuals, meaning they have the ability to do whatever it is in their path. I want curators broadly, Black curators specifically, to be able to navigate this field while changing it, all the while acknowledging the spaces that aren't changing and our ability to continue to work in them effectively. To me, mentoring is providing the support to allow people to do their absolute best, and sometimes what that looks like varies.

But what my thirty years have given me is a sense of what it looks like in all its variations. While I'm not at all invested in one way or another, my own values put me squarely in a position to say there is work bigger than the individual to be done. Therefore, our ability to work collectively to support each other to do that is significant and important.

RH: What is the future of institutions? What do you think is the place of arts institutions with a capital *I* twenty years from now?

TG: They remain what they are now, responsive to the moment. In these last couple of years—I am sure I feel like everybody else—a lot of change in institutions has been needed, but I also acknowledge that some of it's not going to happen in the institutions we have, which is why we have to keep creating them. In the late 1960s, when many, many, many people had real issues with museums in this country and the way they excluded Black artists, a group of them got together. While they didn't stop protesting those museums, they also formed the Studio Museum. Another group of them formed El Museo del Barrio. These are all organizations that came at that moment. Today, all the ways we live our life can happen without much action attached—you can be protesting from your social media. I want to see some of that energy go into the next thing that needs to happen.

The Studio Museum is a different kind of museum than the Whitney because we came out of a different moment and with different values. Now, will we still be valid? I hope so because I hope our mission to present and preserve the work of artists of African descent will always be resonant to audiences for time to come. I hope we will always be physically sited in Harlem in a way that is a real cultural anchor for the community and continues to have a global reach, as it speaks to the breadth, depth, power, and ability of Black artists.

But could there be other ways in which institution-making could create a future version of this? Yes. In my support of curators, self-awareness is very important. Everyone has to find their path. One of my closest, closest, truly closest professional colleagues—who was a friend and was really family—was Okwui Enwezor. Okwui and I used to talk about this all the time, how your path can be different but still be aligned. Okwui and I never worked in the same ways but had a deeply, deeply, deeply shared sense of vision. When people say to me now, "Oh, why don't you want to do this?" I'm like, "That's not my path. That is someone else's." I do feel like that kind of self-awareness is important because it's what allows us all to find our way in this field.

RH: I want to dive into some of your exhibitions and bigger picture reflections on where you've been, where you might be going, and where our field is going. Firstly, what is the most meaningful exhibition you have worked on?

TG: The obvious answer is *Black Male: Representations of Masculinity in Contemporary American Art* [1994–95], and because you framed the question as "meaningful to me," I would stick with that answer [figs. 5.3–5.6].

RH: How did *Black Male* come to be? What about *Black Male*—from this vantage point, however many years later—makes it still the most meaningful to you?

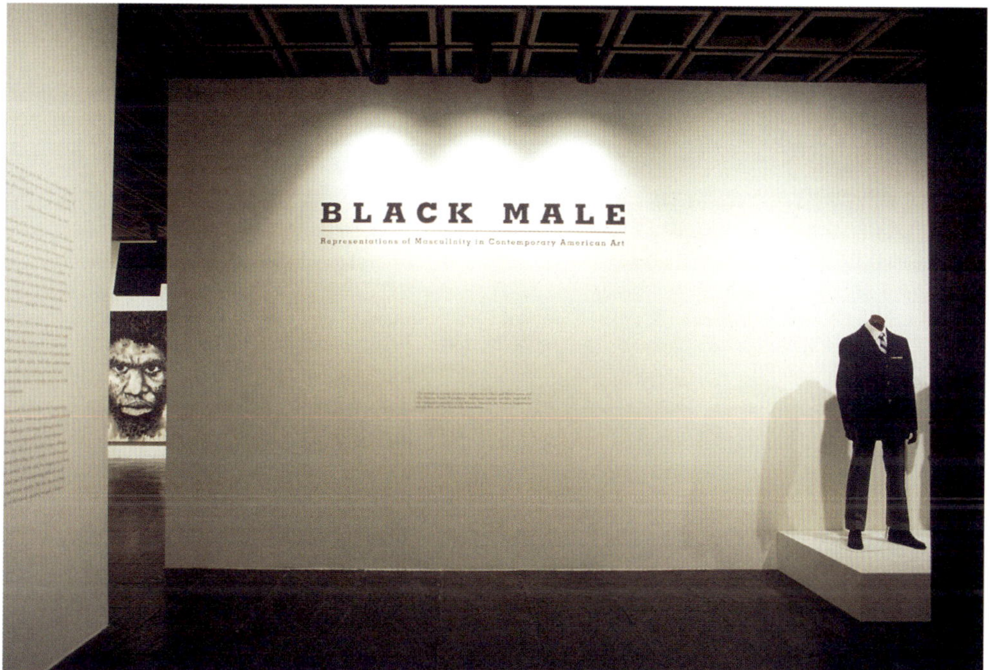

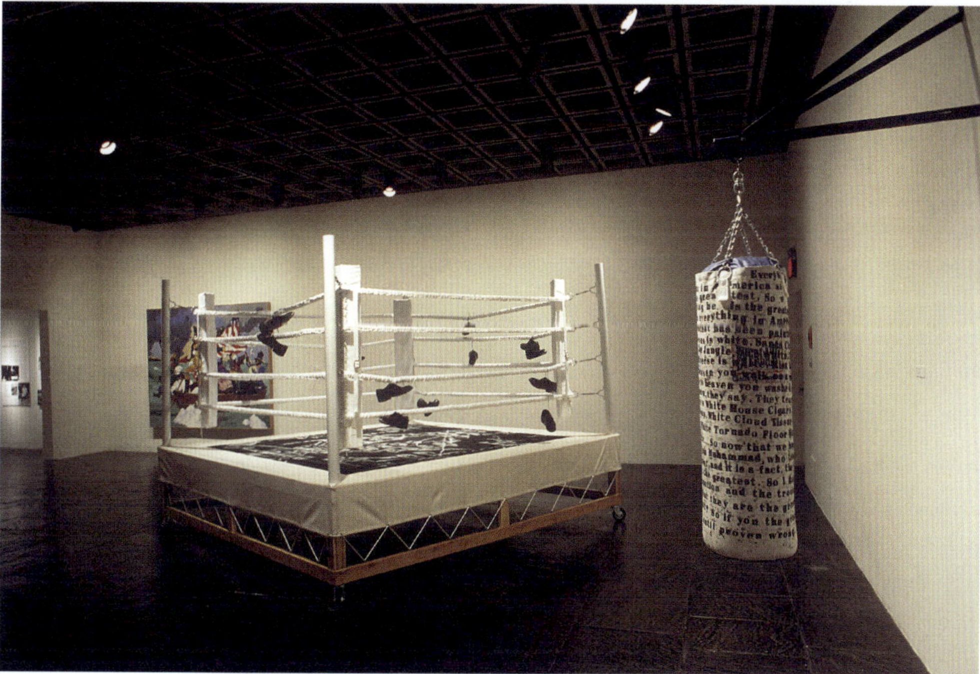

Fig. 5.3 Installation view of *Black Male: Representations of Masculinity in Contemporary American Art*, curated by Thelma Golden, Whitney Museum of American Art, New York, 10 November 1994–5 March 1995. *Left to right:* Robert Arneson's *Special Assistant to the President* (1989) and Fred Wilson's *Guarded View* (1991).

Fig. 5.4 Installation view of *Black Male: Representations of Masculinity in Contemporary American Art*, curated by Thelma Golden, Whitney Museum of American Art, New York, 10 November 1994–5 March 1995. *Left to right:* Robert Colescott's *George Washington Carver Crossing the Delaware: Page from an American History Textbook* (1975), Gary Simmons's *Step in the Arena (The Essentialist Trap)* (1994), and Byron Kim and Glenn Ligon's *Rumble Young Man Rumble (Version #1)* (1993).

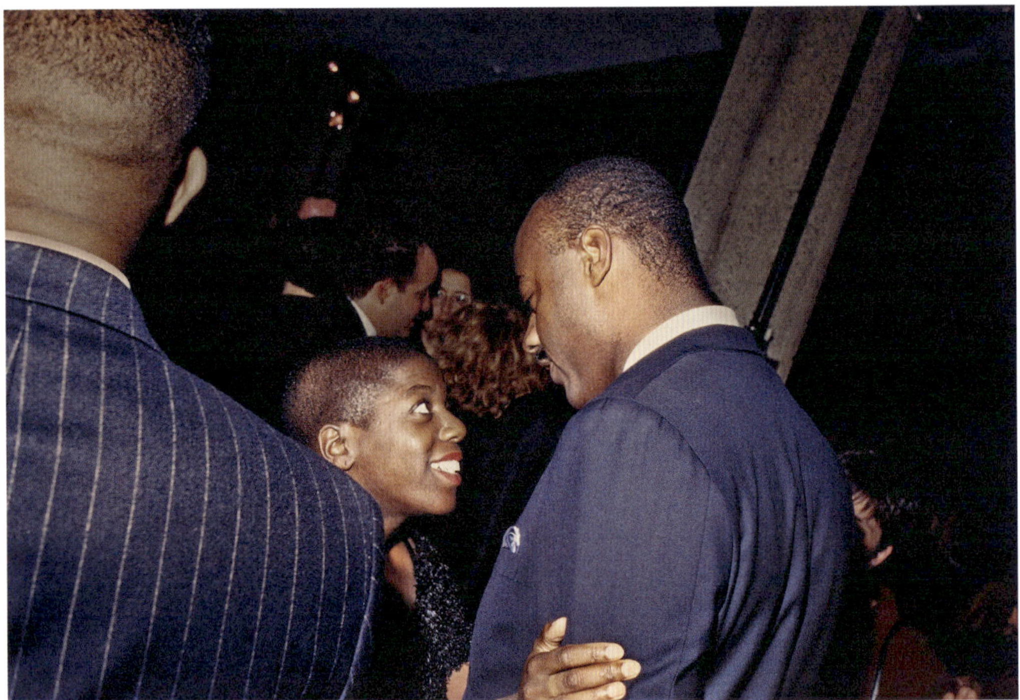

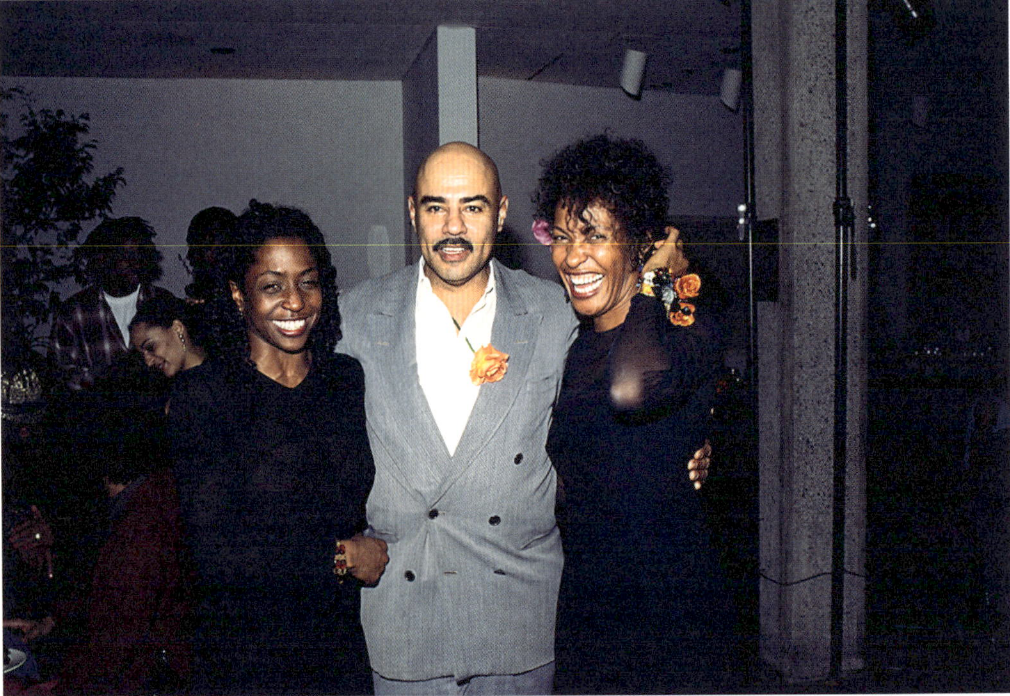

Fig. 5.5 Thelma Golden and Ray McGuire at the exhibition dinner for *Black Male: Representations of Masculinity in Contemporary American Art,* New York, 1994.

Fig. 5.6 *Left to right:* Lorna Simpson, Papo Colo, and Carrie Mae Weems at the exhibition dinner for *Black Male: Representations of Masculinity in Contemporary American Art,* New York, 1994.

TG: November 2024 will be thirty years. Most meaningful because it was the first major exhibition I ever made. I consider the 1993 Whitney Biennial a group effort, in which different people added their voices, so I do not claim authorship of that edition of it. *Black Male* was my first exhibition on my own, and it came as an idea during the 1993 Biennial, which coincided with the uprisings in Los Angeles and the beginnings of my engagement in looking at the relationship between popular culture and contemporary art.

Organizing several single-artist exhibitions at the Whitney at Philip Morris, like Ligon and Simmons, put me in a position to think about their work through art history, conceptual art practice, and biography. *Black Male* was also an exhibition that formed out of living in the world at that moment. For me, what specifically gelled the idea for this exhibition was the inclusion of George Holliday's video of Rodney King being beaten by police in the 1993 Biennial and the decision and conversation that happened as part of that process.

That is, at its core, where some of the curatorial premise came from: thinking about the way Black masculinity had been understood through our relationship to media and pop culture and the way contemporary artists reflected on that. But there wasn't a day when it was like, "Here is the exhibition." It was all these experiences coming together, combined with conversations with artists, that made this exhibition happen.

RH: *Black Male* lives on in many different ways. It's still extremely relevant, including the conversations you started then and picked up coming out of the 1993 Biennial. In that thirty-year time span, how do you see the world of a Black curator or of a curator who's interested in these questions? One of the ways the art world has changed is that many more people are interested in these questions. But, for our purposes, how do you see the world of a Black curator having changed in these thirty years?

TG: The world for Black curators has opened so profoundly. There are so many ways I understand *Black Male.* At its core, it was an exhibition informed by a generation of artists who formed me. It was inspired by a group of artists, namely Robert Colescott, David Hammons, Adrian Piper, and Charles Gaines, who completely informed the way I understood art.

The other reason the exhibition is meaningful to me is because there were many expectations of me as a Black curator at the Whitney Museum—from outside the institution, from many different quarters, and from many different people. Those expectations were to make a certain kind of exhibition. Many wanted the kinds of exhibitions I would make to be correctives to the histories of exclusion, both inside the Whitney and the art world more broadly. I quickly acknowledged that I had some autonomy to make exhibitions. The pressure for that was profound. *Black Male* was a huge disappointment to many of the people who wanted a corrective because that's not what it was at all.

With *Black Male,* I was also trying to create some space for myself and, perhaps, for other Black curators to exist within the context of curatorial practice in more open ways. I wanted it for myself, but I also felt like, "Oh, let me try and do this for other people." When people ask me about my own relationship to the response to *Black Male* all these years later I feel like it was worth it. What hurt me and happened to me was worth it for the community as a whole. Once it was done, then no one else had to go through that again.

RH: What happened to you?

TG: I was in the crosshairs of unrelenting critical response to the exhibition that did not stop. It was focused on me, the exhibition, and museum as a whole.

RH: Did you feel supported by the museum?

TG: Completely, 100 percent. However, it wasn't something the museum could control.

RH: I want to jump a couple years ahead to when you returned to the Studio Museum in this position of leadership. What were you thinking when you came back to the Studio Museum and what did you understand your charge to be?

TG: I left the Whitney in November 1998 without an idea of what I would do. Leaving was not my choice, so therefore I hadn't planned it. Leaving unplanned, I spent a year figuring out what my next steps could and should be. For a moment, I really considered what it might mean to not work in museums. I tried to consider what it would mean to be a freelance curator. I tried to consider what it would mean to engage in the academy. I tried to consider what it would mean to maybe even work in the commercial world. I quite literally thought that maybe there was another place for me. And that's because museums were different than they are now; there weren't as many opportunities as there are at this moment.

When I started working at the Whitney, Ray [Raymond] McGuire became a Whitney trustee in that same year, or maybe the year after. He is a primary source of support, mentorship, sponsorship, interlocutor, friend, biggest cheerleader, coach, critic, all of it. About six months after I left—even though I was talking to Ray every day—he said, "An opportunity has arisen, and the Studio Museum is in search of a director." Ray was on the Studio Museum board for maybe five years at that point. He was not chair, but was tasked with a strategic planning exercise that led to thinking about the future. When Kinshasha resigned to go work in Washington, DC, for Lonnie Bunch at what we now call the National Museum of African American History and Culture, Ray was tasked with a search. He said, "The Studio Museum's looking for a director, and I have been in serious conversations with Lowery Stokes Sims, and Lowery is seriously considering this possibility. We, the Studio Museum Board, would be thrilled if Lowery considered this. This could be an amazing move. And I'd like you to consider what it would mean to be—you name it, chief curator, deputy director." There were a couple different roles. Because I didn't really believe in that first call that Lowery was going to do it, I was fairly open.

RH: Because you didn't think it was real. You were like, "I'll think about it."

TG: Like, "Yes, sure. That would be great." I was fully unemployed. Lowery at that point had been at the Met for twenty-seven years and had a legendary but deep career in the Modern and Contemporary Art Department. So, I thought, "Okay, this is interesting. Lowery's considering this, so I'll consider it." The idea of what it would mean to work for Lowery meant that all the other factors I would normally consider did not matter to me. My number one priority was getting to work with Lowery. I've often said, if all these other things did not happen, that alone would have been major for me.

When Lowery took on the position at the Studio Museum, she knew the museum required reimagining in the space of all the great work that had been done. This is really the Studio Museum's secret—this planned, steady succession. When Mary was director, Kinshasha was her deputy director. Kinshasha then became director. After her came Lowery, and I was deputy director. All of this creates continuity. The person who made me aware of this was Nancy Lane, who at her passing had been on our board for forty-seven years. She watched this happen. The museum had this incredible legacy that each director had built further. With Lowery, the idea was, "Okay, can we envision a future?"

When I first came on as a curator, I was eager to make exhibitions at a scale and size that was different from what I'd come from. Many curators would come into their curatorial life making shows of a small-to-medium scale, doing things on a fast turnaround. My beginning was the opposite.

I had lived a certain kind of curatorial dream. I had also lived a certain curatorial nightmare. And it made me super free. Although the Studio Museum didn't have certain kinds of resources, there is a lot of possibility when there are not a lot of resources. I came in January 2000, Christine Y. Kim joined me in May 2000, and *Freestyle* opened in May 2001 [figs. 5.7, 5.8]. Literally, all of that was just boom, boom, boom. At the Whitney, I made three major exhibitions in a ten-year career. In my first five years at the Studio Museum, I probably did fifteen projects.

I did a lot in a very short time during those first five years when I was chief curator. When I became director, I stopped curating, which was a conscious decision and necessary for me. But those first five years were incredibly intense. I came with my intuitive belief that *Black Male* had to take on a different exhibition form. In ways that I am not proud of now, there was a youthful sense of wanting to discard entire pasts; it was simply because I knew if I went down that road, I'd never get out of it.

RH: Meaning making historical and recuperative exhibitions?

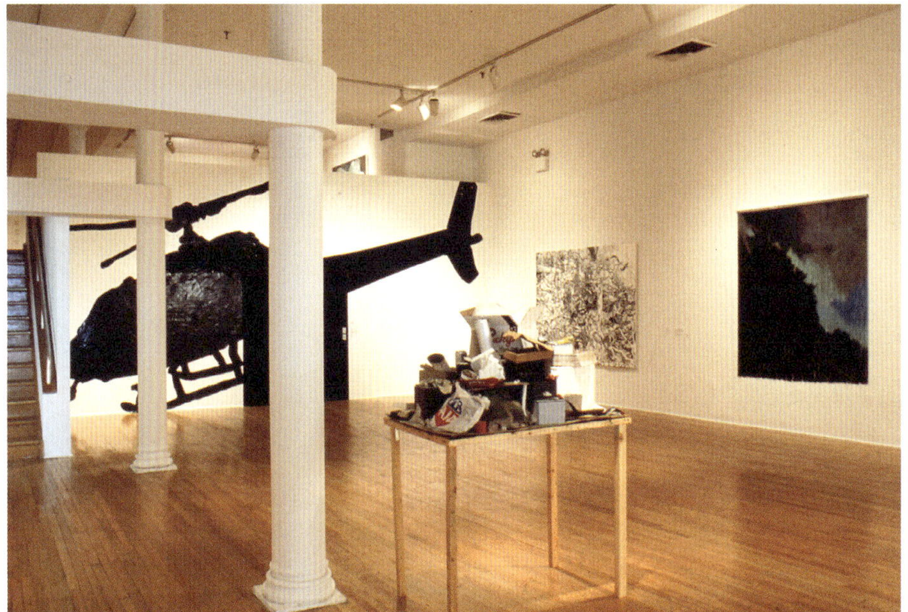

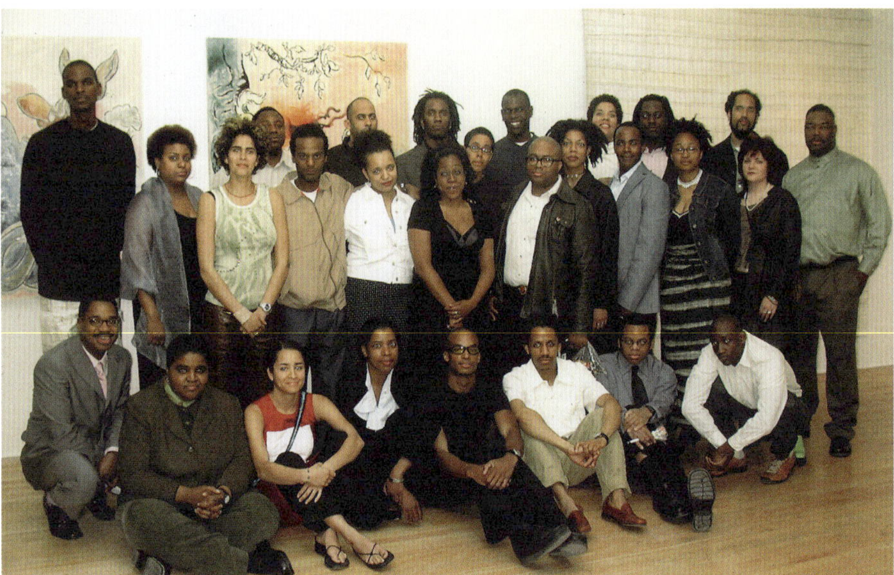

Fig. 5.7 Installation view of *Freestyle,* curated by Thelma Golden, Studio Museum in Harlem, New York, 28 April–24 June 2001.

Fig. 5.8 Artists featured in *Freestyle,* Studio Museum in Harlem, New York, April 2001.

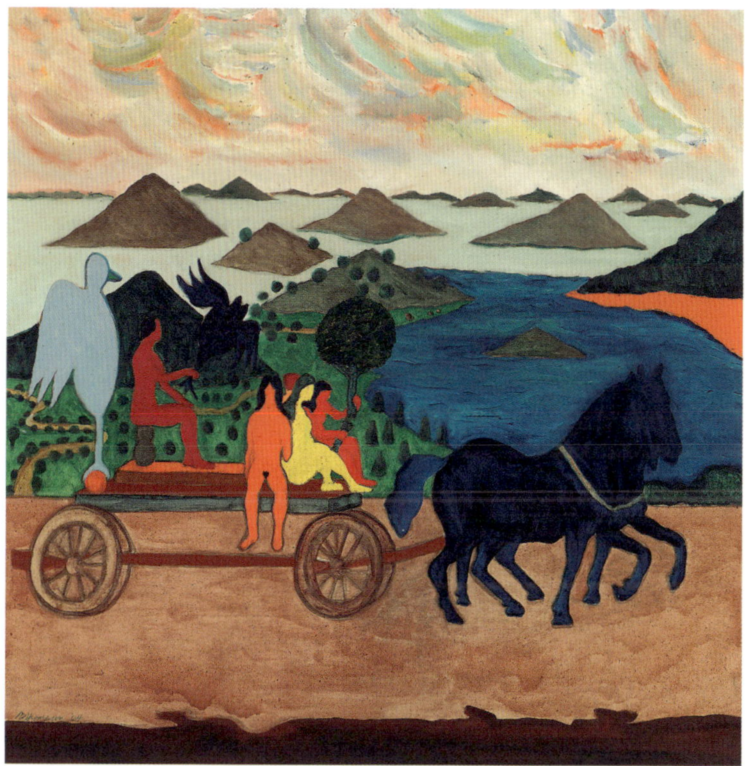

Fig. 5.9 Bob Thompson (American, 1937–66). *An Allegory,* oil on linen, 121.9 × 121.9 cm, 1964. New York, Whitney Museum of American Art, 72.137. Artwork shown in *Bob Thompson,* curated by Thelma Golden, Whitney Museum of American Art, New York, 5 September 1998–3 January 1999.

TG: I mean historical survey show mode because it was so desired. There was so much pressure on me. Everybody saw me as the linchpin toward what could happen in this museum context. There was also a lot of pressure on the Whitney, specifically, as the "Museum of American Art" that had not lived up to what that fully meant. The artists of the generation who were at mid- and late career when I got there—people like Jack Whitten, Gilliam, Mel [Melvin] Edwards, and Faith Ringgold—had complicated relationships with the Whitney and had all been activists in the change of museums. In many ways, when I got into the position at the Whitney, everyone had assignments.

When I got to the Studio Museum, some people were nervous because I was seen as someone who wasn't holding the same values. I found that problematic because, at the Whitney, I'd done a Jacob Lawrence show with Jake at his request. I did a beautiful Romare Bearden project after Romare died. I did the Bob Thompson show, which was a sort of connector between Judith Wilson's work about Thompson and the reality of making an exhibition [fig. 5.9]. When I got to the Studio Museum, I had all those forms, but I also had the form that said, "What if we, as a Black institution, break open some of the models of exhibition-making to create more possibility for what we can do for and with Black art and Black artists?"

RH: I'm curious, you opened *Freestyle* fifteen months after you started at the museum. When did you start thinking about *Freestyle*?

TG: I started thinking about that show in 1998 when I left the Whitney. I had been asked by David Ross to curate the 2000 Biennial and, in 1998, had begun looking at art and artists. That work still lived with me when I left. When I got to the Studio Museum, I began to think about some of those artists. Though there'd been a break in time, I kept in touch with many of those artists.

I also was keenly aware of this switch in institution and location. I wanted to give myself the gift of reimagining what it would mean for me to make an exhibition with emerging artists. I wanted to signal what I thought were some important ideas among emerging Black artists as a way for the Studio Museum to reinvest in that space and to open the museum to a new generation of artists. For me, it was also a way to begin. I thought, how could I make a space that would be open and generative and echo the past of the museum—the great legacy—but also position us toward the future?

We made this show in a way that, to this day, I still don't quite know how it happened. But when it was happening, it was very real. The moment it opened, it signaled many different things, and one of them was that this was a space curatorially we needed to stay in. It became a model that could then be replicated, and it has been by different groups of curators over time. After *Freestyle,* it became *Frequency* [2005–6] [fig. 5.10]*;* after *Frequency, Flow* [2008]*;* after *Flow, Fore* [2012–13]*;* and then after *Fore, Fictions* [2017–18]. *Fictions* was the show on the walls when we closed in January 2018.

RH: It's almost like the Studio Museum's version of the next one would be specific and incredible in its own way. Many other institutions have taken on what these shows initially inaugurated, so it's very interesting to see that percolate out. This pivot or shift in the focus of the institution's vision to embrace emerging artists in a different way is really important about what has happened and what you did at the Studio Museum. But the other thing that never gets talked about is the expansion of the mission to include a global perspective. Can you talk about that decision—how you came to think through the solution to one of the knots that a culturally specific, nationally specific, or community/neighborhood specific institution, might find itself forty years into its existence?

TG: The Studio Museum, from its founding, always showed artists of African descent from around the world. It's just that our mission was written in a way that didn't necessarily indicate that. It said something like: "A museum of African American art and artifacts of the African diaspora." That formation, at the time of our founding, would have matched the thinking of African American studies and the Black arts movement.

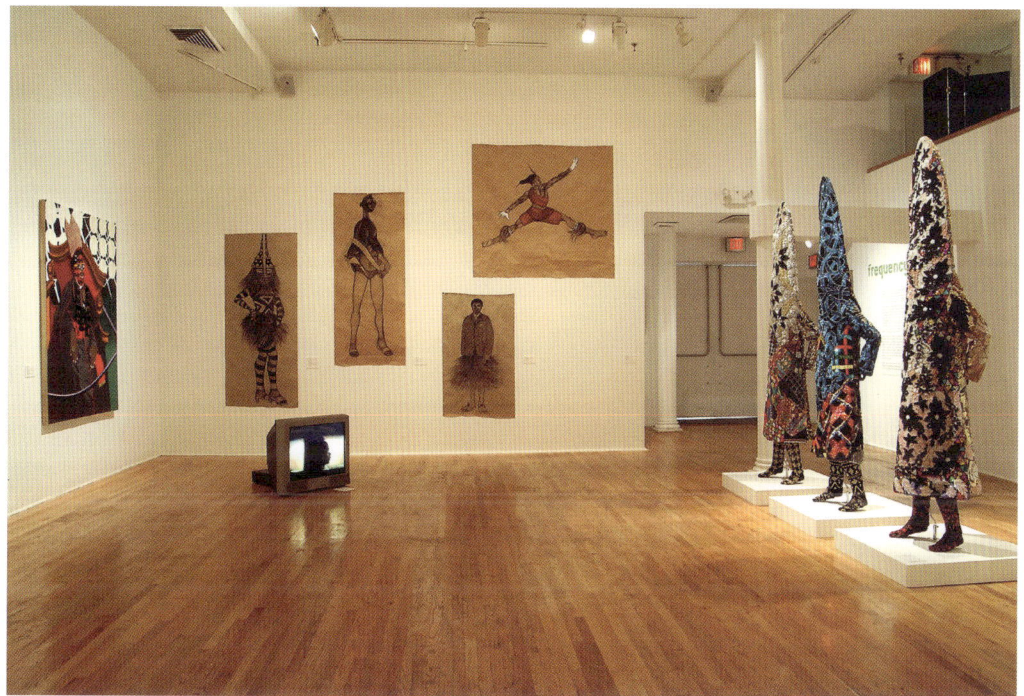

Fig. 5.10 Installation view of *Frequency,* curated by Thelma Golden and Christine Y. Kim, Studio Museum in Harlem, New York, 9 November 2005–12 March 2006.

Even though that was the mission, the museum had shown and had artists in the artist-in-residence program from the African continent, the Caribbean, North America, and South America—all of that happened but it wasn't named. The rewriting of the mission happened around 2004. I invited Okwui to a board retreat to discuss this. It's probably the only time I thought, in my Studio Museum career, I was going to be fired. Okwui, in his ultimately erudite, elegant, and brilliant way, told my board that African American people had to get over the idea that the Black American story is the central Black narrative in the world. Okwui saying this was fundamentally blasphemous in so many ways. But, of course, he then unpacked it in ways that were transformative. What he was positioning was an idea of what it meant to consider the museum's mission in acknowledgement of a global Black presence. I'm grateful to Okwui for this because the complexity of it all is real, interesting, and important. He brought out something else that had been present in our collection, which is that this collection had work by artists who were not Black but whose work was inspired by, resonated with, or existed within some relationship to Black culture.

We have an absolutely incredible work by Louise Nevelson [*Homage to Martin Luther King, Jr.* (1974–85)] that she had in her studio when the United States made Martin Luther King Jr.'s birthday a holiday. She was so moved by this act, having been someone who lived through his assassination, that she called her dealer, Arne Glimcher, and said, "I read about this museum in Harlem, and I want them to have this work." Mary accepted it, and I'm glad she did. We have photographs from Aaron Siskind's *Harlem Document* series [1932–40], which is an incredible group of images of this community. There's other work as well. So, we have works by artists of African descent and work that is inspired by Black culture. That was the rewrite. The second half of that rewrite was also one that Okwui and I formed to allow for complexity within the space of a culturally specific institution.

RH: Because Blackness and Black people are everywhere.

TG: Exactly.

RH: Thinking now about this critical moment we're at in the Studio Museum's trajectory, and thus your trajectory, how has the building campaign been going? What do you see and hope for at the reopening of Studio Museum?

TG: In some ways I see the same, meaning that we still commit to creating important and significant exhibitions and projects that allow us to educate, inspire, entertain, and engage. I am so thrilled we'll be able to do it in a space that can accommodate us at the highest level. I have a lot of nostalgia around this because our old building was a bank building made into a museum. J. Max Bond Jr. lovingly—through the deep principles of adaptive reuse—took that old building and made it into a museum.

RH: I love that. Once you have the building, what are you going to do?

TG: Let me say something else about building this building. To build this building requires a lot of money. Part of what my job has become is working hard with our team and board to secure those funds. I bring that up because it has to do with what it means for our institutions to be sustainable and have a future. So, in addition to raising money for the building, raising money for an endowment is also important for me. Therefore, I'm not thinking so much about what I'm going to do next because a lot of the next for me is about sustainability, which I feel is necessary to take the Studio Museum through its next half century.

Now, what will I do? I don't know. My career as a curator has been one that has been filled with incredible experiences [fig. 5.11]. Being a curator and a Black curator committed to Black artists and Black culture has not just allowed me to work in these two incredible museums but it has also allowed me to work with our first Black president, Barack Obama, and First Lady Michelle Obama on art- and artist-involved projects. In this role, I was able to work with the first lady on what it meant to expand the White House Collection and personally think deeply about what that could be. I was able to find and secure Alma Thomas's *Resurrection* [1966], which Mrs. Obama, with the White House Historical

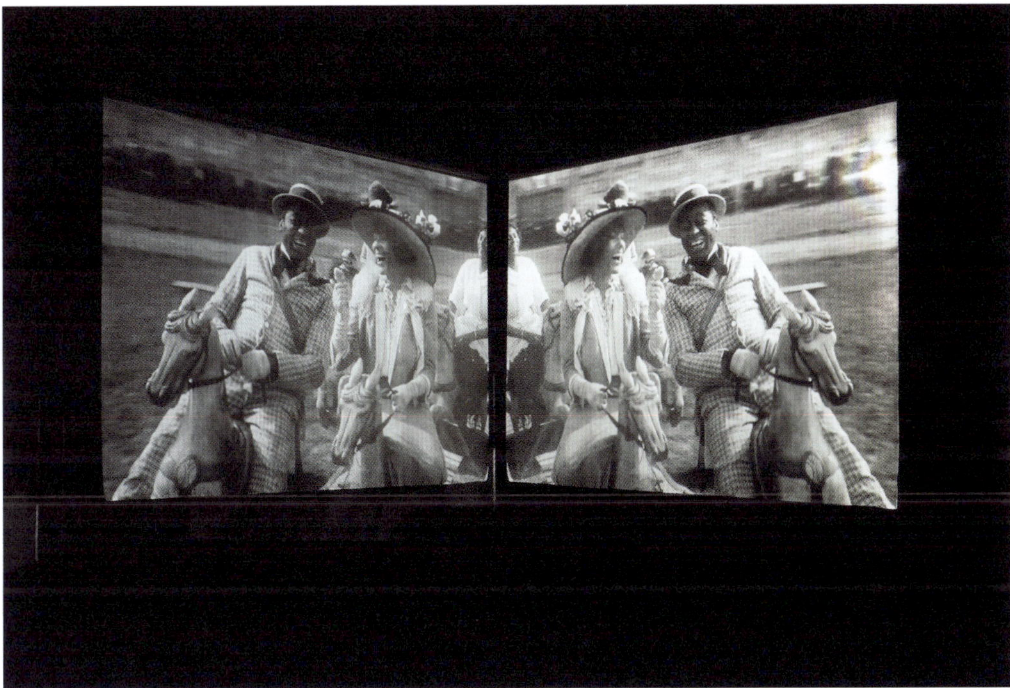

Fig. 5.11 Installation view of *Projects: Garrett Bradley,* organized by Thelma Golden with Legacy Russell, Museum of Modern Art, New York, 21 November 2020–21 March 2021.

Association, acquired and hung in the old family dining room. It all still fills me with an incredible sense of awe and pride, especially knowing that Thomas, a 1924 graduate of Howard University—their first art graduate—and a District of Columbia public school teacher who, in retirement, painted in her kitchen, had her work hanging in the White House. In these ways, art can be a part of a larger conversation about what it means to think about this country and our democracy in its fullest way. What I do next, I don't have any predictions because I've gotten to do so many incredible and amazing things in this role, in my Whitney role, and in all the work I've done around it. Who knows.

My hope is that my legacy as a curator is not simply in the exhibitions I've made. I'm very proud of them, and I love being an exhibition-maker. To me, being able to create curatorial opportunities for others has been as significant as exhibition-making and building relationships with artists. That's really why I stopped curating. Early on, I had the ability to work in a deeply critical, crucial, and supported way. I've always wanted to make that possible for others. That's what I hope my own curatorial legacy will be.

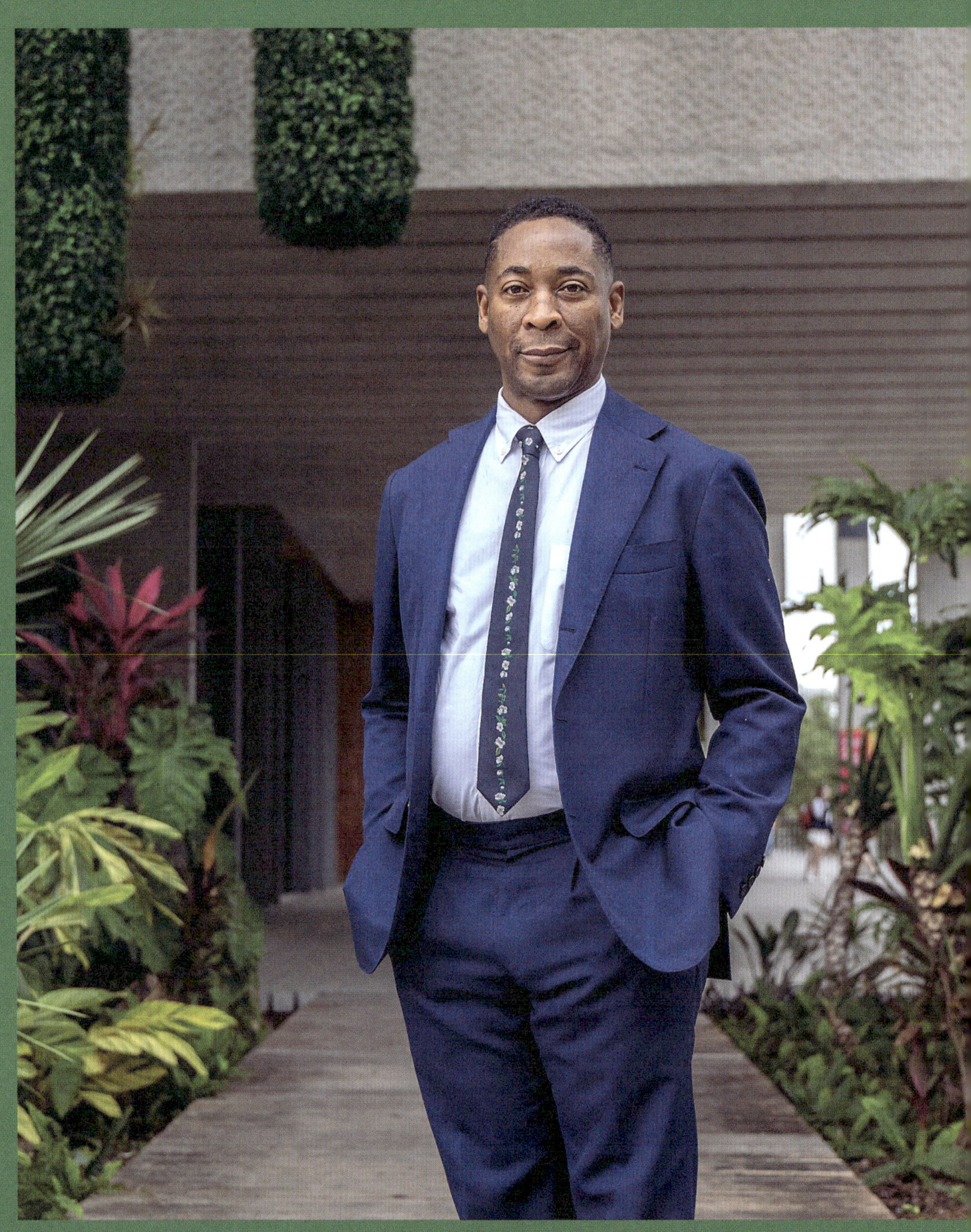

Franklin Sirmans

INTERVIEWED BY LERONN P. BROOKS
11 April and 6 June 2023

LERONN P. BROOKS (LPB): So, Franklin, where are you from?

FRANKLIN SIRMANS (FS): I'm from New York. I was born in Queens, but I actually never lived there. My father was in the Navy at the time, so I was born at the naval hospital and came home to Harlem—you know, a place where art was cherished. I moved to Albany for a few years as a child of divorce, came back and "graduated" eighth grade from Manhattan Country School, and then went to New Rochelle High School in Westchester County.

LPB: Yeah, I'm from Rosedale, Queens. And I moved to Harlem. What was it like growing up in Harlem?

FS: Oh, man, it was fun. I'm sure everybody would say the same about their earliest years of running around and having fun, with not a lot of cares in the world at seven-to-ten years old! If we're talking about the 1970s, this was post–Vietnam War and post–civil rights. But, as a kid, who would have known? It was a real enjoyable place to be. I was never in the apartment, always running around, and there was always someone looking after us even if we didn't know who it was. I was in the Lenox Terrace apartment complex, and we had a lot of green space. I went to school down on Fifth Avenue and Ninety-Sixth Street, so I was in Central Park all the time, used to go ice-skating there. It was a regular upbringing.

LPB: You know, being a New York kid, you had access to all the culture, too. How did museums factor into your early life?

FS: I definitely went to the American Museum of Natural History first. What I most remember is later, during high school, being at events for the Studio Museum in Harlem. But, by that point, I at least had a reference point to the Metropolitan Museum of Art and Museum of Modern Art [MoMA].

LPB: What pulled you in?

FS: To be honest, as for many children, it was a place of absolute wonder. It was a place of creativity. It was a place to be taken outside of your everyday life, your normal thoughts. It was more a sense of art and artists are cool—it was more a sensation in the 1980s than it was necessarily a specific location or event.

LPB: In what spaces did you find community? Was it the Studio Museum or another space?

FS: My father was interested in art and artists and was inspired by David Driskell. Driskell had an informal collectors' group, and my father learned about art and artists through that in a significant way. He became very, very, very passionate about it to the point where our social spaces were usually populated by friends like Al Loving, Ed Clark, Corrine Jennings, and Joe Overstreet, among many others. Cinque gallery was another regular spot, as was the Kenkeleba House, Wilmer Jennings Gallery, Peg Alston Fine Arts and later Eric Robertson Gallery. Ruth Jett, the director of Cinque for many years, lived around the corner from me also in the Lenox Terrace complex in Harlem. It was that kind of accessibility, without a doubt, that made museum-going more every day and very natural. Going to the Met or MoMA, okay cool. But we've got our own thing over here. Obviously, that wouldn't happen everywhere. Being in Harlem, you kind of took it for granted. The Schomburg Center for Research in Black Culture was catty corner to Lenox Terrace, right across the street from the Harlem Hospital Center. The Adam Clayton Powell Jr. State Office Building was across from the Studio Museum. These museums had accessibility to everyday people at least I thought.

LPB: You mentioned Driskell, so in my mind, I'm picturing a generational situation. You enter this field and Driskell is there and he's active. With that generation still being active in the art world when you were there, what was it like to see Driskell and these pioneers?

FS: I did not see Driskell; I got to know him later. That was more my dad's space. Probably the closest for me was Lowery Stokes Sims; going to one of her events at the Met was the real umbilical cord. Then during college, that cord extended to Thelma Golden and Kellie Jones in a much broader sense. Lowery was the real bridge for me. Driskell was a generation removed in some sense. By the time he did the big show in 1976–77, *Two Centuries of Black American Art,* I was seven. Driskell was still a huge figure for me though, especially after I won the Driskell Prize in 2007, which was an amazing show of faith from that community.

LPB: The same with Lowery for me. There was accessible mentorship there. She and others were making space, with Lowery being one of the only Black curators and working at that tier in New York City. It was the first time I had ever talked to a Black curator. That began a relationship that led to my dissertation defense fifteen years later. What did a mentor structure of curators look like for you back then?

FS: It was a combination. It's Thelma I'm closest to, but also Kellie, Lowery, and Leslie King-Hammond. Leslie brought me to the Maryland Institute College of Art to teach for a couple of years. My teaching would not have happened without her.

It's all of that but most importantly it was the Studio Museum for giving us all a space to think, believe, and find fellowship and mentorship amongst ourselves, putting us in conversation together so that no matter how little representation there might have been in other museum spaces at that moment, we knew each other and to some degree looked out for each other. That was huge. There were countless people who remain allies.

I wouldn't be here without them. Of course, we're compressing time, so I would say that I got out of eighth grade in 1983 and was way more interested in sports and hip-hop than anything that had to do with art. I eventually learned that hip-hop was art. I graduated from New Rochelle High School in 1987 and from Wesleyan University in 1991 with a degree in English and art history, so by that time the support system was stronger. Thelma was at the Jamaica Arts Center—brought there by Kellie. I arranged for Thelma to visit Wesleyan University when I was an undergraduate and talk to our class. Kellie was more of a family friend. I was probably reading Lisa Jones more at that point than I was Kellie's work because of Lisa's relationship to writing about music and cultural criticism.

LPB: In *Vibe* magazine?

FS: In *Vibe,* but especially in the *Village Voice* first. So, that was the backdrop. When you say there was a support system there, it can't be understated. Lowery, Leslie, and then Deborah Willis all provided generosity and leadership. To call Lowery and Leslie mentors, and say that with love, is not quite accurate. Along with Deborah, they were more fairy godmothers.

LPB: You bring up the *Village Voice, Vibe,* and there was also *Source* magazine. You had all these publications with so many giants contributing. This idea of fine art, but also popular culture and writing—all the stuff was coming together. Because you worked as a writer and were curating, did you see yourself at the intersection of these worlds?

FS: I entered the curatorial space from literature and writing. I have a reference to Driskell, but then there's also an interest in writers like Frank O'Hara. In addition to writing poetry and criticism, O'Hara was a curator at MoMA. I studied art history in school. Whatever I didn't know about the Harlem Renaissance, I certainly learned in that context as well, thinking about Alain Locke, Arna Bontemps, James A. Porter, and others. Those kinds of writers who provided a foundation for us in the discussion of Black art history was certainly significant. Kinshasha Holman Conwill was also an important figure. I interned at the Studio Museum when I was in high school; Valerie J. Mercer was there and I worked for her during a summer. Patricia Cruz was deputy director and Kinshasha Holman Conwill was director. John Hutton was the registrar. I worked with him as well and learned so much about the logistics of the movement of art objects.

LPB: I remember what it felt like for me to be in your presence when I interned at Studio Museum and Thelma was director. It was you, Glenn Ligon, and Thelma. I felt a certain bond but also a power there, an institutional power. I felt like in the selection process for Studio Museum interns, there was a great amount of respect between you three. Because Thelma brought the interns into the weekly staff meetings, I got a sense that there was some kind of power in Black infrastructures.

FS: Absolutely, that's her leadership, and those are important moments. I was an intern while Kerry James Marshall was in the artist-in-residence program and being a fly on the wall in meetings was powerful.

LPB: W. E. B. Du Bois, Locke, and Porter represented that African American art infrastructure, that kind of history at an earlier moment. Generationally, you were also a part of something that was a continuation but different. At that moment, you were also working with Jean-Michel Basquiat.

FS: Being a part of the Studio Museum community that was so supportive and accessible also meant figuring out how to find yourself within that. If my father was excited to support artists whom he was a little bit younger than, then what is my generation talking about? Of course, to already have the backdrop of the music and art created under the idea of what would become known as graffiti, as well as to see dance, movement, everything that related to it, and then to see Basquiat on the cover of the *New York Times Magazine* in 1985—it was like, "Oh, *this* is it." This is us. This is different. This is of the now in a way that was different from the work of other artists—particularly the abstract artists I met through my dad. Although they were creating work in the moment, the roots of their work felt like they existed elsewhere in an earlier era. Basquiat exploded that idea. He, of course, was all those things I mentioned in regard to hip-hop: the dance, style, and writing. So, yeah, that really blew my mind.

LPB: I remember that show at the Brooklyn Museum—was it in 2005?

FS: In 2005, Kellie and I, along with Marc Mayer and Fred Hoffman, curated the exhibition at the Brooklyn Museum, but the Whitney Museum of American Art organized a Basquiat show in 1992 and I did the chronology for the exhibition catalog with the curator Richard D. Marshall. I did my undergraduate thesis on Basquiat with professors Robert O'Meally and Peter Mark at Wesleyan University. I had the accessibility I had because of the support system you're talking about. Thelma was working at the Whitney's Philip Morris branch at this point. She spoke with Richard, the curator at the Whitney who was about to work on the first retrospective of Basquiat. She told him all about my work, showed him my chronology, and end of story. Although I was working a pretty lucrative job just out of school at Shearson Lehman/

American Express and paying my own rent most importantly, the Whitney contacted me about this retrospective and asked if I would like to be involved. I quit the job at Shearson Lehman—I have been filled with regret many times for doing that. But all in all, it worked out. Thanks to Thelma, Richard took me in, and I worked out of the Whitney while researching and writing the chronology, which has been translated into many languages and published many times in variations. That's how it happened.

You mentioned cultural criticism. I have to tell you, I sat in Richard's office in 1992, along with Greg Tate and Arthur Jafa. A mind-boggling experience. Can you imagine? The two of them, geniuses. I was twenty-two and just out of school. They were respectful, but by all means I was not really in their conversation. I was listening to these two gigantic heads on different planes and just trying to absorb as much as possible. I was asking myself whether I belonged there. They talked to me—so yes, I belonged. Those kinds of moments change everything.

LPB: It's exposure. It's very interesting being within that context and people working to give you exposure to put you in a room. What happened in that room is something you still remember to this day. Leaving that day job for the art world, now that's a decision. I don't want to skip over that. That's a decision.

FS: We weren't from wealth. On one hand, you're rolling the dice. But, on the other hand, who cares? You're in your early twenties and you've got a degree for what it's worth, a BA. If it doesn't work, it doesn't work, and you can figure out a way to do something else. But within that moment, you feel like you can fly. A lot of it was luck and a lot of it was being able to say, economically, I'm going to take a chance. I realize not everybody can say that. I was able to say that. For better or worse, it manages to work itself out eventually. I ended up working at Dia Center for the Arts a year after the 1992 Basquiat show. That was the first time I was in a paid museum position full-time other than at the Studio Museum.

The other important thing is that it wasn't a curatorial position. I worked in the Publications Department. The year that I went to Dia was also same time that Gina Dent was editing the groundbreaking book right after *Black Popular Culture* [1992]. The book was a compilation of papers delivered at a conference organized by Michele Wallace in 1991 at the Studio Museum and Dia. It is a classic, and it is amazing to look back and take in all the serious intellectuals who participated, including Cornel West, Angela Davis, Henry Louis Gates Jr., Tate, Jafa, Judith Wilson, bell hooks, and the Black British contingent of Hazel Carby, Stuart Hall, Paul Gilroy, and Isaac Julien.

Black Popular Culture was also part of Dia's larger conversation and book series Discussions in Contemporary Culture, which brought together artists, scholars, and critics to think through different aspects of the cultural landscape and critical theory. Some of the books I worked on included: *Culture on the Brink: Ideologies of Technology* [1994], *Constructing Masculinity* [1995], and *Visual Display: Culture Beyond Appearances* [1995]. My office was next door to Lynne Cooke, the chief curator at Dia, who would do an exhibition that brought together Frédéric Bruly Bouabré from the Ivory Coast and the Italian artist Alighiero Boetti. That was an incredible time, just to be a part of all that was going on at Dia. There were so many linkages and connections to be made across cultural life in New York City; poetry, music, and dance were all an integral part of Dia at that time.

I started writing for several publications around that time. Okwui Enwezor started *Nka: Journal of Contemporary African Art* around that time. Danny Simmons had a magazine called *One World* along with the important gallery Rush Arts. Tate was also a significant connection for me and for so many of us who were trying find a voice that felt like our own. At the time, I was in the Publications Department at Dia, dealing with many writers and scholars and also writing for *Publishers Weekly* thanks to Calvin Reid—talk about people looking out for you! I was doing book reviews and trying to figure it out as it was happening. But because of him, I was allowed to make those kinds of mistakes. I started writing reviews for *Art News* and then for *Flash Art* with my friend Francesco Bonami. My first two reviews for *Flash Art* were on Robert Ryman and Ashley Bickerton. Then, at Francesco's suggestion and invitation, I quit Dia in 1996 and went to live in Italy to work for *Flash Art.* And again, like leaving Shearson Lehman it was like "Oh, man, you're about to lose something." Dia paid well for a museum. The check came every two weeks and then it was gone.

LPB: Now you're in Italy. What was that like?

FS: It was an incredible experience! For somebody who grew up in New York with all that accessibility, you also can be really narrow-minded in your thinking. You can be very New York–centric and especially since I only went to college two hours away. So, I was kind of scared in some ways to go to Italy because it was a totally different experience. But that made it a great time of growth in retrospect. I was there at the perfect time from 1996 to 1998.

I was living in Milan. In fall 1996, Peter Weibel did an exhibition in Graz, Austria, called *Inclusion/Exclusion: Art in the Age of Global Migration and Postcolonialism.* It was an earnest attempt to create an intersectional space to think about globalism as it related to the United States, Europe, Africa, Asia, and across the world. It was absolutely a phenomenal thing and something you weren't going to see in New York at that time. In 1997, I interviewed the celebrated curator Harald Szeemann who was working on the Gwangju Biennale in South Korea that had only begun in 1994. He was organizing another big show in Europe, the Lyon Biennale, as well as a large-scale show in Ljubljana. He also organized all the other big European exhibitions going back to Documenta 5 in 1972. Okwui organized the second Johannesburg Biennale in 1997. We all went there, right? You had to be there. It wasn't about Venice, Münster, and Kassel, it was getting much bigger than that. Dan Cameron was one of the few Americans who traveled in that space heavily; in 2003, he was the artistic director of the Istanbul Biennial. It was incredible to find oneself in that broad global conversation.

If you come from where we come from in New York, you know that the "art world" has willful blinders. How do you all not know Norman Lewis in the 1990s? It doesn't make any sense. If people don't know that, then they don't know a lot of other things. To be able to enter a conversation that was truly global, you can also use a New York centricity as a means of putting on blinders, but it's bigger, way bigger than that. At that moment, globalism also suggested a space where there would be advancement for people of color in a general sense. At least, that was the promise. It wasn't happening in the immediate aftermath of decolonization in West Africa; there was time to grow up a little bit. It was a space in which possibility felt immense. On top of that, as Tumelo Mosaka knows so well, South Africa, and all that was happening there, was also on the verge of change and opening to the world in terms of liberation, not only locally but in a much broader sense. All these things force you to consider: What is my New York? What does it mean? How insular is it in the grand scheme?

There's one moment before that I will never forget. I was working on the 1992 Basquiat show during the trial of the Los Angeles Police Department officers accused of unreasonable force in the brutal beating and arrest of Rodney King. I remember going to the Whitney Museum, then on Madison Avenue on the Upper East Side, and there was nobody on the streets. After the officers "not guilty" verdict, protests erupted on the West Coast, later known as the Los Angeles riots of 1992. Some people thought those protests would erupt in New York City as well. I mean, that's our backdrop. What else is our backdrop in terms of identity? And there was a sense of, not camaraderie, but of possibility in a global space that spoke to me much more than any American thing. Sonically, this moment was accompanied by the hip-hop group Public Enemy.

LPB: How did this expanded field affect your practice?

FS: I came back to New York in 1998, taught at the School of Visual Arts [SVA], and wrote for *Time Out New York,* and then the *New York Times, Art in America, Art News, Grand Street,* and other journals.

For me, *Time Out New York* was really important. I wrote for a great editor named Howard Halle and then the brilliant Tim Griffin. I taught art criticism first at SVA, then at Princeton University with Eve Aschheim, and then at the Maryland Institute College of Art thanks to Leslie King-Hammond.

LPB: Teaching allows you to think about what you're thinking about. The more you teach something, the more you find yourself getting more particular on things you find interesting. Your students benefit. Were you thinking about being a full-time curator at this moment or being an academic?

FS: I was back to the O'Hara dream and trying to figure it out. I had my apartment in Lenox Terrace thankfully. I rented another studio space around the corner to find a rhythm and make a go of being a writer,

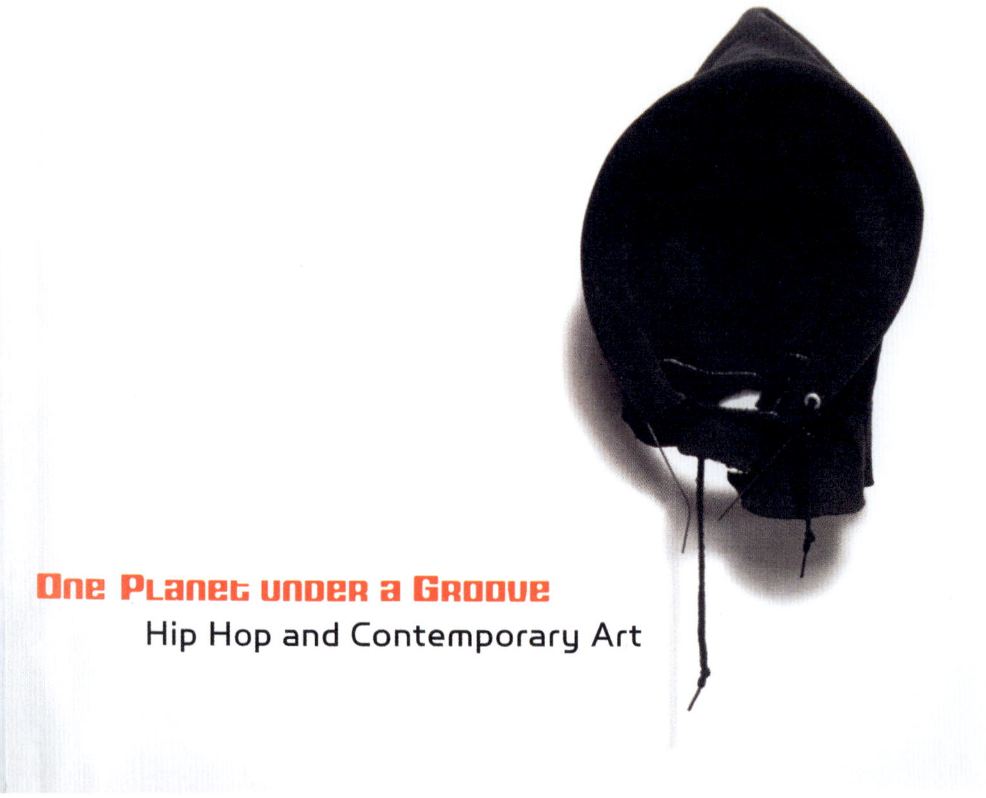

Fig. 6.1 Cover of *One Planet Under a Groove: Hip Hop and Contemporary Art,* exh. cat. (Bronx Museum of the Arts, 2001).

editor, and hopefully an independent curator. That was kind of working until 11 September 2001 when the terrorist attacks on the Twin Towers made things a little more challenging. Still, what a time to be a New Yorker and involved in the arts.

My first real museum show was *One Planet Under a Groove: Hip Hop and Contemporary Art* [2001] organized with Lydia Yee at the Bronx Museum of the Arts, which later traveled to the Spelman College Museum of Fine Art in Atlanta, the Walker Art Center in Minneapolis, and Villa Stuck in Munich [fig. 6.1]. I entered what would be a much more defined curatorial role. It was essentially ten years or more of writing and thinking through art history scholarship before I reached a curatorial moment.

I freelanced and independently curated for four to five years. I was able to curate on the commercial side as well as on the nonprofit side nationally in the United States and internationally in Canada, Italy, and South Korea. One of the big things that happened for many of us was Christian Haye opening the Project gallery space in Harlem in 1998. Now there was a commercial space that spoke out to different generations by embracing diversity, both demographically and intellectually. As someone who grew up seeing the crucial role of gallerists and advisors like Peg Alston, Alitash Kebede, June Kelly, and Corinne Jennings, this felt essential for our generation.

LPB: When the Project opened as a commercial gallery in Harlem, it meant a lot.

FS: Yes, because Christian took the approach we were talking about of participating in a global conversation that had a level of intersectionality and allowed us to thrive and support each other across the world, not just across New York City. He represented Elmgreen & Dragset very early in their career. Michael Elmgreen and Ingar Dragset came to Harlem and made work for their show. Christian also represented artists like Edgar Arceneaux, Julie Mehretu, William Pope.L, and Tracey Rose for the first time in New York. He is brilliant. Prior to the gallery, he worked at the Jack Tilton Gallery and wrote criticism for *Frieze* magazine and, of course, poetry!

LPB: How did you feel around this particular moment in terms of the ways in which you could move through the world?

FS: Post–September 11, I was in my early thirties and figuring out a way to pay rent and was traveling a lot. I started working as editor in chief for a magazine called *ArtAsiaPacific*, published by my friend and fellow Harlemite at the time, Zhao Gang. I was going to Japan, Korea, and China. The world opened in so many ways. I definitely benefited from that and tried to share that global mindset in New York, but, at a certain point, it was like, "All right, time to grow up. I'm thirty. Time to get a job." I started to think that way after September 11, but by 2005, it was time. In 2005, I worked on two exhibitions in New York that opened within a few months of each other. One was at the SculptureCenter; it was a show called *Make It Now: New Sculpture in New York* [2005]. I co-organized that with Mary Ceruti and Anthony Huberman. It was like a roundup of new sculptural work in New York. The Basquiat show opened in spring 2005 and I knew it was time to get a real job. I got married the following year as well to my amazing, incredible wife Jessica. We grew up with a group of friends who were all pretty much in New York City. It was time for a change—time to get out of the bubble again.

New York started to feel different too. Maybe it was the economic rebound. I don't know. But it was changing. I didn't feel like I could work as intuitively. It was time to go. Having grown up in New York City and Westchester, and having all the same friends and family around, I felt it was good to breathe a little bit. Then the perfect position came along: to work as a curator in modern and contemporary art at the Menil Collection and move to Houston. There was a connection to my very first museum position at Dia a decade earlier because the children of the Menil family that started the museum in Houston started Dia in New York. There was this direct tie. The other tie for me was that during my time at Dia, Michael Govan became the director and eventually became my friend, confidant, mentor, partner in crime, and more. He was working on big projects with all the artists who were connected to Dia and the Menil Collection. So, it made sense to go to a place that really was ensconced in many of the things that concern us both, which is the idea that art can be a catalyst for difficult conversations, can bring people together, and has a spiritual inclination. The Menil Collection started with a couple, John and Dominique de Menil, who began collecting art with an art adviser named Father Marie-Alain Couturier. They commissioned the Rothko Chapel with Mark Rothko before he passed away. They believed deeply in the power of art and tried to give Barnett Newman's *Broken Obelisk* [1963–69] to the city of Houston in the name of Dr. Martin Luther King. But the city said, "No, we don't need that." The Menil Collection's commitment to liberation politics was deep. The painter Peter Bradley was there working with Clement Greenberg on the *De Luxe Show* [1971], which was one of the first group exhibitions outside New York that had many of the Black abstract painters we all know and love. Larry Rivers also did a show there called *Some American History* [1971] and it was pretty raw regarding American politics from a racial point of view. It made perfect sense for me to land there. The Cy Twombly Gallery, part of the Menil Collection, became a refuge. It felt so right.

LPB: Did the Menil context spark anything in you as a creative person?

FS: Walter Hopps, the founding director and curator at the Menil Collection, has this famous phrase: "The job of the curator is to find the cave and hold the torch." Like, get out of the way, in some sense. I honestly, deeply, and personally think about curating in that way. But, yes, there's also an artistic level to curating as a form of poetry and creativity that doesn't exist in any other space. I always try to find the balance that prizes the work but is also level-headed and sober about one's position in relation to the artists. Some of the shows I organized for the Menil Collection while I was there between 2006 and 2010 were *NeoHooDoo: Art for a Forgotten Faith* [2008], *Vija Celmins: Television and Disaster, 1964–1966* [2010–11], *Steve Wolfe on Paper* [2010], and *Maurizio Cattelan: Is There Life Before Death?* [2010].

In 2010, I joined the Los Angeles County Museum of Art [LACMA], reuniting with Govan, and became the Terri and Michael Smooke Department Head and Curator of Contemporary Art. At LACMA among the shows I curated were *Human Nature: Contemporary Art from the Collection* [2011] with Christine Y. Kim, *Variations: Conversations in and Around Abstract Painting* [2014–15], and *Fútbol: The Beautiful Game* [2014] [figs. 6.2, 6.3]. I also co-curated *Noah Purifoy: Junk Dada* [2015–16] with Yael Lipschutz [figs. 6.4, 6.5].

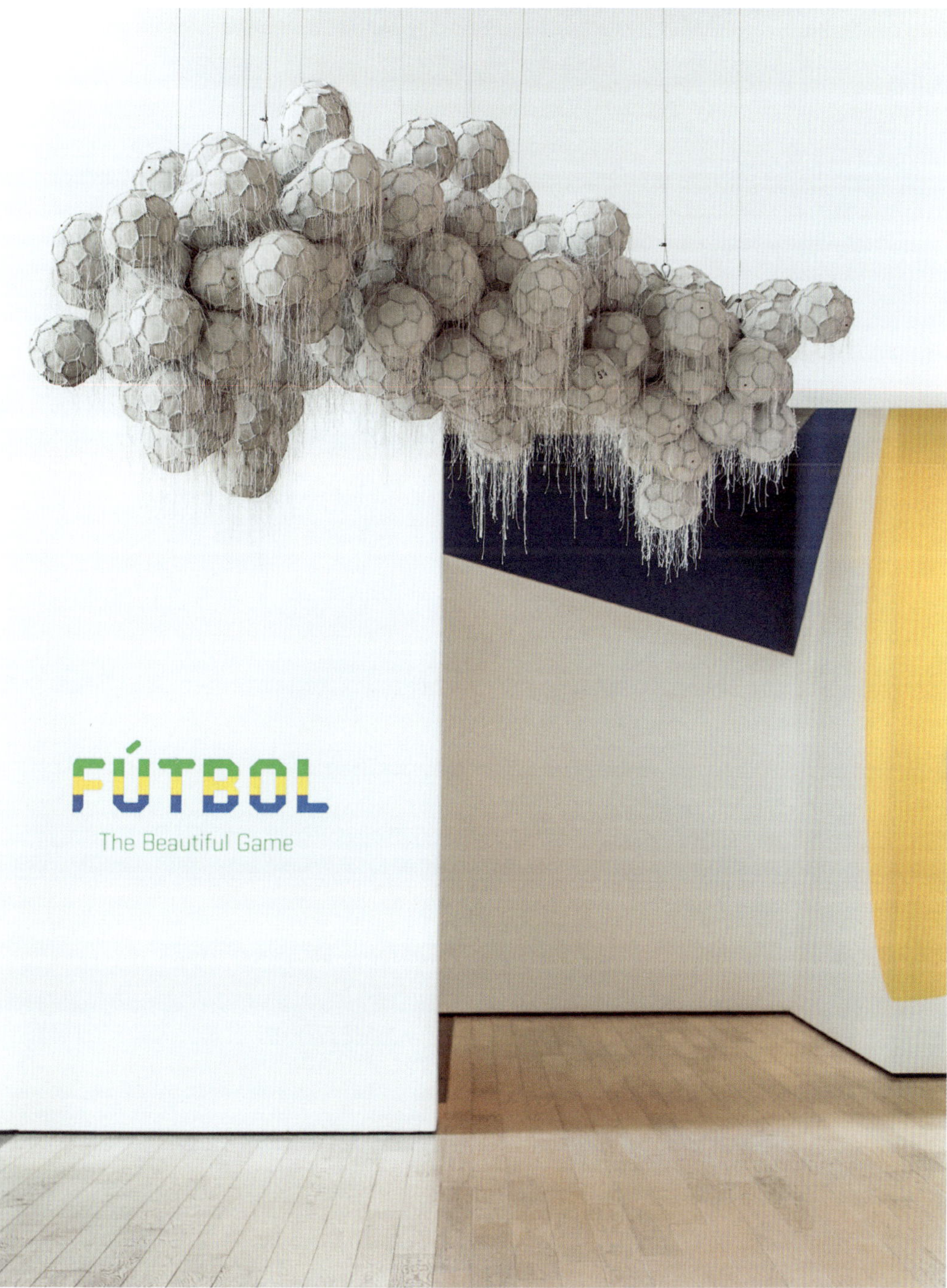

Fig. 6.2 Installation view of *Fútbol: The Beautiful Game*, curated by Franklin Sirmans, Los Angeles County Museum of Art, Los Angeles, 2 February–20 July 2014.

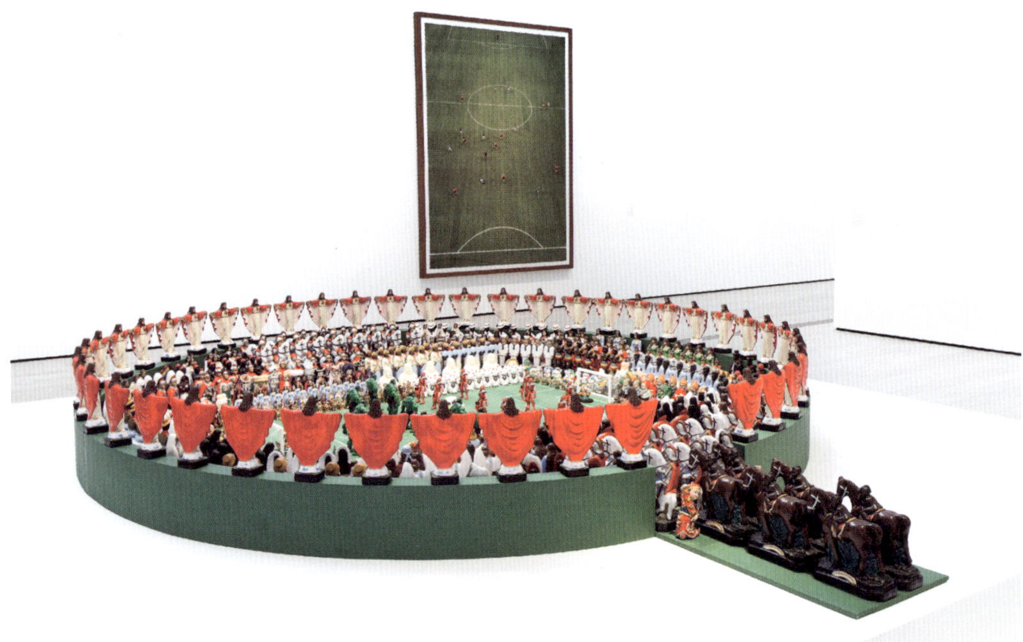

Fig. 6.3 Installation view of *Fútbol: The Beautiful Game,* curated by Franklin Sirmans, Los Angeles County Museum of Art, Los Angeles, 2 February–20 July 2014.

Fig. 6.4 Installation view of *Noah Purifoy: Junk Dada,* curated by Franklin Sirmans and Yael Lipschutz, Los Angeles County Museum of Art, Los Angeles, 7 June 2015–3 January 2016.

Fig. 6.5 Installation view of *Noah Purifoy: Junk Dada,* curated by Franklin Sirmans and Yael Lipschutz, Los Angeles County Museum of Art, Los Angeles, 7 June 2015–3 January 2016.

During my time at LACMA, I also served as artistic director of the American contemporary art triennial known as Prospect that takes place in New Orleans. *Prospect 3: Notes for Now* [2012–14] was spread over eighteen venues, including traditional spaces for art such as the New Orleans Museum of Art and Dillard University, but also many nontraditional spaces like the Mississippi River itself. The show included fifty-eight artists and many site-specific works. My time in Italy taking in all those grand shows from Venice, Gwangju, and Johannesburg shaped my thinking on *Prospect 3* and art as a way to encounter the world and culture of a specific place all at once.

Within *Prospect 3,* I also organized the exhibition *Basquiat and the Bayou* [2014–15] for the Ogden Museum of Southern Art in New Orleans [figs. 6.6–6.8]. Though Basquiat only visited New Orleans once toward the end of his life, several of his paintings celebrated Southern Black culture as well as its connection to the larger African diaspora and, specifically, New Orleans as a repository of an African aesthetic. I had worked with the esteemed scholars Robert O'Meally and Robert

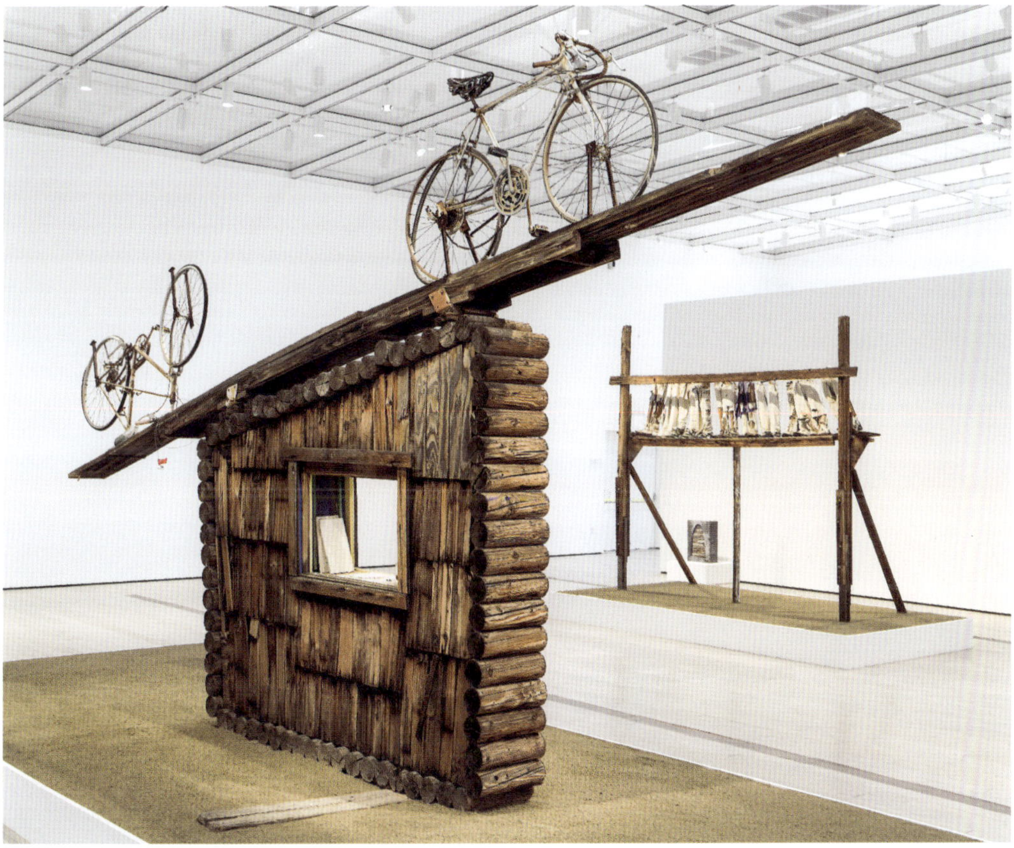

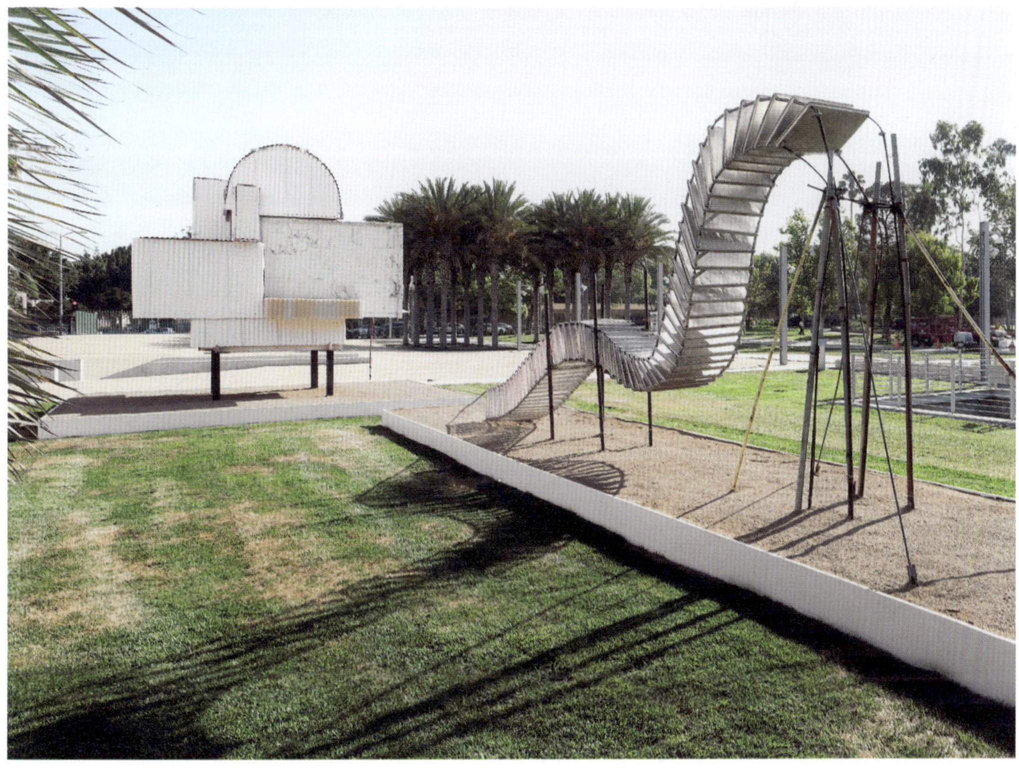

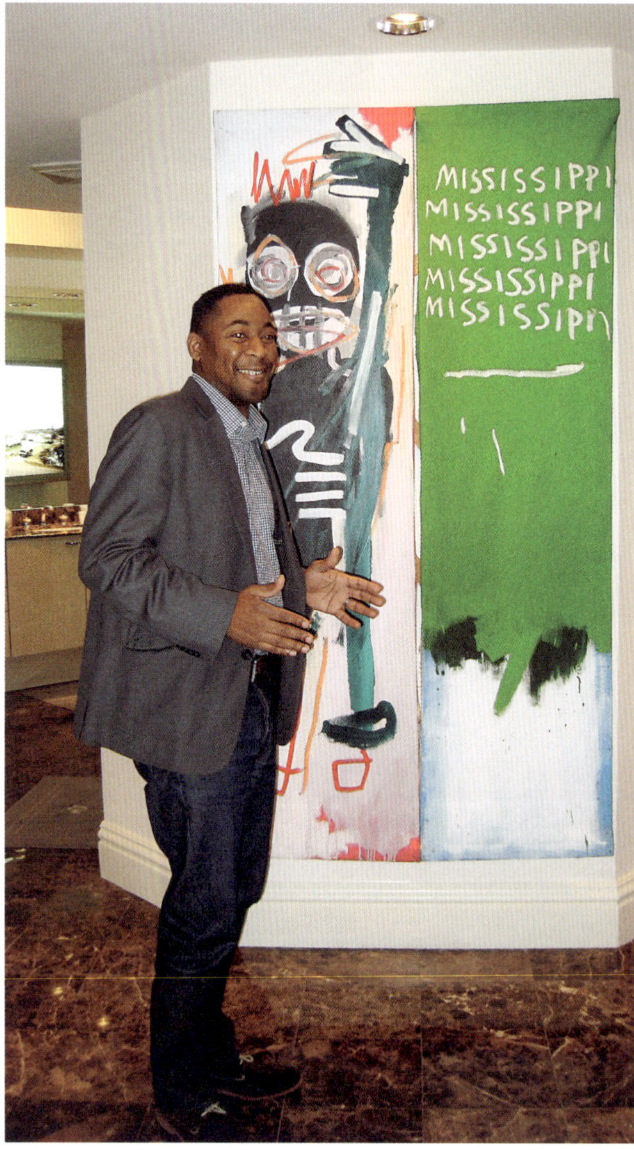

Fig. 6.6 Franklin Sirmans with Jean-Michel Basquiat's *Mississippi* (1982), at the home of Joan and Michael Salke, Naples, 2011.

Fig. 6.7 Installation view of *Basquiat and the Bayou,* curated by Franklin Sirmans, Ogden Museum of Southern Art, New Orleans, 25 October 2014—25 January 2015.

Fig. 6.8 Jean-Michel Basquiat (American, 1960–88). *King Zulu,* acrylic, wax and felt-tip pen on canvas, 202.5 × 255 cm, 1986. Barcelona, Museu d'Art Contemporani de Barcelona, R.0412. Artwork shown in *Basquiat and the Bayou,* curated by Franklin Sirmans, Ogden Museum of Southern Art, New Orleans, 25 October 2014—25 January 2015.

Farris Thompson over the years and was thrilled to include their writing in the exhibition catalog. Also, my friend and colleague Brooke Davis Anderson was the executive director of *Prospect 3*, and her view was crucial to the whole project for me. O'Meally was my teacher at Wesleyan University and encouraged an interdisciplinary approach to studying history. *Prospect 3* also hosted a conference celebrating Thompson's groundbreaking scholarship on art of the African diaspora.

LPB: What also sticks out is that you're deeply rooted. Sometimes people meet you and they know of your name but have no idea how deeply rooted you are in the field. Do you think that for the younger people today, who are in their

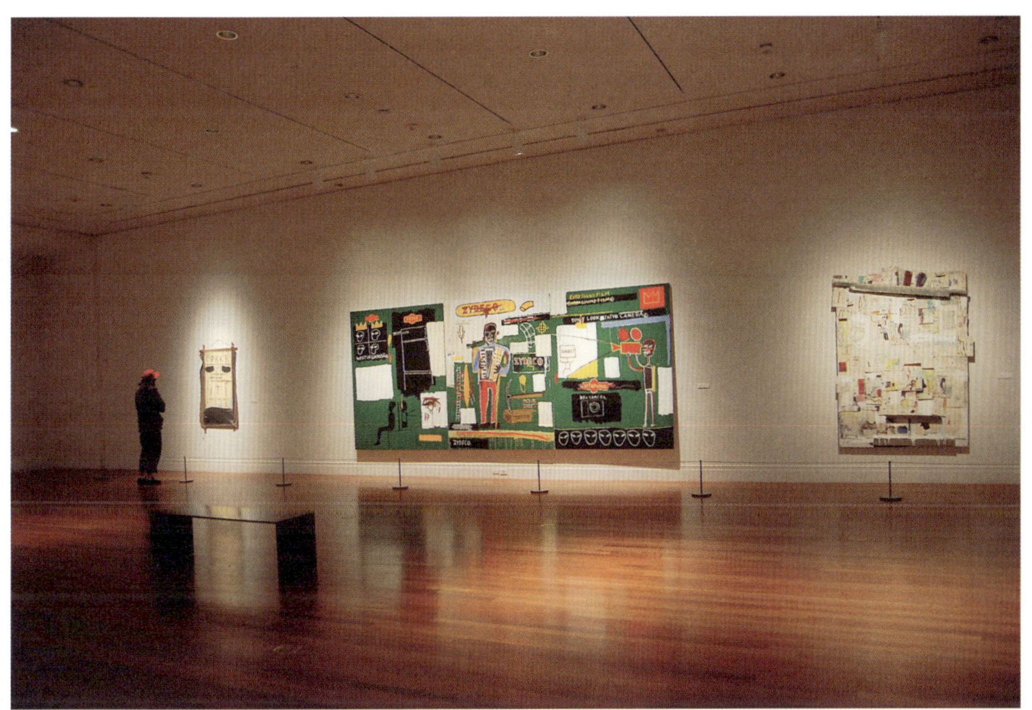

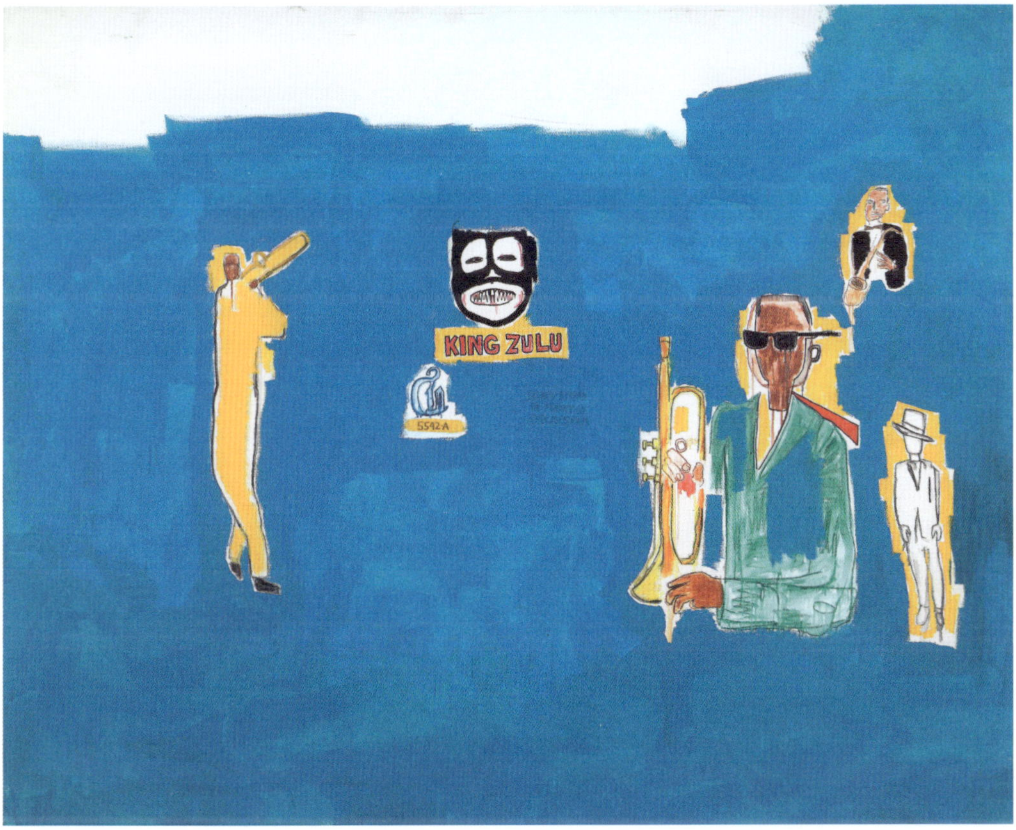

early twenties, it's possible to still have that deep rooting like you had?

FS: Absolutely, I think it's even more possible. Because of the prevalence of social media, you know who is in a position to help you regardless of where you are. I love the fact that you're in L.A. now. You've got to be at a certain point where you feel like, "All right, I'm going to go wherever." There are more of us in the field, but we still have to be responsible in at least thinking about others who may come in our footsteps. Everyone we've talked about has done just that. You and I wouldn't be here without Kellie. There's a natural way that that happens, especially if you think about the people we've mentioned. I mean, nobody does more for the next generation than Thelma.

LPB: You said a minute ago, "I always try to find the balance that prizes the work but is also quite level-headed and sober about one's position in relation to the artists." I get the feeling that that's also important to your practice as a director.

FS: Exactly. Even more so now, in a way. There is a distance sometimes from what was a much more intensive curatorial aspect. Now, I love working with curators and artists but not as intensely as the curators working with the artists. I love that space. I also love working with patrons who support these projects. We can cherish those relationships on both the curatorial side and artist side. That's where I find myself now, and I really enjoy that.

LPB: Let's back up a bit. You were in Italy. You traveled the world. How did you get to the Pérez Art Museum Miami [PAMM]? What was the trajectory that led to that?

FS: In 2005, I was working on a show at MoMA PS1 with Alanna Heiss and Klaus Biesenbach as part of a curatorial committee. Nick Stillman, who runs Prospect, was on it, and some other brilliant minds like Neville Wakefield. I presented *NeoHooDoo* there [fig. 6.9]. That show started at MoMA PS1 and then went to the Menil Collection. It also came to PAMM in 2009. The show was about spirituality and its relationship to the Americas. Subjects included Candomblé from Brazil, Santería from Cuba, and Vodou from Haiti. I felt like that show had to come to Miami and, in 2009, it did. I knew about the museum from that standpoint. One of the things that struck me about that moment in the context of our conversation today is that a lot of the people I met who were affiliated with the museum just so happened to be Black. They were on the board of trustees. There were other trustees from different backgrounds and that representation was good to see. I had come down for the show and spent some time in Miami. Terry [Terence] Riley was the director at that time. But I knew some of the players. I knew our chief curator, René Morales, from that earlier experience.

My hire wasn't completely out of nowhere. I imagine that having done an exhibition that traveled to the museum was helpful. I had

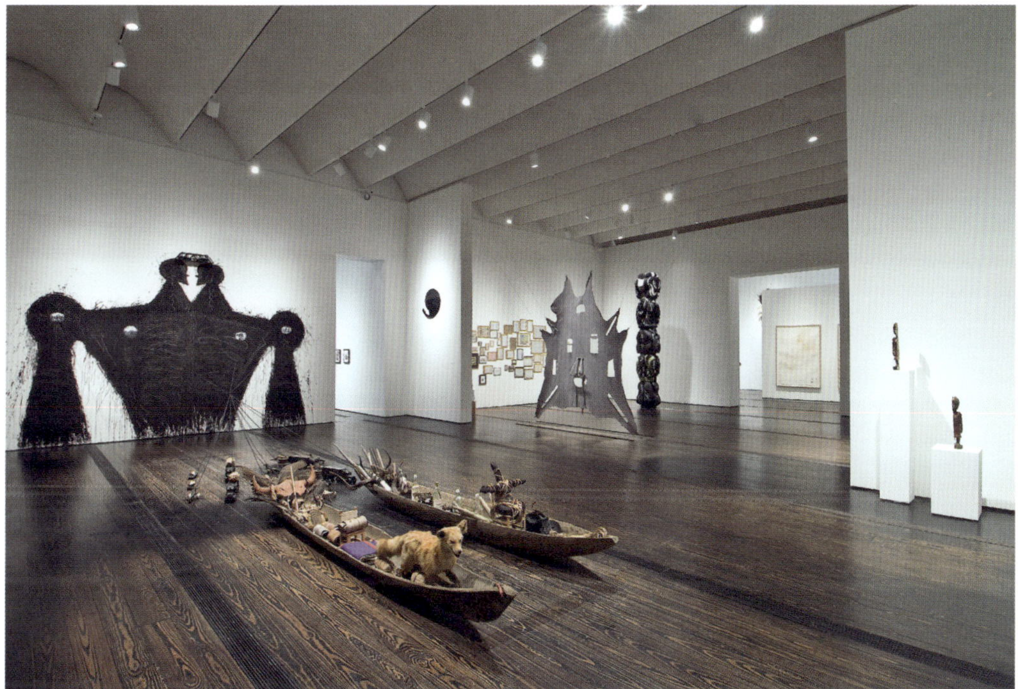

Fig. 6.9 Installation view of *NeoHooDoo: Art for a Forgotten Faith,* curated by Franklin Sirmans, Menil Collection, Houston, 27 June–21 September 2008.

worked at LACMA with encyclopedic content. The Menil Collection was not encyclopedic but had a very broadly defined sense of historical periods, reaching as far back as the Byzantine era. PAMM is aligned with a modern and contemporary remit. It was ideal in that regard. It was also housed in a building that had just been built. Watching the things that people like Michael and Thelma go through in creating buildings, I didn't need to try and build a building as a first-time director. I love building collections and teams. I think we've done that here.

LPB: It really makes me think about how, in your position as director, you must have a sense of place. Your sense of place and priorities for that institution define that particular moment. Lowery, and then Thelma at the Studio Museum, kept defining their moment. How do you think that extends, if at all, to PAMM in Miami?

FS: Oh, it's paramount. That's what we've tried to lean into: to recognize how many museums of international modern and contemporary art there truly are, to emphatically embrace our role as an example, and to highlight what sets us apart. We have been explicit that, although we are global in scope in our collections, exhibitions, and programs, we want to be the best at presenting the art and artists of Latin America and the Caribbean and we look toward the African diaspora.

One big event happened before I arrived. In 2013, Alberto Ibargüen—a giant thinker who led the Knight Foundation for many years—and Jorge Pérez started funding what would be the PAMM Fund for Black Art. They gave half a million dollars each, which was spent down to around three hundred and fifty thousand dollars on some great works of art, including Loving's *Untitled #32* [ca. 1975], Faith Ringgold's *Black Light Series #1: Big Black* [1967], and Nari Ward's *Homeland Sweet Homeland* [2012]—just great works of art. We also took some chances, like on Leslie Hewitt's early work.

LPB: This is also an interesting moment in terms of the art world, considering Robin Pogrebin's recent article in the *New York Times,* "What Does It Take to Run a Museum? The Job Description Is Changing" [2023]. Post-George Floyd, historically white institutions were under a certain kind of duress, right? There was a call for what are you doing in terms of diversity. Has that made a difference?

FS: Where I'm coming from right now, where you are, and what Tumelo has done from a big global perspective, I think has made a difference. Has it made enough of a difference? I don't know. There are degrees and levels to the conversation. It's weird to say, but I was coming off this conversation about the early 1990s, with the Whitney Biennial in 1993 and Thelma's *Black Male: Representations of Masculinity in Contemporary American Art* [1994–95] exhibition. You used the phrase "post-George Floyd," but there was a post-Rodney King moment too. I don't know how much has changed, but, certainly, we can say that some things have changed. I try to be optimistic.

Especially in a place like PAMM, where the history of the institution is relatively young and so many young people are coming into the museum for the first time and never had that kind of experience, it's immensely important to be optimistic. When you come into PAMM now, two things happen. One is that there's a conversation on abstraction in one room that is about changing canons. There are a couple of names that many people know, like Sol LeWitt, but those are surrounded by artists like Loló Soldevilla, Carmen Herrera, or Virginia Jaramillo. That's happening in one gallery. In the other gallery, it's more about a figurative or representational presence, with artists like Jordan Casteel, Kehinde Wiley, Lynette Yiadom-Boakye, Bisa Butler, and on and on. We know it's important, but when you stand there and watch people engage with the work, it's so evident. The presentation allows for people to be represented visually and intellectually. To use that as a source of inspiration, moving about one's life, is the ultimate thing that the engagement with art provides.

That's huge. That's what we're trying to do. In some ways, we have a default within museums where it's an educational or programmatic priority to provide an interpretation of the work. That's the fun part of what we do. We're fortunate to be able to think of art in that way as a malleable tool and in service of a greater degree of humanism or social cohesion.

We have a group called the PAMM Teen Arts Council and I get to engage in that conversation periodically. It's amazing to be able to hear those viewpoints from people who are sixteen years old. What I try to offer is a sharing of experience and stress the idea of being open to possibilities. I try to make sure the teens are aware of the varied paths and highlight the importance of critical thinking skills. At the end of the day, your experience with the museum, specifically your experience of thinking about curating and its relationship to the museum, is going to aid your ability to think for yourself and to think critically no matter what you do. It's not limited to a museum space. At the end of the day, what I'm trying to do isn't that different from running a good and successful company. Our product is "experience," and it's driven by art and culture.

We are in a position to move conversations forward around diversity and its relationship to simple humanism in a positive way. That's what I look forward to. I still believe in the power of art and the discussion around art to lead us to a better place. It may take a long time, but the potential exists. We want to provide a space for people to think differently all the time and to think in a way that is more open to others, new ideas, and humanist ideals all the time.

ACKNOWLEDGMENTS

Black Curators Matter: Conversations on Art and Change has been a labor of love, coalescing a larger community that continues to expand and encompassing generations of Black curators whose work and influence spans some five decades. First and foremost, we would like to thank the amazing curators who offered their stories and queries for the record: LeRonn P. Brooks, Kalia Brooks, Aaron Bryant, Thelma Golden, Rujeko Hockley, Ashley James, Thomas Jean Lax, Richard J. Powell, Lowery Stokes Sims, Franklin Sirmans, and Deborah Willis.

This oral history, part of Columbia University's Mellon Arts Project launched during the 2020–21 academic year, was made possible by the Mellon Foundation to whom we express gratitude for understanding why Black curators matter. The partnerships created through the Mellon Arts Project are designed to sustain the centrality of the arts in African American and African diaspora studies and its broader intellectual community in collaboration with departments at Columbia University, Harlem-based organizations, and national and international cultural institutions. The exceptional faculty and staff of Columbia University's African American and African Diaspora Studies Department have provided us with a warm home and unwavering support for which we are grateful. We are deeply grateful to Kalia Brooks who served as the project's inaugural director and would also like to thank Farah Jasmine Griffin and Josef Sorett, the principal investigators of this initiative. We would also like to extend our gratitude to the graduate fellows who provided critical research and support: KJ Abudu, Scarlett Olivia Croft, Brooke Lin Finister, Jennifer Harley, Jasmine Kouyaté, Chloe V. Powers, Irene Denise Ross, and Ardel'Paschal Sampson. Special thanks as well to Sinclair Spratley who helped craft a design that not only provided a blueprint for the oral history as a whole but also served as a template for this volume's introduction.

We are also deeply grateful to the Columbia University Center for Oral History Research for providing personnel for the recording and auditing of all the oral histories as well as helping us set up a rubric for the project. We would like to especially thank Mary Marshall Clark and Michael Falco-Felderman who oversaw the recordings and trained the curators in oral history methods. We would also like to recognize the Oral History Master of Arts fellows involved in the project who oversaw the recording, auditing, transcription, and formatting of the interviews: Ornella Bagazini, Chris Pandza, Jarrett Payne, Kayleigh Stack, and Auriana Woods.

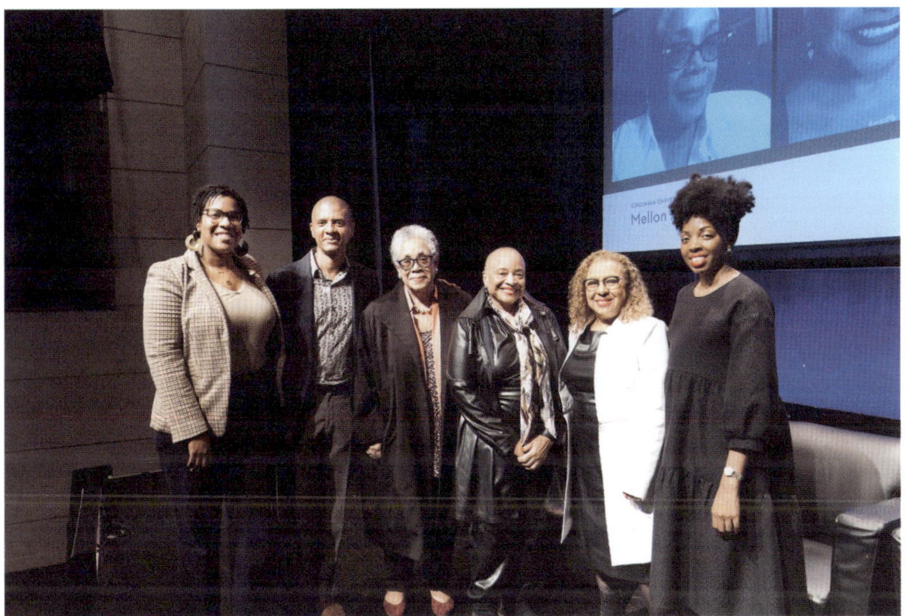

Fig. 7.1 *Left to right:* Joy Bivins, Tumelo Mosaka, Lowery Stokes Sims, Deborah Willis, Kellie Jones, and Novella Ford, "Black Curators Matter: Oral History Project Part I," Schomburg Center for Research in Black Culture, New York, 2023.

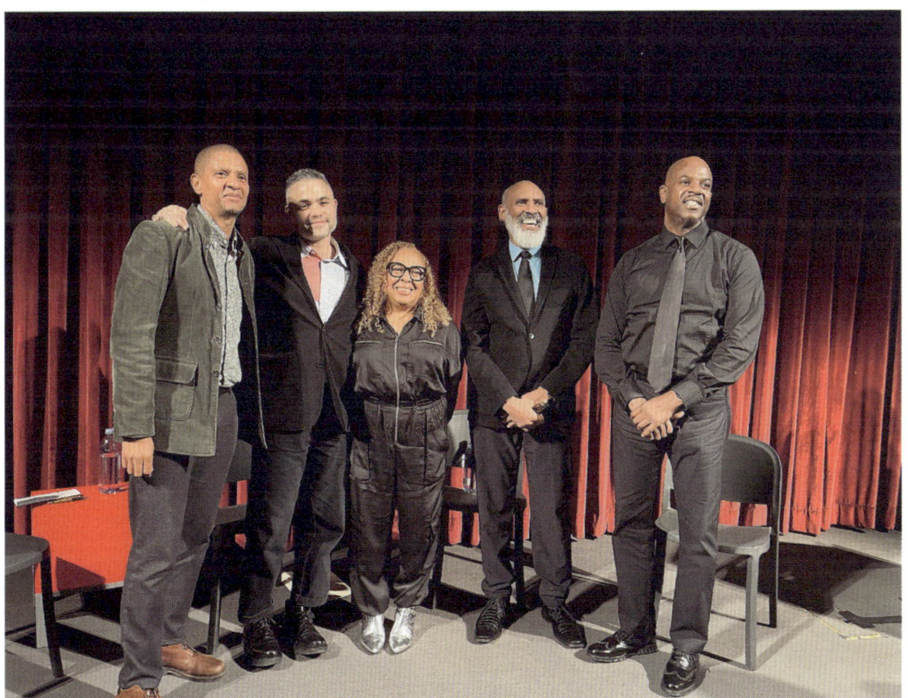

Fig. 7.2 *Left to right:* Tumelo Mosaka, Thomas Jean Lax, Kellie Jones, Richard J. Powell, and Aaron Bryant, "Black Curators Matter: Oral History Project Part II," Museum of Modern Art, New York, 2023.

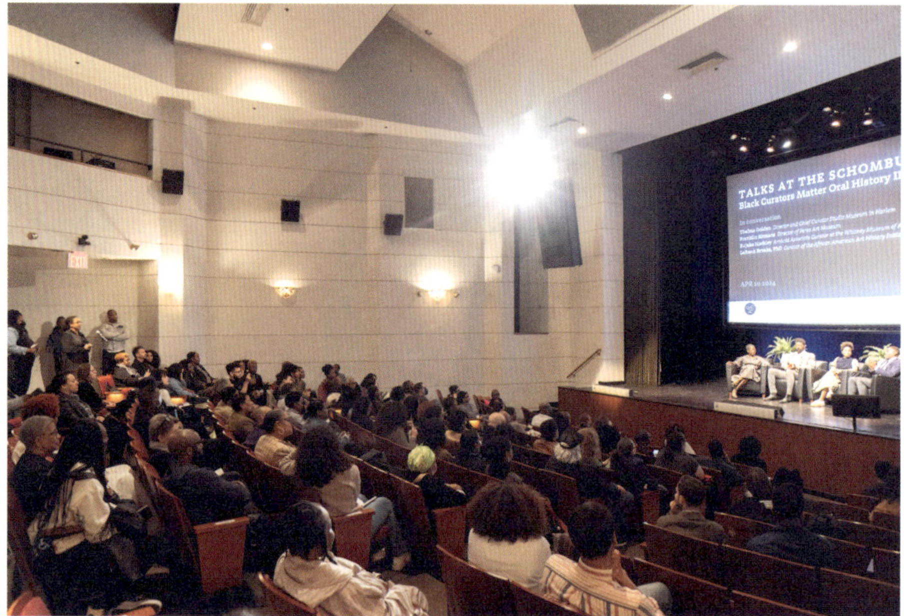

Fig. 7.3 View of the audience with Thelma Golden, LeRonn P. Brooks, Rujeko Hockley, and Franklin Sirmans (*left to right*) on stage, "Black Curators Matter: Oral History Project Part III," Schomburg Center for Research in Black Culture, New York, 2023.

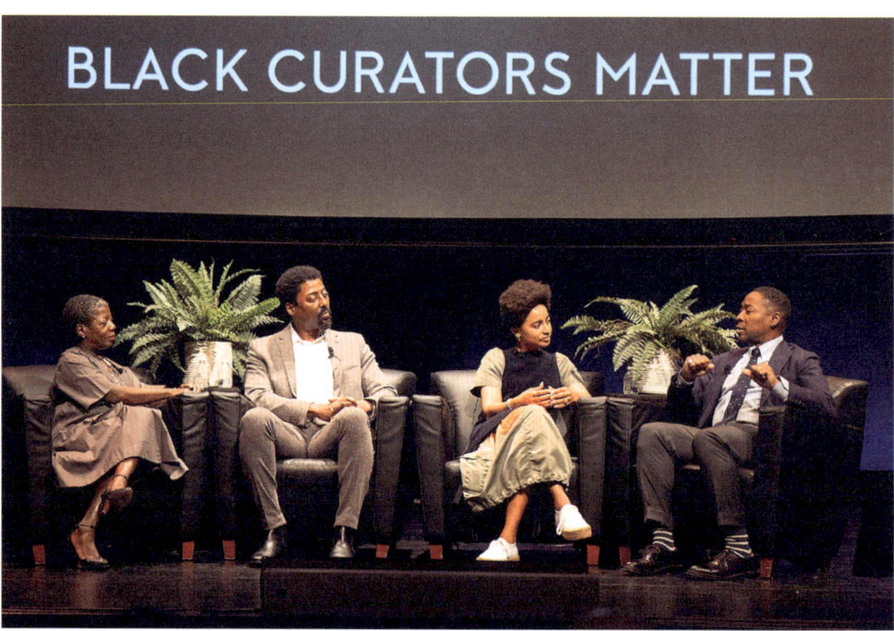

Fig. 7.4 *Left to right:* Thelma Golden, LeRonn P. Brooks, Rujeko Hockley, and Franklin Sirmans, "Black Curators Matter: Oral History Project Part III," Schomburg Center for Research in Black Culture, New York, 2023.

Special recognition is due to our public programming partners: Columbia University's Institute for Research in African American Studies, the Schomburg Center for Research in Black Culture, and the Museum of Modern Art for hosting and supporting the three public programs related to this project (figs. 7.1–7.4). We are also grateful to Duke University, the Guggenheim Museum, New York University, Pérez Art Museum Miami, the Studio Museum in Harlem, and the Whitney Museum of American Art for their continued support and engagement. We thank the Getty Library and the Schomburg Center for Research in Black Culture for agreeing to be sites for the deposit of digital files where they will be accessed by researchers for years to come.

The Getty has also been another wonderful partner. Staff at the Getty Research Institute (GRI), including Mary Miller and LeRonn P. Brooks, have been crucial curatorial interlocuters. The Getty trustee Pamela Joyner was the inspiration behind the GRI's African American Art History Initiative, and Kara Tucina Olidge, GRI associate director of Collections and Discovery, has done a wonderful job growing this significant enterprise. Last but not least, we would like to thank our previous editor Karen Levine for her initial enthusiasm for the project, Michele Ciaccio, head of GRI Publications, and Adriana Romero, our manuscript and project editor, who have been with us all the way.

—Kellie Jones and Tumelo Mosaka

CONTRIBUTORS

Kalia Brooks is a program officer at Fundamental Philanthropy, where she stewards grantmaking for the Hearthland Foundation—an organization that champions justice, equity, and connection through the power of art and storytelling. Previously, she was director of programs and exhibitions at NXTHVN where she was responsible for the design and delivery of curatorial exhibitions, public programs, artist projects, and community engagement initiatives. She was the inaugural director of the Mellon Arts Project at Columbia University. Brooks holds a PhD in aesthetics and art theory from the Institute for Doctoral Studies in the Visual Arts. She is coeditor of *Women and Migration: Responses in Art and History* (2019). She has served as a consulting curator with the City of New York's Department of Cultural Affairs and the Gracie Mansion Conservancy. Brooks was also an ex-officio trustee on the Board of the Museum of the City of New York.

LeRonn P. Brooks is an art historian and curator of the African American Art History Initiative at the Getty Research Institute (GRI) as well as curator of African American collections and acquisitions at the GRI. Previously, he was assistant professor of Africana studies at Lehman College and curator for the Racial Imaginary Institute founded by the poet Claudia Rankine. He received his PhD from the Graduate Center of the City University of New York. Brooks is also the curator and co-curator of several archives, including the Johnson Publishing Company Archive, Paul Revere Williams Archive, Richard Hunt Archive, and Robert Farris Thompson Archive. His interviews and essays on African American art and poetry have been featured in *Callaloo, The International Review of African American Art,* and *Aperture* as well as in many exhibition catalogs including *Dawoud Bey: Elegy* (2023), *Torkwase Dyson: A Liquid Belonging* (2023), *A Long Arc: Photography and the American South Since 1845* (2023), and *Faith Ringgold: American People* (2022).

Aaron Bryant is a curator at the National Museum of African American History and Culture and co-curator of the Johnson Publishing Company Archive. Prior to joining the Smithsonian, he was a curator at Morgan State University's James E. Lewis Museum of Art. Bryant's research and work in social justice has received honors from various institutions, including the Lyndon B. Johnson Presidential Library, the Library of Congress, the New York Public Library, the US Department of Justice, the US Congress, the Center for Black Equity, the Smithsonian, and the Royal

Anthropological Institute. Additionally, Bryant has lectured for the US State Department at universities and cultural institutions throughout Barcelona, Seville, and Madrid. He is chair of Baltimore's Public Art Commission and a commissioner for Baltimore's Commission for Historical and Architectural Preservation. He also served as chair of a special commission to review Baltimore's confederate monuments. Bryant earned his PhD from the University of Maryland, College Park, an MFA from Yale University, and a BA from Duke University.

Thelma Golden is the Ford Foundation Director and Chief Curator of the Studio Museum in Harlem, the world's leading institution devoted to visual arts by artists of African descent. She began her career in 1987 as a fellow at the Studio Museum, then joined the Whitney Museum of American Art in 1988. Golden returned to the Studio Museum in 2000 as deputy director for exhibitions and programs and was named director and chief curator in 2005. Golden serves on the board of directors for the Barack Obama Foundation, the Crystal Bridges Museum of American Art, the Los Angeles County Museum of Art, and the Mellon Foundation. In 2010, she was appointed to the Committee for the Preservation of the White House by former President Barack Obama. She holds a BA in art history and African American studies from Smith College.

Rujeko Hockley is the Arnhold Associate Curator at the Whitney Museum of American Art. She co-curated the 2019 Whitney Biennial. Additional projects at the Whitney include: *Amy Sherald: American Sublime* (2025), *Inheritance* (2023–24), *2 Lizards* (2022–23), *Jennifer Packer: The Eye Is Not Satisfied with Seeing* (2021–22), *Julie Mehretu* (2021), *Toyin Ojih Odutola: To Wander Determined* (2017–18), and *An Incomplete History of Protest: Selections from the Whitney's Collection, 1940–2017* (2017). Previously, she was assistant curator of contemporary art at the Brooklyn Museum, where she co-curated *Crossing Brooklyn: Art from Bushwick, Bed-Stuy, and Beyond* (2014) and was involved in exhibitions highlighting the permanent collection as well as artists like LaToya Ruby Frazier and Kehinde Wiley. She is co-curator of *We Wanted a Revolution: Black Radical Women, 1965–85* (2017), which originated at the Brooklyn Museum and traveled to three US venues in 2017–18. She serves on the boards of Art Matters, For Freedoms, and Museums Moving Forward, as well as the advisory board of Recess.

Ashley James is associate curator of contemporary art at the Guggenheim Museum. She is the curator of *Going Dark: The Contemporary Figure at the Edge of Visibility* (2023–24) and *Off the Record* (2021), and co-curator of *The Hugo Boss Prize 2020: Deana Lawson, Centropy* (2021). Prior to joining the Guggenheim, James served as assistant curator of contemporary art at the Brooklyn Museum, where she curated *Soul of a Nation: Art in the Age of Black Power* (2018–19), organized *Eric N. Mack: Lemme Walk Across the Room* (2019), and co-curated *John Edmonds: A Sidelong Glance* (2020–21). James also served as a Mellon-Marron Research Consortium fellow in Drawing and Prints at the Museum of Modern Art, where her work focused on the groundbreaking retrospectives of Adrian Piper (2018) and Charles White (2018–19). She also has held positions at the Studio Museum in Harlem and at the Yale University Art Gallery, where she co-organized the exhibition *Odd Volumes: Book Art from the Allan Chasanoff Collection* (2015). James holds a BA from Columbia University and a PhD from Yale University in English literature and African American studies.

Kellie Jones is the Hans Hofmann Professor of Modern Art in the Department of Art History and Archaeology and professor of African American and African diaspora studies at Columbia University. Her research interests include African American and African diaspora artists, Latinx and Latin American artists, and issues in contemporary art and museum theory. A member of the American Philosophical Society and American Academy of Arts and Sciences, Jones was named a MacArthur Fellow in 2016. Her writings have appeared in many exhibition catalogs and journals. She is the author of *EyeMinded: Living and Writing Contemporary Art* (2011) and *South of Pico: African American Artists in Los Angeles in the 1960s and 1970s* (2017) and editor of *October Files: David Hammons* (2025). Jones has also worked as a curator for over four decades and has numerous major national and international exhibitions to her credit. The exhibition *Now Dig This! Art and Black Los Angeles, 1960–1980* (2011–12) at the Hammer Museum was named one of the best exhibitions of 2011 and 2012 by *Artforum.* Jones has received numerous awards, including from the Hutchins Center for African and African American Research, Harvard University; Creative Capital, the Andy Warhol Foundation for the Visual Arts; and the Terra Foundation for American Art in Giverny, France.

Thomas Jean Lax is curator of media and performance at the Museum of Modern Art (MoMA). They organized the exhibition *Ceremonies Out of the Air: Ralph Lemon* (2024–25) and co-organized the exhibition *Just Above Midtown: Changing Spaces* (2022–23) with Lilia Rocio Taboada in collaboration with Just Above Midtown's founder Linda Goode Bryant. They worked with colleagues across MoMA on a major rehang of its collection in 2019 and co-organized the exhibition *Judson Dance Theater: The Work Is Never Done* (2018–19) with Ana Janevski and Martha Joseph. Their other collaboratively organized exhibitions include the Projects series for emerging artists with Lanka Tattersall; *Unfinished Conversations: New Work from the Collection* (2017), inspired by the cultural theorist Stuart Hall; MoMA PS1's contemporary art quintennial Greater New York; and commissions with artists including Neil Beloufa, Maria Hassabi, and Steffani Jemison. Previously, they worked at the Studio Museum in Harlem for seven years, where they organized *When the Stars Begin to Fall: Imagination and the American South* (2014) and participated in the landmark F-show contemporary art series. Lax holds degrees in Africana studies and art history from Brown and Columbia Universities and is a PhD candidate in performance studies at New York University.

Tumelo Mosaka is the Mellon Arts Project Director in the Department of African American and African Diaspora Studies at Columbia University. Mosaka has worked within and outside museums exploring global transnational artistic practices especially from Africa, the Caribbean, and North America. He has curated numerous exhibitions including *Between Distance and Desire: African Diasporic Perspectives* (2025), *Fragmented Worlds/Coherent Lives* (2023), *Usha Seejarim: A Solo Exhibition* (2020), *Turning Tide* (2017), *Andrew Lyght: Full Circle* (2016), *Poetic Relations* (2015), and *Otherwise Black* (2014). His previous positions include chief curator for Investec Cape Town Art Fair (2016–19) and curator at the Krannert Art Museum (KAM) at the University of Illinois Urbana-Champaign, where he curated several exhibitions including *Blind Field* (2013), *OPENSTUDIO* (2011), and *MAKEBA!* (2011). Before joining KAM, Mosaka was associate curator of exhibitions at the Brooklyn Museum, where he curated *Infinite Islands: Contemporary Caribbean Art* (2007) and *Passing/Posing: Kehinde Wiley Paintings* (2004). He was born in Johannesburg and lives in New Jersey.

Richard J. Powell is the John Spencer Bassett Distinguished Professor of Art and Art History at Duke University. Along with teaching courses in American art and the arts of the African diaspora, he has written on a range of topics. Some of his publications include: *Homecoming: The Art and Life of William H. Johnson* (1991), *Black Art: A Cultural History* (1997, 2002, and 2021), *Cutting a Figure: Fashioning Black Portraiture* (2008), and *Going There: Black Visual Satire* (2020). His latest book, *Colorstruck! Painting, Pigment, Affect* (forthcoming 2026), traces the visual and conceptual pathways of particular colors as strategically employed by selected African American painters. Powell has also organized numerous art exhibitions, most notably *Rhapsodies in Black: Art of the Harlem Renaissance* (1997), *To Conserve a Legacy: American Art at Historically Black Colleges and Universities* (1999), *Back to Black: Art, Cinema, and the Racial Imaginary* (2005), and *Archibald Motley: Jazz Age Modernist* (2014). From 2007 until 2010, Powell was editor in chief of *The Art Bulletin.* Powell received his MPhil and PhD in the history of art from Yale University.

Lowery Stokes Sims is a specialist in contemporary art, craft, and design. She served on the education and curatorial staff of the Metropolitan Museum of Art (1972–99) and as executive director and president of the Studio Museum in Harlem (2000–2007). She retired as curator emerita from the Museum of Arts and Design (2007–2015). More recently, she has worked as an independent curator and consultant for numerous exhibitions at various institutions, including the Contemporary Arts Center in Cincinnati, Craft Contemporary in Los Angeles, and the Baltimore Museum of Art. She was visiting professor at New York University's Institute of Fine Arts (2018–20) and was appointed the Kress-Beinecke Professor at the National Gallery of Art's Center for Advanced Study in the Visual Arts (2021–22). Sims has published extensively and has had a longtime commitment to working with and writing about modern and contemporary art and artists. Since the 1970s, she has fostered opportunities for many artists, having been a witness to and participant in the Black arts movement, the feminist art movement, and the politics of postmodernism and beyond. She received her PhD in art history from the Graduate Center of the City University of New York and holds numerous honorary doctoral degrees, awards in art criticism, and distinguished professorships.

Franklin Sirmans is the Sandra and Tony Tamer Director of the Pérez Art Museum Miami since fall 2015. Prior to his appointment in Miami, he was department head and curator of contemporary art at Los Angeles County Museum of Art (LACMA) from 2010 until 2015. From 2006 to 2010, he was curator of modern and contemporary art at the Menil Collection. After internships at the Studio Museum in Harlem, Sirmans's initial museum position was at Dia Center for the Arts in the Publications Department (1993–96). After serving as editor at *Flash Art* magazine in Milan from 1996 to 1998, Sirmans began curating exhibitions. Since 1998, he has organized numerous exhibitions, including *One Planet Under a Groove: Hip Hop and Contemporary Art* (2001), *NeoHooDoo: Art for a Forgotten Faith* (2008), *Fútbol: The

Beautiful Game (2014), and monographic shows such as *Vija Celmins: Television and Disaster, 1964–1966* (2010–11), *Noah Purifoy: Junk Dada* (2015–16), and *Maurizio Cattelan: Is There Life Before Death?* (2010). Sirmans was the artistic director of the third iteration of Prospect in New Orleans (2014). Sirmans was born in New York City and raised in Harlem, Albany, and New Rochelle. He earned his BA in English and art history from Wesleyan University with an honors thesis on Jean-Michel Basquiat in 1991.

Deborah Willis is professor and chair of the Department of Photography and Imaging at Tisch School of the Arts at New York University (NYU) and founding director of NYU's Center for Black Visual Culture at the Institute for African American Affairs. She is the recipient of the MacArthur and Guggenheim Fellowships. She is the author of *Reflections in Black: A History of Black Photographers 1840 to the Present* (2000, 2025), *Posing Beauty: African American Images from the 1890s to the Present* (2009), and *The Black Civil War Soldier: A Visual History of Conflict and Citizenship* (2021). Willis's curated exhibitions include: *Let Your Motto Be Resistance: African American Portraits* (2007), *Out [o] Fashion Photography: Framing Beauty* (2013), and *Reframing Beauty: Intimate Visions* (2016). In addition to making art, writing, and teaching, Willis has served as a consultant to museums, archives, and educational centers. She holds honorary degrees from the Pratt Institute and Yale University. She is currently researching projects on photography, the Black arts movement, and how artists reimagine history.

ILLUSTRATION CREDITS

Page ii Installation view of *Frequency,* curated by Thelma Golden and Christine Y. Kim, Studio Museum in Harlem, New York, 9 November 2005–12 March 2006. Courtesy Studio Museum in Harlem. Photo: Adam Reich.

Page 6 Portrait of Lowery Stokes Sims, 2021. Photo: Grace Roselli, Pandora's BoxX Project.

Page 32 Portrait of Deborah Willis, 2022. Photo: Laylah Amatullah Barrayn. Courtesy of Deborah Willis.

Page 56 Portrait of Richard J. Powell, 2021. Photo: J. Caldwell. Courtesy of Richard Powell.

Page 82 Portrait of Kellie Jones. Photo: Daniel Jackson. Courtesy of Kellie Jones.

Page 108 Portrait of Thelma Golden, 2015. Photo: Julie Skarratt. Courtesy Thelma Golden.

Page 132 Portrait of Franklin Sirmans, 2023. Photo: Lazaro Llanes. Courtesy of Franklin Sirmans.

Lowery Stokes Sims

Fig. 1.1 Courtesy the Archives of American Art. The Lowery Stokes Sims Papers, 1967–2019.

Fig. 1.2 © 2025 Estate of Stuart Davis / Licensed by VAGA at Artists Rights Society (ARS), NY. Image © The Metropolitan Museum of Art / Art Resource, NY.

Fig. 1.3 Artwork on cover: Jacob Lawrence, detail of *The Shoemaker,* 1945. Courtesy of the Metropolitan Museum of Art.

Fig. 1.4 Photo: Howard Ehrenfeld, Baltimore, MD. Courtesy of Archives of American Art, Smithsonian Institution, Washington, DC.

Fig. 1.5 Artwork on cover: Kehinde Wiley, *Unity,* 2010. Portraits of Samuel Eto'o, John Mensah, and Emmanuel Eboué. Book design: Zach Hooker.

Figs. 1.6, 1.7 Photo: Jenna Bascom. Courtesy the Museum of Arts and Design.

Fig. 1.8 Courtesy the artist and New Museum Archive. Photo: Fred Scruton.

Fig. 1.9 Courtesy New Museum. Photo: Sowon Kwon.

Fig. 1.10 © 2025 Romare Bearden Foundation / Licensed by VAGA at Artists Rights Society (ARS) NY. Image © The Metropolitan Museum of Art. Image source: Art Resource, NY.

Deborah Willis

Fig. 2.1 © Richard Presha. Courtesy of Richard Presha.

Fig. 2.2 Courtesy of and copyright The Gordon Parks Foundation.

Fig. 2.3 Schomburg Center for Research in Black Culture, Photographs and Prints Division, the New York Public Library.

Fig. 2.4 Courtesy of Deborah Willis.

Fig. 2.5 Photo on cover: Ken Ramsay, *Susan Taylor as a Model,* ca. 1970s. Book jacket design: Evan Gaffney Design.

Fig. 2.6 © Carrie Mae Weems. Courtesy of the artist and Gladstone Gallery, New York, Fraenkel Gallery, San Francisco, and Galerie Barbara Thumm, Berlin.

Fig. 2.7 Photo: Donaldson Collection / Michael Ochs Archives / Getty Images.

Fig. 2.8 Photo on cover: Christian Walker, *Performance Counts #2,* 1988, Collection of Lucinda Bunnen. Book design: Elizabeth Woll and Alison Jones.

Fig. 2.9 © Adama Delphine Fawundu. Courtesy Adama Delphine Fawundu.

Richard J. Powell

Fig. 3.1 Restricted gift of Mr. and Mrs. Robert S. Hartman. The Art Institute of Chicago / Art Resource, NY. © 2025 Mora-Catlett Family / Licensed by VAGA at Artists Rights Society (ARS), NY.

Fig. 3.2 Courtesy Studio Museum in Harlem.

Fig. 3.3 © 2024 Richard J. Powell. Courtesy of Richard J. Powell.

Fig. 3.4 Smithsonian American Art Museum, Washington, DC / Art Resource, NY.

Fig. 3.5 © 2024 C.T. Woods-Powell. Courtesy of Richard J. Powell.

Fig. 3.6 Art © Michael Rosenfeld Gallery LLC, New York, NY, Courtesy of Michael Rosenfeld Gallery LLC, New York, NY. Image © The Metropolitan Museum of Art. Image source: Art Resource, NY.

Fig. 3.7 Cover artwork: Frederick C. Flemister, *Man with a Brush,* 1940, collection of Clark Atlanta University Art Galleries. Book design: Katy Homans.

Fig. 3.8 Gift of Reba and Dave Williams, 1999. © The Metropolitan Museum of Art. Image source: Art Resource, NY.

Fig. 3.9 Mary Swift Papers, 1974–2004. Archives of American Art, Smithsonian Institution. © 2024 Estate of Mary Swift. Image courtesy of Richard J. Powell.

Fig. 3.10 Photo: Matthew Hamilton. Courtesy of Williamstown + Atlanta Art Conservation Centers.

Kellie Jones

Fig. 4.1 Photo: Daniel Jackson. Courtesy of Kellie Jones.

Fig. 4.2 Photo: Sarah Wells. © Martin Puryear, Courtesy Matthew Marks Gallery.

Fig. 4.3 Gift from the Junior Volunteer Committee. © Rebecca Belmore. Photo: Art Gallery of Ontario.

Fig. 4.4 Courtesy of Kellie Jones.

Fig. 4.5 Courtesy of Tumelo Mosaka. Courtesy of Kellie Jones.

Fig. 4.6 Courtesy of Kellie Jones. Used by permission of Berni Searle.

Fig. 4.7 Courtesy of Kellie Jones. Used by permission of Wangechi Mutu.

Fig. 4.8 Courtesy Walker Art Center, Minneapolis.

Fig. 4.9 The Modern Women's Fund and Committee on Painting and Sculpture Funds. © The Museum of Modern Art / Licensed by SCALA / Art Resource, NY.

Fig. 4.10 Courtesy Studio Museum in Harlem.

Fig. 4.11 © Lorna Simpson. Courtesy the artist and Hauser & Wirth. Photo: James Wang.

Thelma Golden

Fig. 5.1 © Glenn Ligon. Courtesy the artist and Hauser & Wirth. Photo: George Hirose.

Fig. 5.2 Artwork © Lorna Simpson. Courtesy the Whitney Museum of American Art. Photo: George Hirose.

Fig. 5.3 Digital image © Whitney Museum of American Art / Licensed by SCALA/ Art Resource, NY. Photo: Geoffrey Clements.

Fig. 5.4 Digital image © Whitney Museum of American Art / Licensed by SCALA / Art Resource, NY. Photo: Geoffrey Clements. Courtesy the Whitney Museum of American Art.

Figs. 5.5, 5.6 Photo: Lyle Ashton Harris. © Lyle Ashton Harris Studio. Courtesy Lyle Ashton Harris Studio and the Whitney Museum of American Art.

Figs. 5.7, 5.10 Courtesy Studio Museum in Harlem. Photo: Adam Reich.

Fig. 5.8 Courtesy Studio Museum in Harlem.

Fig. 5.9 Gift of Thomas Bellinger. © Whitney Museum of American Art / Licensed by SCALA / Art Resource, NY.

Fig. 5.11 Digital Image © The Museum of Modern Art / Licensed by SCALA / Art Resource, NY. Photo: Robert Gerhardt.

Franklin Sirmans

Fig. 6.1 Cover artwork: David Hammons, *In the Hood,* 1993. Book design: Paul Mittleman. © Bronx Museum of the Arts.

Figs. 6.2, 6.3 Courtesy of Los Angeles County Museum of Art © Museum Associates / LACMA.

Figs. 6.4, 6.5 © Noah Purifoy Foundation 2020, photo © Museum Associates / LACMA.

Figs. 6.6–6.7 © Estate of Jean-Michel Basquiat. Licensed by Artestar, New York. Image courtesy of Prospect New Orleans.

Fig. 6.8 © Estate of Jean-Michel Basquiat. Licensed by Artestar, New York. Image courtesy of Prospect New Orleans. Museu d'Art Contemporani de Barcelona Collection. Government of Catalonia long-term loan.

Fig. 6.9 Courtesy of Menil Archives, the Menil Collection, Houston.

Acknowledgments

Fig. 7.1 Photo: Kevin Dale. Courtesy of Columbia University.

Fig. 7.2 Photo: On White Wall. Courtesy of Columbia University.

Figs. 7.3, 7.4 Photo: Lucas Hoeffel. Courtesy of Columbia University.

INDEX

Page numbers in *italics* refer to illustrations.